I0148400

THE REWARD
of
RELIGION

Edward Topsell

Edification Press
Culpeper, VA

The Reward of Religion
Copyright © 2013 by Edification Press
All rights reserved

Edification Press
Culpeper, VA
www.edificationpress.com

This edition is based on the text of *The Reward of Religion* published in 1613 and the text was compared with the 1596 printing. The text has been revised to reflect modern spelling. Words in brackets [ ] were supplied to aid the reader in understanding some of the more obscure words that were used in the text.

Cover photograph: "Cornfield before Thunderstorm" by Rene Schwietzke

ISBN 978-1-936473-02-1

THE
REWARD OF
RELIGION
DELIVERED IN SUNDRY
LECTURES UPON THE
BOOK OF
RUTH.

Wherein the Godly may see
their daily both inward and outward
trials, with the presence of God to assist
them, and his mercies to recompense them.

Luke 12.32
*Fear not little flock, for it is your Father's will to
give you a kingdom.*

Cyprian in the end of the 6·· Epist. lib. 4.
Dearly beloved Brethren, let this be rooted in your hearts,
let this be the preparation of your weapons, let this be
your Meditation day and night, to set before your eyes,
and consider with mind and senses, the punishments of
the wicked, with the rewards and deserts of the righteous:
what penalty he threateneth to them that deny him; and
what glory he promiseth to them which confess him.

TO THE RIGHT
Honorable, virtuous and
Christian Lady, the Lady Margaret,
Baroness Dacre of the South, grace,
mercy and peace, be multiplied, in
this life present and eternal felicity
in the life to come.

ight Honorable Lady, it is reported that the inhabitants of the mountain *Cassius* by *Seleucia*, at the third watch of the night do behold the Globe of the Sun: so that on the one side they see our accustomed darkness, covering the face of the whole earth, on the other side the glistering beams of the shining light, displaying these shadows of the nightly darkness. In my opinion this hill doth very fitly resemble the excellency of the word of God, and the inhabitants thereof, the professors of Religion: for long since the Sun of righteousness, the Son of God, departed from the sight of the world, and declined like the Sun of the firmament, hath left the universal Orb of the whole earth in palpable darkness. Yet to us living in this world, the beams of his brightness, the light of his spirit, the power of his person, and the glory of his godhead, is most evidently manifested by the Scriptures and preaching of his holy word: so that there we behold infinite thousands walking in darkness, and standing on the left hand of God, ready for damnation: but here we see a few persons, professors of Religion, like the men of *Cassius*, living in the sight and presence of our Savior, (whom they behold shining in the Scriptures) and standing on the right hand waiting for salvation. For this cause, the voice of the eternal God soundeth so often unto us in the Scriptures, that we were under the Prince of darkness, that we were darkened in our cogitation, that it was night, but now the day-star from on high hath visited us, and therefore we must cast away the deeds of darkness, and put on the armor of light: and the Scriptures everywhere testify, that the Church of God is in the top of the mountains, meaning that the dignity of our calling, as far excelleth the fancies of the world, as the hills arise above the valleys of the earth. This is the infallible word of life, and all the writings of men are but the Apes hereof: from hence they heard of their golden ages, their fearful wonders, their strange inventions, and their incredible fictions, which they have broached concerning heaven and earth. When *Ptolemaeus Philadelphus*, king of Egypt, built his famous library, and had furnished it with all the writings of the heathen, he also by Ambassadors to the high Priest in Judah, obtained the old Testament, and six men of every Tribe, to translate it out of Hebrew into Greek: then *Demetrius Phalereus*, one of the Scholars of *Theophrastus*, certified the King, that among all the writings of their learned Philosophers, they only were divine, and the Celestial Oracles of the everlasting God. For their truth the secret nature of every heart is forced to confess for their substance, it is altogether occupied on heavenly things, for their sincerity, it is established in the promise of him, who never changeth, for their style, neither their principles of *Plato*, the demonstrations of *Aristotle*, the inventions of *Hippocrates*, the sleights of *Carneades*, the exclamations of *Cicero*, or the conceits of *Seneca*, were uttered in so plain eloquence or commendable phrases, as the Scriptures of our salvation. Also if your Honor consider the often changes of the laws of godless Gentiles, you shall perceive that they have had as many Religions as generations: but you shall find that we have now the Religion of *Adam*, the faith of *Enoch*, the Ark of *Noah*, the sacrifice of *Abraham*, and all the true worship of God, as the Church possessed it many thousand years ago: and all because the rule hereof, the heavenly word of God remaineth forever. *Lycurgus* the best lawmaker that ever was among the Gentiles, when he saw his laws to be amended of the *Spartans*, for very grief thereof famished himself at *Crissa*. The laws which *Papius* and *Julius* gave to the Romans, were disannulled by *Severus* the Emperor: all the world erreth, some one way, and some another, mutually condemning each other's superstition; only the Church of God, in every age retained one God, one faith, one Baptism, and one substance of Religion, because it followeth one voice of the holy Ghost speaking in the Scriptures. It were infinite to set down all the commodity we receive by this heavenly writing. By it our manners are mollified, our minds instructed, our lives blessed, and we delivered from Atheism, Paganism and Papism: Atheism denieth all things, Paganism corrupteth all things, and Papism confoundeth all things, therefore by the word of God, we are freed from doubting the truth, deceiving our own souls, and confounding Religion. And because this requireth some proof, I beseech your Honor to bear with my tediousness, while I manifest my mind so briefly as I may, omitting Atheism fitter for dogs to believe, than men to profess, I will briefly declare, how the Gentiles (such as we were before the word wrought our calling) have falsified the whole Scripture, and corrupted the tradition thereof with the inventions of their own Poets; and how the Papists are but confounders of Heathenism, heresy and Christianity.

First to begin with the Gentiles, while reason and nature enforced them to confess a God, (which is only and truly learned in the Scriptures,) they imagined a multitude of gods and goddesses; in the Scriptures we find the mention hereof, that every nation had a peculiar God. The Zidonians and Syrians had *Ashtaroth*, or as some call him *Astartes*: the Moabites had *Chemosh*: the Ammonites had *Milcom* or *Moloch*; the Babylonians *Bel*, the Philistines *Dagon*, the Egyptians worshipped many beasts, but especially a sheep: among other writers, we find that the Athenians, had *Apollo* and *Minerva*; the Boetian Thebes, *Bacchus* and *Hercules*; Carthage had *Juno*; Cyprus and Paphus, *Venus*; Rhodes, *Apollo*; Taenarus, *Neptune*; the Cretes, and Ephesians, *Diana*; the Romans *Mars*, the Italians, *Janus*, the Arabians *Diasares*; The Germans *Tibilenus*, the men of Africa *Caelestus*; and the Moors have worshipped the governors of their Country. Thus they turned the glory of the incorruptible God, into the similitude of corruptible creatures, as birds, beasts, fish and serpents, and wandered without God, while they framed to themselves a multitude of gods: and the best they could invent, were sinful and abominable wretches, such as exceeded all others in notorious crimes, as I could easily show, if it were to my purpose: and moreover they have forsaken not only the true God, but have blotted the names of their most famous men, leaving the worthiest in hell, and lifting the worst into heaven. For might not they as well made *Socrates* a God for his wisdom, whom *Apollo* himself honored with this Oracle: *Pantoon, Androon, Socrates Sophotatos*, of all men *Socrates* was the wisest: *Aristides* excelled them all in justice, *Themistocles* for war, *Alexander* in honor, *Polycrates* in felicity, and *Demosthenes* in eloquence: Who was more grave than *Cato*, more valiant than *Scipio*, more affable than *Camillus*, more excellent than *Jul. Caesar*, more happy than *Sylla*, more wealthy than *Crassus*, or more religious than *Numa Pompilius*? truly none among all their devils, I would say gods, with whom all the nations of the earth have committed fornication. In latter times the Romans had only power to consecrate gods, as now the Pope and his Cardinals do challenge the same to canonize Saints. But would not the hearts of the godly break in sunder, to consider that every City invented a new God, yea every family had their houshold gods, committed idolatry with birds of the air, and beasts of the earth, men and women, Moon and Stars, Sun and Angels, even to the Asses head, as commonly as the Serpent liveth on the dust, or as greedily as the Lion raveneth when he findeth a prey. The study of Astronomy verifieth this, for they have imagined signs from the Eagle to the little bird, from the Lion to the little dog, from the Whale to the little fish, and from reasonable creatures to unreasonable monsters: because they would have some color for their impiety, they translated their Idols to be signs in heaven. But now when the light of the word of life once shined in the world, they perceived their own follies, renounced their old errors and received the wholesome doctrine of the only true and eternal God: for as the Lions run at the sight of a firebrand, as the Cockatrice flyeth when she savoreth the Weasel, and the clouds fly away when the Northern wind bloweth; so these subtleties of Satan being once discovered, through the simplicity of the Scriptures, they fall again into the breast of the first Author, and I would to God they were forever buried in his bottomless kingdom. Also that which we find in the word of God, concerning the creation, the flood, the replenishing of the earth, the beginning or confusion of tongues, the destruction of *Sodom* and *Gomorrah*, the delivery of the Israelites from *Egypt*, the miracles of *Moses* and *Aaron*, the overthrow of the Canaanites whom they call *Phoenicians*, the building of *Solomon's* Temple, the scattering of the Tribes of *Israel*, the birth of Christ, the darkness at his death, and the preaching of the Apostles: they have corrupted with fond additions, willful devises, intolerable blasphemies, ignorant relations, wicked subtractions, and accursed depravations, which if I should follow, I might make a large volume: only thus much I will be bold to say, that all the wisdom of the Gentiles was nothing but the doctrine of devils, and that all the world before the coming of Christ, was without the true knowledge of God, the Jews only excepted. The learned have noted these four as the general heads of ancient captivity; the first is *Barbarism*, wherein men lived under no guide, preserved no peace, followed no commendable kind of life, but everyone did that which pleased him, to the disgrace of mankind, refusing only that which was good, and altogether embracing that which was accursed. Then one satisfied another with bloody revenge, making no more account of the life of a man than the blood of a beast, then they mingled themselves like brutish creatures in generation, brother with sister, father with daughter, and mother with her son, then their strength was their law, their desire was their counselor, their affections pleaded, their will gave judgment, and their malice was the means to execute their cruelty. The second head or fountain of falsehood among the Gentiles, is called *Schythism*, because it was first practiced among the Scythians, a barbarous and cruel people, differing in nothing from the former, save only because they had one governor or ruler, to whom they were subject, being at his commandment, to execute right or wrong, to save or kill, keeping peace with none, but many times setting the children to drink the blood of their own parents, and the parents to eat the flesh of their own children. The third kind of falsehood which reigneth among the Gentiles for want of the word of God, is called *Hellenism*, which consisteth in the worship of Idols; this began among the Grecians, who are called in their own tongue *Hellenes*, and therefore was the superstition called Hellenism; this detestable canker so prevailed, that not only the Grecians, Babylonians, Egyptians, Syrians, Phoenicians, Phrygians, and many other nations were infected therewith, but the Israelites, the people of God, were poisoned therewith, which in the end was their utter subversion, and this hath reigned a long time in the Church of Rome, and in all those kingdoms where she could plant her chair, which all the godly do perceive will be her everlasting destruction. But this Hellenism prevailed mightily, for the space of two thousand years, under which time sprang up all the sects of the Philosophers: as the Pythagoreans, which taught that men might not sacrifice to the gods, that the souls of men departed do go into other men, and also into brute beasts, that whatsoever was above the Moon was immortal, with such like fantasies, and in the end this Pythagoras would be called a God. Next unto him arose the Platonists, who affirmed that the world was created of the Angels and little gods, that of one God there came many other Gods, that all women ought to be common, and that no man ought to have a wife peculiar to himself in a well ordered commonwealth. After these succeeded the *Stoics,* who affirmed this world to be God, that all flesh shall perish, and that the souls departed from one into another. Then also began the Epicures to grow like serpents, born only to destroy others, they would have all things to end in pleasure, that there is no God or providence, that none are blessed but in this present life. And thus your Honor may perceive how miserable were those days, when men ran headlong into so great extremities, that their profession of wisdom was the confession of folly, and for all their light of learning, they groped in a Cimmerian darkness, being shadowed with ignorance like the Country *Odessa* in Greece, which by reason of mighty hills thereto adjoining, never felt the beams of the Sun. The fourth head or fountain of ungodliness is called *Samaritanism,* of the Samarians which mingled themselves with the profession of the Jews, and received some part of the Bible; yet like the Anabaptists of our days, without any difference or conscience, kept company with Jews and Gentiles. Of these came many accursed sects, from whom sprang many detestable opinions, and thus the world labored with damnable devises, while the Devil laughed at their daily destruction; whereby this is evident, that Philosophy or Paganism is the corruption of our Religion. But some peradventure will object unto me, that they had very excellent and worthy men, who Crowned their Country and kindred with endless memory. *Mutius* left his right hand on the Altar. *Empedocles* willingly cast himself into the burning flames of the mountain. *Aetna*, one of the builders of Carthage, to avoid a second marriage, cast herself into the burning grave. *Regulus* being freed from the Carthaginians, chose rather to suffer death himself in most cruel torments, than to discharge their prisoners at Rome. *Menocaeus*, seeing his City of the *Thebes* besieged by the Grecians, which they threatened to destroy, except one of them would give himself for all, did ascend to the wall of the City, and there piercing his body with a sword, fell down dead among his enemies, wherewith they contented, departed. *Alcestis* the wife of *Perilaus* seeing (as she supposed) the fiends come for her husband, who lay sick, slew herself, bidding them to take her shadow and spare her husband's life.

To speak nothing of *Lucretia; Dyrachia, Aria, Cyane* and many others, only let this suffice; *Eleates* being asked of *Dionisius* the Tyrant, what was better than Philosophy, answered death, whereupon he was commanded to be scourged to death, which for the defense of his speech, and contempt of death he most patiently endured. Yet *Tertullian*, a Christian father, speaking of such like actions, hath these words; O lawful commendation because human, to whom neither willful presumption, nor desperate persuasion is imputed, to whom it is permitted to die in contempt of death, and all manner of cruelty: to whom is given more liberty to suffer for his country, kingdom or friends than for God.

Who is he that cannot with one eye espy the meaning of this father? Improving this kind of death, as presumption or desperation which may never have any harbor in the hearts of the faithful: what shall we then say of all these worthy persons? Surely, whatsoever is not of faith is sin, and without faith it is impossible to please God. We must not regard what man doth, but what God commandeth, as the Emperor *Constantine* once said, it is not death, but the cause of death that deserveth commendation; as *Agesilaus* the best Grecian Prince that ever was wont to say, The purest Adamant is not worn with iron, nor wasted with fire, yet a little Goat's blood will consume it: even so, if one man could suffer all the trials in the world, and abide many thousand deaths by fire and torture, yet it shall no whit profit him, except the blood of Jesus Christ loose the fetters of sin, and break the chains of the Devil; now the mercies of God in Christ, are not communicated to any, but to such as know them, and who can know them without the word of God? This is the fountain of water of life, and all other are but poisoned puddles, stinking more filthily in the presence of God, than the Lake of *Camarina* in the nostrils of men. They report that in *Sicilia* there are two springs, whereof one will make a fruitful woman barren, the other, a barren woman fruitful: if this were so, I think all the world would have recourse unto it. Yet in this word of God, there is a greater commodity declared unto us, for here we learn the true cause of barrenness; which being known, the disease is the more easily removed: here we learn the means whereby it is cured, as in *Rebecca, Hannah, Elizabeth* and others, which might as easily be practiced, as true Religion unfeignedly professed. Moreover they tell us, that in *Epirus* at the foot of the hill *Tomarus*, there is a holy Well, which of itself will kindle a Torch, being put unto it, and quench it being brought burning thereto; grant this to be true, and it will represent unto us the nature of this holy Well, the word of God, which with the water of our Baptism doth fire our hearts by the holy Ghost, but coming unto it, burning in the heat of our own lust, quencheth the flame of our own concupiscence. Also we find in *Varro*, that there are two streams in *Boeotia*, whereof if sheep drink, the one burneth their color in Russet, and the other maketh them white again, if this be possible as all things are possible to the Creator of the world, what marvel though we are regenerated, (not new colored) by the immortal seed of his heavenly word. Which are his sheep, and the corruptions of our nature so washed in the same, that our garments of righteousness are as white as snow in his presence. *Solinus* telleth that at the City *Debris* among the *Garamantes*, there is a spring which at the rising of the sun congealeth to ice, but at the setting thereof resolveth to water again, which is contrary to all the world beside freezing with heat, and thawing with cold: yet we may make this use thereof, that it is no wonder to see our heavenly Well to work these contraries, to be the savor of life unto life, or else the savor of death unto death, that unto some it is a two edged sword to give them mortal wounds, unto other, a broad target to defend them from danger, that it wrought so effectually in the days of persecution, when it was oppressed in darkness, but now freezeth and hardneth in these days of peace, when the sun of prosperity shineth to all. Surely as the Albeste stone once set on fire, can never be quenched, so if we could but once burn in love unfeignedly with the Gospel, our profession should not be so lukewarm, nor our devotion so small in the cause of Religion. And thus I have been bold with your Honor to prove my first assertion, wherein if I have been too long, let me crave pardon, and I will promise greater brevity in my second proposition, which is this, that Popery is a confusion of Heathenism, Heresy and Christianity.

And that I may methodically proceed, I will begin at their highest degree, and so in order lightly touch so many things as may certify your Honor of the truth of their Religion. *Numa* appointed one to be a high Priest, at whose judgment all temporal and spiritual things were administered: the same is retained in the Church of *Rome*, for the Pope obtained of *Phocas* the Emperor and murderer of *Mauritius*, that the Bishop of *Rome* might be the head of all Churches, to whose judgment all the world in spiritual matters must be subject: by which in time it came to this, that he corrupted the whole Church of Christ, that he got both swords into his hand, and made himself a triple Crown, after the manner of the late Roman Emperors, who had three Crowns at their inauguration. And as the triple lightning was the Ensign of *Jupiter*: so the triple Crown is the badge of the Pope, through the honor or terror thereof, he threateneth what thunderbolts he pleaseth in the world. The Cabalists imagined two Keys, whereby Paradise was opened and shut; from hence the Pope hath in his banner the Cross Keys, telling us that he hath power, to open and shut Paradise, for, and against whom he pleaseth. Being thus exalted into the highest place, as it was reported, the God *Terminus* would not give place to *Jupiter* standing both in the Capitol, no more the Pope giveth place to Christ, although he stand in the midst of his Church, and sit at the right hand of his Father in heaven. For this cause, as the Emperors had their Senate, so he hath his Cardinals: as the Egyptians bound the Priests of *Isis* or *Apis* to live in perpetual virginity; so he forceth the sacred shavelings [*monks*] of his unholy seat, with the vow of perpetual chastity, and that he might help their weakness in this behalf, as *Caligula* suffered the whores of *Rome* in his days, so the Popes have granted the toleration of a Stews [*brothel*], built by a Pope, *Sixtus* the fourth, which in short time so prevailed, that the Pope received for Rents thereof forty thousand Duccats by the year. And *Paul* the third had the names of forty and five thousand Tenants belonging to that most filthy and damnable kind of life. Furthermore he furnished, or rather poisoned the Church of Christ, with Friars, Monks, Nuns. The Friars and Monks are the successors of the *Essaean, Dosithaean, Nasachaean* and *Cynical* heretics, which like these take upon them the vows of willful poverty, and perpetual chastity, placing their Religion in abstinence from meats, in outward and hypocritical fasting, affirming that they are the successors and followers of the Apostles, like the heretics called by *Augustine* Apostolics, defending that the Apostles lead a single life, and had no wives, so these Romish heretics account marriage but filthiness, like the Marcionites, Tacians, Adamites, Platonists, and Valesian heretics, and are not ashamed to make the holy Apostles of Christ breakers of wedlock, and willful departers from their own wives, contrary to the writings of the Evangelists and Saint *Paul*. The Nuns or women Monks are the natural successors of the vestal Virgins instituted by *Numa*, and as these were dedicated to *Vesta, Apollo; Juno, Argiva, Diana* and *Minerva*, so are the Romish Nuns to *Mary* the mother of Christ, and other holy women. Then also did he begin to dress and adorn the Temples with Images, which he learned of the Gentiles, as I have already declared, and herein he joined with the Gnostics and Basilidian heretics, who defended images to be lawful for Christian people; and as the Gentiles had their sacrifices for the dead, called *Inferiae*, so he instituted prayers for the dead, lest he should seem to want anything, which he should not have. Then also he took the Scriptures from the common people, least they should espy his lewdness, and as *Lysis* the Pythagorean blamed one of his fellows for making known abroad their Master's precepts, so he blameth all those that shall open the mysteries of the Gospel to the common people: and as the Magicians of *Persia* were wont to sing to their Idols in a strange tongue, so the Pope commanded all things to be done in the Church in an unknown language, wherein they also join with the Basilidian heretics, who gave this as a principle, that their mysteries must be concealed, and revealed only to a few, being worse than the Pythagoreans, who commanded but five years silence to their Disciples, but the Papists keep men all their lives from reading, speaking and conferring on the Scriptures. By this means he deceived the world with juggling, like the heretics called *Mirabiliary*, and affirmed that faith cometh by nature, like the Basilidians and Gnostics; they taught that every one that would be saved must be anoiled [*anointed with oil*] in their sickness; like the Heracleonite heretics; that it is lawful for women to Baptize like the Marcionites; that children unbaptized are not under the covenant, and that grace is given with the outward sign, like the Arians and Heracleonites; that children must be anointed with oil in Baptism, like the heretics *Marcus* and *Marcosus*; that Baptism washeth away original sins, and such actual as are committed before, like the Novatians, and Messalian heretics; that the Sacrament of the Supper of the Lord, after the words of Consecration spoken, is the very body and blood of Christ, so the heretics called *Marcites*, said, they made by conjuration, and for this cause the Pepuzian heretics baked the blood of man with the bread ordained for this supper; that wine must be mingled with water, as the *Artotyrites* said, they must offer cheese with the bread in the Sacrament; that good works merit eternal life, like the Pelagians, Catharites, and Mahumetistes; that a man since the fall of *Adam* hath free will, and that God hath Predestinated none, like the Pelagians, that it is lawful for us to swear by creatures, as the Virgin *Mary*, Saints and Angels, so do the Manicheans and Mahumetistes; that some sins be mortal and some venial, so doth *Mahomet* affirm: with a thousand like, most vain, wicked, wretched, blasphemous and damnable assertions, which were most easy to be proved if there were any question of it. By this your Honor may perceive, that their Religion is but patched of many condemned heresies, defended by unwritten traditions, and maintained by violent and forcible dealing: like the *Chameleon* they have often changed and poisoned the world, but the Scriptures are as a bay-leaf, to cure the contagion of such mortal confusion. And thus in some sort I have performed my promise, in delivering the vanity of the world which hath refused the wisdom of the eternal word of God. The end of this my speech is to show the wonderful and incomparable treasure of the holy Scriptures; for as the gold hath the brightest beams, being laid to the Copper: as the Adamant is of greatest force, when the loadstone is beside it, and the purest color hath the best hue, when the counterfeit is compared with it; so the blessing of God in his word, doth most magnificently appear, when we behold before our eyes the counterfeit colors of superstitious conceits, the crooked devises and cursed opinions of the condemned crew, which have refused the way of life declared herein, and chose the path of damnation for the hire of their superstition. The Scriptures are not only a Castle to keep us from heresy, but also a salve or remedy, if we have been poisoned by falsehood. The sting of the Scorpion is cured by applying the Agate stone, the grass Alimos preserveth the famished person from death, the Bear having eaten Mandragora saveth his life by the little Emmet, and the poison of the Chameleon is expelled by a bay-leaf: even so the word of God, cureth the heresies of Popery, which are compared to the stinging of the Scorpions in the Scriptures, it is the fruit of the tree of life, and whosoever eateth and digesteth it shall never die, it is a preservative against all poison, and the leaves thereof shall cure the nations. By this alone the Lord hath wrought the calling of his children, the confusion of his enemies, the comfort of his Saints, and the replenishing of his kingdom. All the Kings of the earth have been in arms against it: yet the ministers thereof, who never bore arms against them, by their only preaching have won a glorious field. All *Egypt* could not resist *Moses* and *Aaron*, because they came on the Lord's message: no more shall all the world overcome the preachers of peace, so long as they faithfully perform their heavenly Ambassage. Words have wrought more than weapons; the Spirit hath pierced more than the Spear; the walls of Paper and the ordinance of feathers have battered down the stately kingdom of the Whore of *Babylon*, learning hath done better service than Lances, Gowns have conquered more than Guns; Books have done more good than Bullets; and the prayers of the faithful have prevailed more than the Pikes of horsemen; the stone which the builders refused, is become the head of the corner, this is the Lord's doing, and it is marvelous in our eyes, the blood of the dead Martyrs hath given greater wounds in this quarrel, than the swords of the living soldiers. But thus I have too long troubled your Honor with that which you knew before, and have presumed on your favor for the acceptation of these my slender labors upon one part of Scripture, the book of *Ruth*; which as the holy Ghost hath vouchsafed to call by the name of a woman, to the praise of the whole sex, and everlasting commendation of her Religion: so am I emboldened to Dedicate it to so Honorable a Lady as yourself, whom I know to be a *Ruth* by Religion, though a Noble woman by birth. For many witnesses can testify this also if I should be silent, and the ordinary exercises at *Seuenoke*, will sound your name, because your presence and diligence at them, hath stirred up many meaner persons, comforted some godly people thereabout, and much every way countenanced, and encouraged the preachers of the same. There are many causes which might compel me, (though unwilling) to commit my labors to the Press, yet willingly to present them to the world under the name of your Honor. For I am assured of the acceptation of any small thing that shall be offered in the name of Religion, much more of this which comprehendeth the recompense and reward of our profession. Your Honor knoweth that better is it to see the smoke of one's own Country, than the fire of another: so I trust my slender studies, which are but as smoke, being compared with the burning coals of others' knowledge, such as daily you hear, shall be the better accepted, because there I had my being, where your Honor hath your dwelling. Also I am hereunto moved, that I might have any occasion, to testify my bounden duty, which I owe unto that Noble and worthy Gentleman, Sir *Henry Leonard* your son, of whom I have received especial encouragements in the course of my studies, and to whom I must remain a debtor to the end of my days, being no ways able to recompense his wonted kindness, but only by this, daily to pray for the life and prosperity, that he may be as the heir of your Honor, so an ornament of the Noble house of the *Dacres.* And the God of all peace bless your own person, with such blessings as you daily desire, that you may still live to the comfort of the godly in this present life, to the enlarging of your own Honor, to the rejoicing of your whole family, and to the endless salvation of your own soul with Jesus Christ the Savior of all them which have unfeignedly embraced true Religion. London this first of October, 1596.

Your Honor's to command
in the Lord,

EDWARD TOPSELL.

To all them that unfeignedly embrace true Religion

early beloved in Christ, when I consider that comfortable Oracle of the Apostle, when he saith that godliness hath the promises of this life, and of the life to come; it cometh into my mind, that Religion is none of the meanest professions that is labored for in the world: for the greatest rewards are promised to the chiefest exploits; and the worthiest enterprises are crowned with glorious benefits. *Joseph* for his wisdom was made the governor of *Egypt.* *Othniel* for his service received *Achsah* the daughter of *Caleb* for his wife. *Jephthah* for his victory was made judge of Israel, and *David* for his Music was made one of the Courtiers of *Saul.* In so much as it seemeth an ordinary practice that every knowledge is rewarded with some courtesy: whereby we are certified, that it is no marvel to hear and hope for so excellent blessings as are promised to the Religious. For they are the house of the Lord, and as he dwelleth with all majesty in heaven, so he reigneth with all authority in the righteous; they are a chosen generation born of God, a royal and holy priesthood, a holy nation, a peculiar people, the freemen of Christ, the inheritors of the earth, the judges of the world, the coheirs of Christ's kingdom, and the Citizens of heaven. If we look for their Nobility, they are the Sons of God; if for their instruction, they are taught of God; if for their tuition, the heavenly Angels are their servants;

if for their degrees they are kings and priests for the eternal God, if for their calling they are Saints; if for their life it is heavenly; if for their wealth it is the whole world; and finally their death is the birthday of all felicity. For this cause *David* desired rather to be a doorkeeper in the house of God, than a dweller in the stately tents of the wicked; as if the meanest condition among the professors of Religion, were more excellent than the chiefest estates among the worldlings, their Crosses excel the other's Crowns, their barrenness, the other's fruitfulness, their humility the other's honor, their ignorance the other's knowledge, their simplicity the other's wisdom, their weakness the other's strength, and a little thing that the righteous hath, is better than the great possessions of the ungodly. When there is famine they are satisfied, when there is war they are delivered, when there is plague they are without danger, if fire fall from heaven it shall not burn them, if the waters arise above the mountains, they are not drowned, if the earth quake and rend asunder, yet they are not swallowed up, if the wild beasts fall upon them they are not devoured, and if the Devil himself would oppress them, yet he shall not overcome them. Then how glorious is our calling, that live under the wings of God, that feed with the flock of Christ, to whom are revealed the secret counsels of the Lord, speaking unto us by his Ministers, giving us the evidence of our salvation by his Testament, regenerating us by the immortal seed of his holy word, sealing us with the spirit of promise, lifting us up from the dust of worldly misery, to the thrones of heavenly Majesty. *Solomon's* servants were happy that stood in his presence and heard his wisdom. *Daniel* was happy when the Lions could not destroy him, his fellows were happy when the fire could not consume them, the Israelites were happy when the Egyptians were drowned, *Job* was happy when his wealth was restored, and the Disciples were blessed when they heard Christ preach. How many blessings belong to the religious? Satan that roaring Lion, cannot overcome them, the fire shall have no power on them, their enemies shall never hurt them, the riches of the grace of God shall be poured upon them, and the word of life is daily preached unto them. Consider therefore, my beloved, what is the hope of our profession whereunto we are called, the dignity of our condition wherein we stand, and the reward of our Religion prepared for our souls. Call to mind the examples of the Fathers, the promises of the Gospel, the oath of the Lord himself, the price of our redemption, and the place of our salvation: you shall find nothing wanting in Religion, that might increase your blessedness. Therefore how happy are the ears that hear the things which we hear, the eyes that see the things which we see, the hands that handle the things which we touch, nay the souls that are assured of the favor of God. If all the world would go about to set down the felicity of the godly, and the dignity of the chosen, they could never achieve it: no, not that which they enjoy in this life, for their thoughts are heavenly, their hearts the throne of the holy Ghost, their hands feel the Lord of glory, their tongues talk of his praise, their feet stand in his Temple, their words are acceptable before him, their prayers like sweet savors of incense, their worship like evening sacrifices, their eyes behold his glory, their ears hear his wisdom, and their names are written in the kingdom of heaven. Would not any man become religious, that he might be rewarded with this excellent honor? To eat his meat with the King of heaven, to wear the Crown that never shall have end, to have the Angels his attenders, the Saints his fellows, the heavens his dwelling place, the stars under his feet, the everlasting light to walk in, the presence of God to delight him, and the pleasures of Paradise for the recompense of his religion. For this cause I have given this title unto these my slender labors upon this book of *Ruth*, wherein (beloved in Christ) you shall find the matter to agree with the title, and the hope of all the faithful concerning the end of their profession, so profitably deciphered, as hath comforted many troubled souls, confirmed many wavering minds, confounded many obstinate Atheists, encouraged many godly persons; and therefore I hope will offer the same favor unto you in reading, as it hath unto many other in preaching. Herein the holy Ghost (I mean in the book of *Ruth*) hath laid open whatsoever can be expected of them that fear the Lord: here are afflictions to humble us, death to prevent us, and examples to admonish us; here is the zeal of the godly, the virtue of an effectual calling, the vizard [*mask*] of hypocrisy declared unto us; here is the love of the faithful, the obedience to parents, and the benevolence of godly persons commended unto us; here is the care of our parents, the gifts of the spirit, and the holiness of the religious committed to the Church; here is the office of Magistrates, the prayers of our brethren, and the calling of the Gentiles expressed, in the marriage of *Ruth* with *Boaz*, who was made a mother of many Kings, but especially of the King of glory, the Son of God, the Savior of the world, and the gatherer together of the heirs of grace. My desire therefore is this, that you try it by perusing and reading this treatise: for it is but superfluous labor for me, any farther to trouble you with the argument hereof, seeing the whole matter lieth before your consideration. I will pray for your success, and commend the end of my travels, (which is the comfort and instruction of the members of Christ) to the fountain of mercy, by whom the heavens water the earth, and the earth multiplieth with increase, and the increase thereof preserveth the world, that by the same power, your souls may be edified, your faith may be strengthened, my labors may be blessed, that his name may be glorified, his Word may evermore be taught among us, that many generations may embrace his Gospel, and the course thereof finished, our Religion, by the mercy of the Father, in the Son with the holy

Ghost, may be rewarded with eternal salvation. To whom let us evermore give thanks, because he hath vouchsafed us the dignity thereof, and walk worthy of our calling, lest our secure lives, our idle faith, our vain hope, our cold profession, and our common conversation with the ungodly, bring upon us everlasting damnation.

Your loving brother, who desireth
your prayers,

EDWARD TOPSELL.

Lo here what guardian godliness doth get,
And how the cross doth come before the crown:
Lo widows twain before our eyes are set
Not rais'd aloft, before they be cast down.
And thou O *Ruth* renouncing native town,
   And *Baal-peor* God of *Moab* land,
    Art set at rest, and blest by God's own hand.

The love of friends and country overpoised,
With love of sovereign Lord behold in sight:
The antique age, and life of Patriarchs praised,
How liberal, frugal, chaste, pure, and upright.
But now this mold of earth is turned quite,
   Alas that naught in perfect state should sit,
    The world is chang'd, and we are chang'd in it.

Art thou a maid? Learn here of *Ruth* thy mate,
To choose whom God inspires with grace divine,
A widow thou to pains and labor late,
In each degree thy self with *Ruth* resign,
Or art a wife? To righteous *Ruth* incline.
   If maid, or wife, or widow then thou be,
    Thy self in *Ruth*, thou as in Glass shalt see.

Go little Book, display thy golden title,
(And yet not little, though thou little be:)
Little for price, and yet in price not little,
Thine was the Pain, the gain is ours I see:
(Although our gain, thou deem'st no pain to thee)
   If then O Reader, little pain thou take,
    Thou greatest gain with smallest pain shalt make.

The hungry stomach feeds with full desire,
Whereby the vital spirits soon renew:
So if thine heart shall burn with heavenly fire,
Hereby great fruit shall to thy faith accrue.
Try ere thou trust, and then give sentence true,
    If reading once, be pleasant to thy taste,
    Next pleaseth more: yet sweetest comes at last.

WILLIAM ATTERSOLL.

The Analysis, or Resolution

The Book of Ruth containeth the lively view of the Reward of Religion in the family of Elimelech wherein must be considered their

{

Affliction, as
{
- Famine, which bringeth {
- Sojourning and wandering in strange countries, to {

Deliverance by
{
Receiving
{
- Hospitality, as {
- Plenty, { Among / Among

Returning
{
- To their own country, where they are
- With company gained to the Lord, for the

of the Book of Ruth.

Intolerable wrath and misery to the
{
Utter decay and loss of worldly prosperity.

Selling and forsaking their patrimonies.
}

Fearful and pining death.

Forsake the people of the Lord with the
{
Temple and place of sacrifice,

Lord's Ministers and Word.
}

To remain with their enemies, infidels,
{
Many years together.

To die and be buried among them.
}

Houses and lands,

Marriage.
{
For themselves.

For their families.
}

strangers in the time of their pilgrimage.

their own friends at home, the famine being ended.

{
Joyfully received of their friends,
{
To the praise of God in his Word.

To their own comforts in the Lord.
}

Readily restored by the Magistrates
{
To their liberty:
{
1. To be present at the Temple.

2. To have justice.
}

To their lands, livings.
}
}

{
Increase of the Church, by
{
Wholesome doctrine.

Sanctified and holy conversations.
}

Reviving of their own that be dead,
{
To stir up their names
{
In their houses.

On their inheritance.
}

To multiply their Father's family, for
{
Worldy honor.

The Reward of their Religion.
}
}
}

THE
REWARD
OF RELIGION

Ruth Chapter 1. verses 1-6

1 *In the time that the Judges ruled, there was a famine in the land: and a certain man of* Bethlehem Judah *went for to sojourn in the country of* Moab, *he and his wife, and his two sons.*

2 *And the name of the man was* Elimelech, *and the name of his wife* Naomi, *and the names of his two sons* Mahlon *and* Chilion, *Ephrathites of the land of* Judah, *and when they were come into the land of* Moab, *they continued there.*

3 *Then* Elimelech *the husband of* Naomi *died there, and she remained with her two sons.*

4 *Which took them wives of the* Moabites, *the name of the one was* Orpah, *and the name of the other* Ruth: *and they dwelled there about ten years.*

5 *And* Mahlon *and* Chilion *died also both twain, so the woman was left destitute of her two sons, and of her husband.*

6 *Then she arose with her daughters in law, and returned from the country of* Moab: *for she had heard said in the country of* Moab, *that the Lord had visited his people, and given them bread.*

lthough the author of this book of *Ruth* hath not expressed his name, yet there is no doubt but it proceedeth from the spirit of God, as well as the books of the Judges, Kings, and Chronicles, which have not the names of their authors described: but if it may be lawful to judge or give any sentence thereof, it was either *Samuel* or some other godly prophet under the reign of *Saul*, which is proved by the genealogies in the last chapter, where *David* is by name mentioned, testifying unto us, (that it was then written) when he was chosen from his brethren and anointed king over *Israel*, and yet before his reign, or else there had been added unto it, the title of a King, for the advancing of the name of *Ruth*, who was his grandmother, upon whom this history following dependeth, for the sum and scope hereof is to show the pedigree, or ancestry, the natural progenitors of Christ from *Judah* the fourth son of *Jacob*, until the time that he began to challenge the princely seat, the royal scepter, and the right of government over the people of *Israel*, which was at that time when *David* was chosen from his father's house, and anointed king by *Samuel*. Again, in this history, there is delivered unto us; the hope which the fathers had concerning the calling of the Gentiles, for this marriage of *Ruth* into the kindred of Christ, who was a Gentile, and by nature none of the people of God, did plainly foretell that the Gentiles should be called in Christ: for as he took part of his human nature of them, so he showed us that he would give the same for them, that there might be no difference in his body, between Jews and Gentiles, but that the power of his death, the graces of the spirit, and the knowledge of redemption might redound to all. Now the occasion of this history is delivered unto us in this first Chapter, which is the sojourning of a certain Jew in the land of *Moab*, (by reason there was a famine in the land of *Judah*,) with his family, and the return of them that lived, which were only *Naomi* his wife, and one other, *Ruth* the Moabitess the widow of his eldest son.

This wandering or sojourning is described with all the circumstances thereof, in these first six verses lately read: and generally contain in them these two parts, the first, is their travel to the land of *Moab*: the second, those things that happened unto them, after they came thither. The first part is expressed in these two first verses, first, by the occasion, which is declared by the time, and by the thing that moved them thereunto, in these words: *In the time that the Judges ruled there was a famine, etc.* Secondly, by the persons that traveled, who are described by the place from whence they were, namely of *Bethlehem Judah*, these were the parents and the children which are named in the second verse. The second part of these words, is in the four other verses following, and it concerneth either the parents or the children, the parents, that one of them even *Elimelech*, the father of the family died there shortly after their arrival: the children, first that they married, verse 4. Secondly, that they likewise died, verse 5. Then remained only *Naomi*, with her two daughters in law, and the time of her abode in *Moab*, is set down to be ten years, verse 4. Secondly, the occasion of her departure because she heard say, that God had visited his people, and given them bread, verse 6: of these parts let us speak in order, as the spirit shall give utterance, and the time permit.

In the days that the Judges ruled. In these words the holy Ghost after his accustomed manner, for the more certainty of the history, beginneth at the time as *Moses* beginneth his book of *Genesis*, from the first creation of the world, so the prophets in the beginning of their books set down under what king or kings they prophesied, so also in the new Testament we may see

Gen. 1.1
Isa. 1.1
Jer. 1.2

how three of the Evangelists begin their Gospels from the preaching of *John Baptist* and the reign of king *Herod.* The which order they undoubtedly learned of the old writers, the same spirit guiding them to one and the same truth, useth but one and the same manner of speaking. For the almighty desiring to meet with the wrangling objections of human inventions, so tempereth the text of every Scripture, as if question were made who did such a thing? He nameth the persons where it was done? He quoteth the place, and when it was done? He mentioneth the time. The cause hereof is, that he might stay the waves of our fickle minds, upon the pillar of truth, his everlasting word. We are much given to enquire the times, although they be to come, as we may see in the Apostles, Mark 12.4. who enquired of our Savior when should the Temple be destroyed: for time which is the true measure of things enflameth men's minds with the knowledge thereof. And for this reason to save our longing, hath the Scriptures chronologized the world, so, as to a day, the experienced Divine can collect the ages from the first day of the world's creation, to the last Act of the Acts of the Apostles. But in this place he chiefly mentioneth the time of the Judges, to show unto us, that when religion was corrupted, the worship of God decayed, and idolatry advanced: when the Lord was forgotten of his own people, when his laws were no more observed, but every man did that which seemed good in his own eyes, yea, when there were almost as many Gods among them as there were men, then even then did the Lord send this plague of famine among them. For, *Solomon* saith the blueness of the wound serveth to purge the evil, and the stripes within the bottom of the belly: as if he had said, as the ripeness of a wound calleth for a corrosive, so the fullness of sin cryeth for vengeance.

By this therefore we note, that the corruption of religion, and neglect of the worship of God, is the cause of all his judgments that are exercised in the world. For

Matt. 3.1
Mark. 1.3,4
Luke 1.5

Judg. 2.11-13;
21.25

Prov. 20.30

the idolatry of *Jeroboam*, and his sins, whereby he in-   1 Kings 14.16;
duced *Israel* to sin: did the Lord threaten by *Ahijah* the   16.2; 13.4
prophet, to scatter the people: so we may read of *Baasha*
king of Israel, and so *Solomon* prayed at the dedication   1 Kings 8.35-
of the temple: when heaven shall be shut and thou give   37
no rain because they have sinned against thee, etc. where
he comprehendeth the chief and capital worldly punishments of sin, as dearth and famine, sword and pestilence,
blindness and ignorance, which are also the rewards of
sin, and the inseparable companions of all unrighteousness. And what saith the Lord by the Prophet? *Cast
from you all your sins wherewithal you have transgressed,*   Ezek. 18.31
and make you a new heart, for why should you die oh
you house of Israel? as if he had said, either repent or
else be damned, for it is a fearful thing to fall into the
hands of the living God. So we read that the wantonness of the Church of God having procured heresies,
and heresies apostasy; Almighty God hath recalled men
back again by sword and famine: when about the year of
Christ 400 the Churches of *Africa* had flourished, there
came a cruel king among them called *Hunnerichus*, who
abrogated and corrupted the true belief of Christians:
and after many slaughters by him made, wherein the
greatest part of men after their usual manner had ap-
plauded and served the king's cruel mind, and received
his false and heretical faith. The Lord took the matter in
hand, and first of all sending such droughts on the earth,
that the Well-springs and fountains were dried up, and
the earth thereby became barren, and void of all green
things, until all the granaries for men, and the store in
Barns for cattle were consumed and spent, to preserve
the life both of man and beast. And then, there coming
no relief, nor remedy, followed such a famine, that men
were forced to strive with wild beasts for meat, and with
wild Boars for the roots which were in the earth, that
they might eat them. Many of the nobler Vandals, who
were most exorbitant from the faith, wished and desired

Ruth Chapter 1. verses 1-6

that some would buy them, and make bondmen of them to any slavery so they could but give them food, and yet none could do it. Lastly followed a pestilence, wherein the cruel Arian king for his own and his courtiers' safeguard, caused an innumerable number of people to be thrust out of *Carthage* their own City, and their own houses, to the end that death might tarry with the less violence. But all notwithstanding, he himself was stricken and perished by rottenness and worms: for *mors regum aulas, & pauperum tabernas aquo pede pulsat*, death seizeth both upon Courts of Kings and the cottages of beggars all alike, especially when God sendeth it to punish men for forsaking his worship.

And may not we think that all these thunderings out of God his judgments among us, will stir up some rain of punishments upon us? Are we not already put into the wine press to be bruised under the hand of fearful destruction? How many plagues have come upon us within these few years? Where is become the remembrance of the late enemies' pretended invasion? The rumor whereof amazed the hearts of our courageous champions, which spend all their days in pleasure: Oh then they cried, if they might be delivered, they would allot some time of their days to the service of the Lord. Where is the remembrance of the late plague, which was scattered almost in every place of the land? Oh then we cried unto the Lord in our distress, and he delivered us out of all our miseries. Oh that men would therefore confess the Lord, and declare the wonders he doth for the children of men. But what are we now amended? Is the ungodly person turned from his ungodliness, and not rather strengthened in his iniquity? They which were ignorant are ignorant still, and many like *Demas*, who seemed religious, have embraced this present world. As for the profane both of poor and rich, they have made a league with death, and a covenant with the grave, though a sword come through the land, yet (say they) it

Lecture 1

shall not come at them. And therefore who can without
watery eyes and bleeding heart, tell this present plague
of dearth and famine which we now most justly endure,
and yet who knoweth how long it shall continue. Now
(as the prophet saith) we are gathered together, and howl
upon our beds for corn and for new wine, that is, for the
belly and for the throat, but there is a greater leanness
in the soul. Now we bite the stone which the Lord hath
cast at us, but we look not at the hand, which did send it,
and who thinketh it to be a punishment of sin that now
reigneth among us? The papists say it is for our heresies,
the popish atheists say that the world was best when the
old Religion was, for then all things were cheap, like the
idolatrous Jews, which said unto *Jeremiah*, that it was
well with them when they burnt incense and made cakes
to the host of heaven. The ruffians say to the preachers,
as *Ahab* said to *Elijah*, Are not you the troublers of *Israel*? when it is themselves and their fathers' houses, while
they have left the commandment of God and followed
their pleasures, yea, almost the whole country is so vain-
ly addicted, that among those multitudes of preachers
that are abroad, there is not one that faithfully followeth
his vocation, but they are molested by the basest, and
contemned by the best. So that we may say, as our Savior
saith, we have piped unto you, and you have not danced,
we have mourned, and you have not sorrowed, yet wisdom is justified of her children, who are not ashamed to
plead her cause in the gates of the Cities, before the face
of her enemies: the Lord increase the number of them.

 We have long retained the name of Christians,
that is, the anointed of the Lord, and yet our lamps are
empty, and we defer our days in slumber, thinking ourselves as good Christians as the best, till we be utterly
excluded from the bridechamber, we have promised the
Lord oftentimes to work in his vineyard, but yet who
hath entered? we are the vineyard of the Lord, and he
hath dressed us: what fruit have we borne unto him? we

Hos. 7.13,14

Jer. 44.19

1 Kings 18.17

Matt. 11.17

Psal. 127.5

Matt. 25.3
Matt. 21.30
John 15.2
John 10.14
Gen. 31.34

Ruth Chapter 1. verses 1-6

are the sheep of Christ and yet we know not his voice:
and as *Rachel* covered her father's Idols with sitting on
them, and with a lie, so we that are the greatest sinners,
cover our iniquities, with hypocrisy and dissembling.
Such pollution of Sabbaths as never was, yea, even in this
time of dearth and famine, drinking and drunkenness,
dancing and riot, feasting and surfeiting, chambering
and wantonness, swearing and foreswearing, accounting
gain to be godliness, and godliness to be the burden of
the world, with a thousand greater and more grievous
calamities, as if the bird could sing in the snare, or as the

Prov. 7.22
Matt. 3.10

fatted ox that runneth willfully to the slaughter. Then beloved let us look about us, even now is the axe of God his
judgments laid to the root of every man's heart, and he is
accursed that feareth it not, even now the Lord is knocking at the door of our hearts, and if ever, let us open unto
him, that the King of glory may come in. Even these are
the days wherein iniquity hath gotten the upper hand,
and the love of many is waxen cold. Therefore as the

Rev. 18.4

Angel warned the godly, so must we still come out from
among them, my people, be not partakers of their sins,
lest you bear a part of their plagues. This is the harvest
of the Lord, oh let us that be the Lord's servants gather
out the wheat, lest it be burned with the tares. There is a

Numb. 16.
12,32

holy convocation to the Lord, and the Lord's ministers,
sound out the trumpet, if we appear not, the earth will
open her mouth, and revenge our rebellion, and swallow
us up alive. Let us at the length say with the Jews, Come

Hos. 6.1,2

let us turn unto the Lord, for he hath spoiled us and he
shall heal us, he hath smitten us and he shall bind us
up: after two days he shall give us life, and the third day
he shall raise us up and we shall live before him: if with
knowledge we follow him, to know the Lord his rising
is like the morning, and he shall come upon us like rain
in a drought, both the first and the latter rain upon the
earth. Let not our righteousness, be as the dew before
the sun rising, but put on the Lord Jesus Christ and let

none call upon him, but such as depart from iniquity.

Secondly, by this we gather that the Lord is as true in his judgments, as in his mercies, for he threatened by *Moses* saying, *If you forsake me, and fall to worship strange Gods (as now they did) then your heaven shall be as brass, and your earth as iron, and your rain like dust, till they were consumed from the face of the earth.* Of all these miseries you may see in the book of *Judges*, *Samuel*, and *Kings* to which I refer you at your leisure, as of *Saul*, *David*, *Jeroboam*, *Ahab*, *Zedekiah*, and others as in this present place: where they are oppressed ten years together, so that heaven and earth may pass but the word of the Lord abideth forever.

Deut. 28.23,24

For this cause the prophets add to their preaching of judgments: (*Thus saith the Lord*) as if they had said it shall never be altered. And if the laws of heathen men, such as the *Medes and Persians, might not alter,* much less the word of the Lord, *which is like silver purified seven times*, should have any dross or changeable substance in it. We see the law of nature stand inviolable forever, and shall not the law of him which made nature, be also immutable? when the fire ceaseth to be hot, and the water to be cold, then shall be exception taken against God his judgments, and not before. The use of this doctrine is to cast down the presumption of notorious sinners, who to avoid the terrors of God his judgments, deceive their own souls with this, that God is merciful. So that in their most singular sins, they will fly to the mercies of God, as if they were the very bond of all iniquity: yea, and these kind of people persuade themselves to be as good Christians as any in the world, because they can say, the Lord is merciful.

Dan. 6.8

Psal. 12.6

But hear me a little in one word I pray you, I am persuaded that I speak to many these people this day. What hurt hath the Lord done unto you, that you rob him of his justice? Shall the Prophet be found a liar that saith, *The Lord is just in all ways, and holy in all his works*?

Psal. 145.17

Ruth Chapter 1. verses 1-6

2 Thes. 1.6

Or shall the Apostle speak untruth, that saith: *It is a just thing with God to render affliction to them that afflict you, and release to you that are afflicted?* Why shall we then spoil God of his judgments, unless we will deprive ourselves of our own salvation. But you will say this serveth for the wicked, as Atheists, Turks, Pagans, Infidels, and such like, which shall have no part with Christ. I answer, what greater wickedness can there be than to deprive God of his justice? Would a mortal man endure to be accounted without honesty, and shall the everlasting King abide to be spoiled of his righteousness? Nay, the justice of God pertaineth to such as you would be, holy persons, as well as to any. For what saith the Prophet, When the

Ezek. 18.16

just man turneth from his righteousness to do iniquity, he shall die in it. And *Peter* saith, that judgment must begin at the house of God. And a Father once said, God

Cyprian

of his most dear justice hath decreed the sum of all discipline, both in exacting and in defending: as if he had said, there is no correction of the Lord, but it proceedeth from his justice, now the children of God are corrected, for he scourgeth every child whom he receiveth. And therefore the judgments of God must be thundered out

Heb. 12.6

as well for the confirming of the faithful, as the confusion of Infidels. But others there are that are so far past feeling of either mercies or judgments that as soon the deaf adder will hear the voice of the charmer, as they any impression of terror for sin. Hence cometh this custom of sinning, which every sabbath commit their wonted iniquity, every hour vomit out their poison of blasphemies, and every day violate the laws of charity, who through their daily staring on the son of righteousness, are now become stark blind, and with the continual noise of God his waters, are made so deaf, that they can hear no goodness. Unto both these sorts of people, hearken what the

Matt. 24.48-51

Lord saith in his Gospel, But if that evil servant shall say in his heart, the Lord deferreth his coming, and shall begin to smite his fellow servants, and to eat and drink with the drunken. The Lord of that servant shall come in a day that he looketh not for, and in an hour that he knoweth not, and shall separate him, and give him his part with unbelievers, there shall be weeping and gnashing of teeth. This shall be the end of secure Christians, and contemptuous sinners, carnal Atheists, and despisers of wholesome doctrine; which have no part but in this present life, with endless and fearful damnation in the world to come. Thus much of the first part, the circumstance of time.

Now let us go to the thing which is the second part, of the occasion. *There was a famine in the land.* This was the chief cause which moved these persons to travel, the avoiding of the pinching penury of fearful death, by lingering till the end of this pining famine. Of all the punishments of sin which happen in this life, there is none more vehement than famine. Therefore the Lord by the Prophet, threateneth to send his arrows of famine to break the staff of bread. Where he alludeth to a main battle, signifying unto us, first as the arrow is the fittest instrument to break the rank, so a famine is the sharpest weapon to dismay the courageous stomachs of rebellious sinners. For as the arrow is always in sight, so a famine ever in sense, the arrow hurteth, but not with a speedy death, a famine spoileth, yet with tedious misery: the arrow entered doth procure more pain and greater wound at the pulling forth, than the falling in: even so abundance of meat sooner dispatcheth a famished person than lingering hunger. Therefore *David* put to his choice of three plagues, famine, flying, and pestilence, chose the last as the most suddenest, and therefore accompanied with less grief, for that disease by the rule of physic is most dangerous, which is the longest in growing. Now we may read of many famines in the Scripture, one and the first we read of, was in the days of *Abraham*, another in the days of *Isaac*, his son. Seven years famine was in Egypt, where *Joseph* by the hand of God succored

Ezek. 5.16

2 Sam. 24.13-15

Gen. 12.10
Gen. 26.1
Gen. 41.30

Ruth Chapter 1. verses 1-6

2 Sam. 21.1
1 Kings 18.2
2 Kings 6.25
Acts 11.28

the Church in his father's family. And to omit that in *David's* time, and that in *Ahab's* time, with those in the days of *Jehoram* and *Zedekiah*, with many others. We read in the new Testament of a universal famine, in the days of *Claudius Caesar*, prophesied by *Agabus*, when the Church did most notably relieve one another. Unto the which we may add that at the destruction of *Jerusalem*, about forty years after Christ. All which are most worthy spectacles of human misery, and worthy examples of God his Judgments, to terrify all them which say in their prosperity, they shall never be moved. There we may read of the pitiful death of many thousands which starved in the streets, in the face of their dearest friends, and yet were not able to relieve them. There we may see how men were driven to eat dogs, cats, rats, mice, and horse flesh: but that which is most miserable, the mothers to succor their stomachs and bodies, with the slaughter and eating of their own children. What heart of adamant would not weep, yea rather bleed at the sight hereof? And yet behold a greater famine than all these! Is it possible? yea verily, a famine of the word of God, when men shall go from one sea to another, and from the North to the East, running to seek the word of God, and shall not find it. In that day shall fall both the fair virgins and the young men, which swear by the Idols of *Samaria*, and say, As thy God liveth, O *Dan*, and as the God of the way of *Beersheba* liveth, they shall fall; neither shall they ever rise up again. Is not this greater than the famine of bread? There was never famine so great, but if liberty were given, the famine was eased: but in this they shall have liberty to run to and fro, and shall not be relieved. There was never any famine wherewith men were so hunger-starved, but some recovered, but in this, saith the Lord, They that fall shall never rise again. Oh that the open contemnors of God his word, would drink but one drop for a taste of these fearful judgments: I am persuaded that the heat of greedy sin would be so

Amos 8.11

cooled in them, that they should recover the health of their souls, which will never be, till of open profaners they become public professors. But of all these famines there is but one cause, which is the abuse of the creatures of God, for so the equity of justice requireth, that in the same thing wherein they sinned, they should be punished. Like as the thief was bound for that which he stole, to restore four fold. *Fullness of bread* was one of Ezek. 16.53 the sins of *Sodom*, and they understood not from whom they had it, because they were unmerciful to the poor, and therefore abused it by unthankfulness.

And this is a worthy doctrine to be urged in our days, wherein our abuse is greater than our want, and yet our want is such as hath not been heard of these many years. The covetous seller keepeth in his corn, and draweth upon himself the curse of the poor, saying it is scanty, it is scanty, when his garners are full. Is not this to tell that the Lord his hand is shortened, when in deed it is lengthened? Is not this to say, thou openest thy hand and fillest with thy blessing every living thing? Nay, you plainly accuse the Lord of illiberality.

Oh detestable cruelty, who for to fat up their own posterities, will murder the bodies of many thousands of poverty, yea this is more cruel than murder in the sight of God. Why deal you not plainly, and say, the Lord hath given abundance, yet your price must be raised, so you should speak truly, and excuse the liberality of the Lord in accusing your own covetous desires. But oh wretchedness, you will not lay the fault upon the guilty, you justify the covetous, whom the Lord abhorreth, and condemn the innocent liberality of him, who giveth to all freely, and casteth none in the teeth. Another sort there are more viler than these, who of this great want, which if the Lord suffer to endure, will turn to extreme famine, yet they will spend more upon one to make him drunk, than upon one dozen of poor folks, These are the tipplers, ale-sellers, and drunkards, the very caterpillars of our country, who like the horse-leach are ever sucking, and never satisfied, and these only consume much that others should not be contented with it. Of these both cities and countries are replenished, and the magistrates suffer them with little or no punishment at all: but if the poor preachers rebuke the folly, their safety is endangered by this ravenous brood, who are not ashamed to give railing, yea and threatening speeches. And magistrates' servants are in greatest fault, who are not only partakers of this unseasonable drinking, but also deal privately with their masters, that those which are complained, might escape unpunished. Thus are the poor unrelieved, the country unprovided, the people unanswered, the wicked unpunished, the commonwealth unreformed, the godly uncomforted, and the judgments of God hailed down upon us, that we might be everlastingly confounded.

There went a certain man. Now are we come to the persons that traveled, which is the second part of this verse, which we showed you, ended in the second verse: they are first generally described in this verse, and after specially by name in the next verses: They are of two sorts, first the parents *Elimelech* and *Naomi*, secondly, the children *Mahlon* and *Chilion*, who are all described by the place from whence they went, *Bethlehem Judah*: it is so called because there was another *Bethlehem*, in the tribe of *Zebulon*: and this is that *Bethlehem* which in *Genesis* is called *Ephrath*, and therefore these persons are in these two verses, called *Ephrathites*, of the place, where afterward Christ was born. Then it is apparent by the book of *Joshua*, that the tribe of *Judah* had the fruitfullest possession, in all the land of *Canaan*, they were the greatest in number, the wisest in policy, the richest by inheritance: yet we see when the scourge of God came, the famine invaded their country, and crop into the walls of *Bethlehem*: and made the wealthiest among them to fly: yet this *Elimelech*, which was as appeareth by his consanguinity of the princes of the whole tribe, such

Josh. 19.15
Gen. 35.19
Matt. 2.1

Josh. 15

is the vehemency of the Lord's arrows, when he shooteth
them abroad, that if king *Ahab* were in his chariot, in the
midst of his host, yet one of them shall give him a mortal wound. The use of this doctrine is, to teach us that
if the Lord suffer his plague to continue, he will strike
down the chosen men in *Israel*, the chosen men in *England*: yea the noblest among us, who think themselves
in greatest security, can he easily bring to greatest misery. Therefore you whose heads the Lord hath advanced
over your brethren, look to your calling, for the voice
of the Lord shaketh as well the *cedars of Lebanon as the
little shrubs* in the wilderness of *Cades*: it is as easy with
him *to bind the nobles in chains, and the princes in links
of iron*, as to raise up the poor from the dunghill to the
throne. Did not his *darkness cover as well the court of
Pharaoh* as the country of *Egypt*? Was not the first born
of the king destroyed, as well as of the poor peasants of
the dwellings of *Ham*? Yea, when the Israelites were carried captive to *Babylon*, their king had his children slain
before his face, his own eyes put out, and after lead in a
chain, neither was he spared for his throne, nor you for
your dignity and wealth.

    Oh that you would therefore be warned of your
slippery estate, that you might avoid the heavy wrath
of God, when without respect of persons he shall judge
both quick and dead. Let not the lots of your inheritance deceive you, though their soil be as fruitful as this
of *Judah*, and your possessions never so great: he that in
one night destroyed all the fruits of *Egypt*, can also in
one hour blast your corn with dews, and consume your
possession with drought, for a fruitful land maketh he
barren, for the wickedness of them that dwell therein.

    Secondly, we note out of these words, when
he *took his wife and children with him*, an example of a
religious father, and a loving husband: he might (if he
had consulted with flesh and blood) done like our husbands in these days, which had rather in their wandering

Marginal references:
1 Kings 22.34

Psal. 29.6; 6.8

Psal. 149.8
Psal. 113.7

Exod. 10.22
Exod. 11.5

2 Kings 25

shift about for themselves, and leave wife and children in a sea of troubles, to sink or swim to some doubtful relief. But the godly in old time knew that their wives and children were as themselves, and as they were careful to cherish their own bodies, so they were mindful to nourish their own families. This the Lord at the first marriage that ever was, commanded that for a man's wife he should forsake father and mother, and they two shall be one flesh, as if he had said, parents must not hinder fellowship of wedlock, much less poverty or temporal wants: as the bark is joined to the tree, and the flesh to the bone, if one be without the other they both perish: so must husband and wife live and love together, unless they will be the slaughter slaves of their own destruction. We read of this practice in the scripture when *Abraham* by reason of a famine went down into *Egypt*, he took *Sara* his wife with him: when *Isaac* by reason of a famine went to *Abimelech* the king of *Gerar*, he took *Rebecca* his wife with him. How do we read of *Jacob*, how twice he sent into *Egypt* for all his family and the third time he went down with all his household, his son *Joseph* fed him five years of famine: yea the Apostle saith, that he is worse than an infidel that provideth not for his own family, and Christ going from his disciples asked them if they had wanted anything, and they answered, nothing. Against this point of doctrine there are many that offend: some that are married by their covetous parents, who respect nothing but wealth, are so matched, as if a vine were planted in the flowing of the sea, which prospereth best when the water is lowest, even so these are in sweetest fellowship when one is a thousand miles from the other. Others there are which in their marriages, please nothing but their eyes, which as old persons cannot see without spectacles, so they cannot find wives without the spectacle of beauty, and these love as long as beauty endureth, which is till they be sick, for sickness is the cutthroat of beauty. Some take wives and husbands,

Gen. 2.24

Gen. 12.18

Gen. 26.1

Gen. chapters
42-44

1 Tim. 5.8

Gen. 6

as fools find pearls, for as they cannot discern them from pebbles: so these are ignorant of all kind of duty towards one another. From hence proceedeth all the adulteries, which are daily committed, here ariseth the fountain of strife, contention, debate, jealousy, and also the unhappy blows which many give to their wives: hence it cometh, that so many gentlemen and others are seldom at home, but either beyond the sea in wars or in travel, which in their unmarried estate wanted nothing but wives, but now being married, want all things but wives. Hence it cometh, that they termed them by the odious titles of crosses, plagues, troubles and also as I have heard some say the causes of their undoing, whereas they may as well accuse the eye of his blindness, as their wives of their own willful misery: and to conclude, there is not one breach of love or kindness between them, but it springeth from these corruptions, which then were sowed, when they intended their marriage. But oh beloved, let not the godly be drawn away with the crooked conversation of these contentious persons, but let them be armed with the forenamed examples of godly unity that as their troubled days were eased in the joy of their own love, so let our miseries be relieved which you suffer in wedlock, with your comfortable agreement in Christian society, for so saith *Solomon*, Let thy fountain be blessed, and rejoice with the wife of thy youth: and thus much of this Prov. 5.18 second doctrine.

Thirdly, by this we may note that the godly are oppressed when the wicked have abundance: here we see the Israelites which were the Church of God had a famine, but the Moabites, to whom this man descended being a cursed generation, incestuous Gentiles, had plenty and abundance, for else *Elimelech* would not have gone thither to be relieved. This may seem a strange thing that the godly should be oppressed with famine, when worldlings and heathens shall wallow in their wealth. Of these *David* speaketh. I have seen the wicked strong and

Psal. 37.35
Psal. 17.14
Psal. 73.12

Psal. 73.4

Job 21.7
Jer. 12.1

Matt.
25.42,43
Matt. 8.20

Heb. 11.36-38

John 15.19

John 16.20

spreading himself like a bay tree. And in another place, They are enclosed in their own fat: And again he saith, They have their portion in this life, whose bellies thou fillest with thy hid treasure, their children have enough, and leave the rest of their substance to their children. And in another place, there are no bands in their death, but they are lusty and strong, they are not in trouble like other men: and a little after, these are the wicked, yet prosper they always and increase in riches. The very like you may hear in *Job*, and in the prophet *Jeremiah*. But of the righteous he saith and often crieth out of their afflictions, their sorrows and nakedness, their hunger and misery, all the day long are they appointed as sheep to the slaughter, yea, our Savior Christ pronounceth himself in his members, poor, hungry, naked, harborless, thirsty, and imprisoned, the foxes have holes and the birds of the air have nests, but the son of man hath not where to rest his head. And the author of the Epistle to the Hebrews, saith of the godly, Some are stoned, some cut asunder, some slain with the sword, some wandering abroad in goat's skins and sheep skins, destitute, oppressed, evil entreated, of whom the world was not worthy, wandering in deserts, in the mountains, in dens and caves of the earth. Judge now I beseech you, between the outward estate of the godly and the wicked, are they not contrary? That which of the world is condemned, is of the Lord commended; yet I beseech you my brethren, be not terrified from godliness, but rather strengthened in your profession. Then will you say, tell us the cause of all this inequality. Our savior answereth it very well, *You are not* (saith he) *of the world, if you were of the world, the world would love his own*: and *David* saith, that their portion is only in this life, but Christ saith, our reward shall be great in heaven: and again, *you shall weep and lament but the world shall rejoice, but your sorrow shall be turned to joy, like a woman that rejoiceth at the birth of her son*, so as a woman in travail hath no ease till a son is come into the world, neither must we look for any rest till our souls are delivered out of the womb of the body into the kingdom of heaven. Our savior compareth us to the *fruitful vine*, which doth not only abide frost, snow, storm and heat, but also at the gathering time is broken off that the grapes might be reached. The gold must be tried in the furnace, the silver fined in the fire, the wheat purged in the floor, and before it be meat for man, is also ground in the mill, so must we be proved in affliction, fined in persecution, and crushed to pieces, under the burden of our own miseries, that we may be made pre-pared bread for the Lord his own spending.

Why then doth the Lord make such large prom-ises to his Church of plenty, seeing it endureth continual poverty? I answer, the Church of God must be consid-ered after two sorts: the first as it is cleansed in the blood of Christ, and washed pure from all outward and notori-ous offences, unto which estate pertain all those outward promises of liberality in the Scripture. The second is the declined estate, or corrupted condition of everyone in the Church, even unto the world's end: unto this per-tain all the punishments, persecutions, and tribulations, which the godly endure: which the Lord sendeth upon them, that he might by little and little scour us from our transgressions, and weary us with the miseries of this life, that we might the more earnestly desire the life to come, for the Lord doth here scourge us that we should not be condemned with the world. Examples of these are most plentiful in the old Testament of the Church of the Jews, and for as much as this perfection of the church being once lost, is like broken glass, which can never be soldered again: so the Church shall never attain those promises in this life, but they are all referred to the life to come, where shall be no hunger, thirst, nakedness, pov-erty, travail, famine, or sorrow, but all tears being wiped from the eyes of the faithful, they shall then rest from their labors, and receive many thousand times, for every

Ruth Chapter 1. verses 1-6

affliction which they here endured, eternal felicity in the presence of Christ, when all worldlings shall be burned with unquenchable fire.

Fourthly, in that they went down to the wicked Moabites and there tarried, we note that it is lawful for the godly in the time of necessity, to crave help or relief of the very enemies of God, so they be not polluted with their superstitions. For the proof hereof we have the former examples of *Abraham* in *Egypt*, of *Isaac* in *Gerar*, of *Moses* in *Midian*, when he fled from *Pharaoh*, of the spies of *Israel* which lodged in the house of *Rahab*. So did the Lord command *Joseph* in a dream, to take *Mary* and Christ, and to go into *Egypt*, to save Christ from *Herod*. So did Christ ask water of the woman of *Samaria* when he was weary, with infinite other testimonies, which the godly may find in the Scripture. But the use of this point is, that although the Lord hath permitted this liberty, yet we must take heed of two things: first, that we never receive any thing with condition of Religion, or doing the least thing against their own knowledge, for idolaters desire nothing more than to win men's souls to the Devil. Secondly, we may not go unto such when we may be eased of the godly, for it is free necessity that constraineth, not necessary liberty that permitteth: By this we learn what to judge of them which are daily at talk and table with the wealthiest Papists, Atheists, and carnal profane persons, who care not for the loss of Religion, so they may gain by their friendship, esteeming more the feathers of a rich man, though ungodly, than the blood of a poor godly Christian: they use them too commonly for wealth and commodity, not for need and necessity: these are seasoned in the leaven of unrighteousness, baked in the oven of hypocrisy, and shall one day be burned in the fire of everlasting destruction, for they which for gain love their company in this life, shall be partakers of their rewards in the life to come.

Fifthly, by this we note, that the Lord doth ever

Gen. 12.7;
26.1
Exod. 2.22
Josh. 2.1
Matt. 2.13
John 4.7

provide for his faithful servants in all their miseries. We see here, these Jews satisfied with plenty in *Moab*, that were almost famished with penury at home: therefore saith *David, The Lord knoweth the days of upright men, and their inheritance shall be perpetual; they shall not be confounded in the perilous time and in the days of famine they shall have enough.* Most notable is that speech of *Joseph* to his brethren; telling them, that God sent him before to provide victuals for them in that seven years famine. So he stirred up *Obadiah* which hid fifty prophets in one cave, and fifty in another, feeding them with bread and water, during the time of famine. He provided for *Elijah* first by the ravens, and after by the widow of *Zarephath,* multiplying her oil and meal, for *Elijah,* herself, and her son. So he sent *Elisha* to warn the Shunammite woman of the seven years famine, that she should fly for herself, and live where she could. I might be infinite in this point, to declare the bountiful liberality of the Lord, who ever provideth one remedy or other, to satisfy the continual prayers of them that fear him: for we may say as *Paul* saith, We are afflicted, yet we are not in distress, in poverty, yet not overcome of poverty, we are persecuted, and yet not forsaken, cast down but we perish not. This is the merciful kindness of him who giveth food to the young ravens that call upon him, and maketh his sun to rise and shine both upon good and bad. Yea we our own selves have experience in our own country, for we which were wont with our abundance to help other nations about us, yet now in our want we are succored by them. How should the poor in many places be relieved, if it were not for the corn which cometh oversea: therefore as the seven plentiful years in *Egypt,* succored the seven dear years: even so the Lord relieveth the misery of one time by the multitude of another. Therefore my brethren, let us not say, the Lord hath forgotten, for although our desires be not satisfied, yet our bodies are not famished; yea the Lord testifieth that he is as unwill-

Psal. 37.18,19

Gen. 45.4-8

I Kings 18.13

1 Kings 17.4,10

2 Kings 8.1

2 Cor. 4.8,9

Ruth Chapter 1. verses 1-6

ing to punish our deserts, and utterly to deprive us of our maintenance, as we are to depart from our pleasant pastime or dainty belly cheer. Poor *Lazarus* that was not relieved with the rich man's crumbs, yet was he comforted with the licking of the dogs: so much doth the Lord affect liberality and kindness, that he commandeth brute beasts to execute his goodness upon his servants.

Now let us proceed to the second part of this Scripture, and seeing we have brought these strangers to their Inn at *Moab*, let us hear their entertainment, and those things that happened unto them after they came thither, for the parts we have in the beginning set down, which I trust you remember, and therefore we will [*go*] to the words.

And they continued there. This is as much to say, as they found entertainment answerable to their expectation: they had liberty of residence granted, and obtained a place for their dwelling in safety. Where we first note the gentleness or humanity of these heathen Moabites, who had learned by nature this point of courtesy, which is friendly to succor poor harborless strangers: and no doubt but he that watcheth the descending of sparrows on the ground, directed this journey to *Moab*, for the accomplishing of his own counsel, and prepared the hearts of these people, with favor to relieve them. For as before he guided the journey of *Abraham's* servant to the city of *Nahor*, where *Rebecca* was, and framed her answer according to his prayer: even so he conducted these to *Moab* where *Ruth* was, and tempered the hearts of the wicked to give these pilgrims a dwelling place among them. By the which we are taught what friendship or love we owe to strangers which are come among us, yea though we know not the purpose of their hearts, yet we must do good unto them for the proportion of their bodies, that is, because they are men. This is not a law written only in the book of God, but imprinted in the very nature of every one. We see these Moabites do it by na-

Gen. 24.10

ture, and yet they had no religion in them, we know how
the king of *Egypt* gave commandment for *Abraham*, that
none should hurt him or any of his possessions. Read
but the Acts of the Apostles, you shall see how barbarous
nations received the church with courtesy, and some
upon their report believed the doctrine of Christ: nay,
the very brute beasts (if there be any truth in history,)
have observed this part, to love men as men. *Romulus* is
said to be nursed of a she-Wolf, *Hieron* King of *Syracuse*
by bees, *Semiramis* of birds, *Habides* King of *Tartesius* of
a Hind, *Cyrus* the *Persian* of a she-Dog, *Pelias* of a Mare,
Paris of a Bear, and *Aegisthus* of a she-Goat: These are
either true in the letter, or in the moral, that either beasts
or men never so savage, loved not only their own kind,
but even strangers because they were men. What shall
we then say to this beastlike behavior of many among us,
who will hardly permit poor Christian strangers to harbor among us; if it were not for that they are men, and
the children of *Adam* like ourselves, yet because they call
upon the name of Christ, being of the household of faith,
let us do good unto them. But some will say, what shall
we do unto them if they will not join with us in our religion? I answer, none must be of *Abraham's family but
those which will be circumcised*, that is, none must dwell
with thee, but such as will be of thy profession. Yet thou
mayest for humanity or courtesy receive a Turk or a Pagan, a Jew or an Infidel, Papist or Heretic, to talk or table
for a night or a small time, so thou keep thy self from his
pollutions. *So did Jacob feast his idolatrous father* in law
and kinsmen when they pursued him to the mount of
Gilead, with purpose to hurt him, and our Savior Christ
biddeth us to feed our enemies and to give them drink
if they thirst. So did *Elisha*, to the host of Syrians, who
being sent to take him, yet when he had taken them and
lead them to the City, he suffered the king to do them
no hurt, but refreshed them with meat and drink, and
sent them away in safety. For our outward courteous

Gen. 17.10,13

Gen. 31.34

2 Kings 6.23

Ruth Chapter 1. verses 1-6

receiving of infidels is like coals of fire, to draw them in love with our inward religion. We know how the Lord commanded the Jews to be good unto strangers, because Luke 10.30,37 they were strangers in *Egypt*. We know how the Lord commendeth the strange Samaritan beyond the priest and the Levite, because he succored the poor wounded Jew, which had fallen among thieves. And truly we ourselves may be strangers in other Countries, therefore let us do good unto them now that we may receive the like of them again, for this is the law and the prophets.

Then Elimelech: when they had escaped one danger, they fell into another sorrow, when by the merciful kindness of the Lord they were jointly come together into *Moab*, and there quietly seated, escaped the arrows of famine, by the hand of God, the father of the family, the nearest and dearest unto them, dieth in plenty.

Where we note the very lot of all the godly, namely, that the end of one sorrow is the beginning of another, like the drops of rain distilling from the top of a house, when one is gone another followeth, like a ship upon the sea, being on the top of one wave, presently is cast down to the foot of another, like the seed which being spread by the sower is haunted by the fouls, being green and past their reach, is endangered by frost and snow, being passed the winter's hurt, by beasts in summer, being ripe is cut with the sickle, threshed with flail, purged in the floor, ground in the mill, baked in the oven, chewed in the teeth, and consumed in the stomach. This made *David* say, *Great are the troubles of the righteous, but the Lord delivereth out of all.* But be not discomfited O my brethren, for through many afflictions must we enter into the kingdom of heaven, and by affliction we are made like to the son of God. But to the matter. We see here their sweet fellowship is prevented by death, which indeed is the end of all worldly friendship. This is a good lesson for all worldlings to remember, how the Lord disappointeth all their purposes, and overthroweth

Psal. 34.19

Acts 14.22
Heb. 2.10

their counsels, more vainer than vanity. The merchant having obtained his bank, promiseth rest and security to himself; the husbandman having gathered his fruits, never doubteth but he shall spend them, and provideth for more; the Gentleman coming to his lands, thinketh his revenues and pleasant life, will endure alway: like the apostles when Christ was transfigured in the mount; presently they would build tabernacles of residence; but as the cloud came betwixt them and heaven, and bereaved them of their purpose: even so suddenly will death come and deprive you of your profits, call the merchant from his bank, the husbandman from his farm, the Gentleman from his lands, the Noble man from his honor, the Prince from his kingdom, the Lady from her pleasures, as this *Elimelech* was suddenly from wife and children.

Matt. 17.4

Secondly, by these words we note the goodness of God toward both the dead man, and also wife and children: for no doubt but they all desired, to be settled in some place or other; and here the Lord suffereth the husband with wife and family, to be quietly seated before their separation. He might have called him away in his journey, as he was coming, and then oh how would it have grieved both him and them: him, to leave a poor comfortless widow and children behind, without dwelling or maintenance, for home again they could not return, by reason of the famine, and to go forth on the journey without a guide, was like as if a ship were set on the sea without a mariner. Therefore in suffering them all to come safe to *Moab*, and there to live till they got favor and dwellings, and also maintenance, was a singular favor of the Lord towards both; that howsoever they were afflicted, yet they were not left destitute. And this teacheth us, that in all our afflictions we receive especial blessings at the hands of God, for this end that we should not be swallowed up of sorrow. There is no sickness but it is either short and sharp, or else tedious and light, if it

Rom. 2.7

Ruth Chapter 1. verses 1-6

be sudden and very extreme, the continuance of it is but short, if it be long and tedious, it hath some time of ease, some time of more quietness, so that in all our miseries we may say with the godly, If the Lord had not been on our side we had been swallowed quick: he tempereth the suddenest showers with least continuance, and the longest winter hath many fair days. Be strong therefore my brethren and sisters, for sure the Lord will establish your hearts, fear not all the dangers of the world: though as many troubles compass us, as there were *Syrians* about *Elisha*, yet lift up your eyes, there are many thousands more with us than are against us. He that suffereth none to be tempted above their power, will not lay more upon us than we are able to bear: but as he wrestled with *Jacob* with one hand, he held him up with the other, so though he afflict with one arm, he shall sustain with the other.

Which took them wives. Now we are come to the children, and the holy Ghost expresseth the friendship which they received of the Moabites after the death of the father, which is, their marriage with their daughters: Where first of all it may be demanded in this place, seeing the Lord forbiddeth all strange marriages, whether these sons of *Elimelech* did not offend against this law: we know that the unmarried are at liberty, to marry whom they will, only in the Lord: now the Moabites were heathen people, and strangers from God his covenant, and therefore these persons married not in the Lord. To which, I answer briefly, that the Lord forbiddeth marriages with infidels, for two causes, first when we may lawfully and without danger join ourselves to them that are godly, and will presumptuously for worldly respects, run to the daughters of men: secondly, that we should refrain from all such marriages where we are like to be drawn away from our profession, as we see in *Solomon.* But these sons of *Elimelech* offended in none of these. For first they were now strangers and had no other choice, and secondly it appeareth by that which

Psal. 124.3

2 Kings 6.20

Deut. 7.3,4

1 Kings 11.4

Lecture 1

followeth that they were both well persuaded in Religion. For as *Moses* married a Midianitish woman, and was blameless, and *Salmon* the son of *Nahshon*, the prince of the Jews, married with *Rahab*, (which both were the parents of *Boaz*, mentioned hereafter) and was faultless, nay it was done by the permission of *Joshua*, and therefore lawful; even so these strange Jews moved with the same reasons, chose the like marriages. But some will say, the Jews which had married strange wives, in the captivity of *Babylon*, might have alleged this against *Nehemiah*, that they were in captivity, and had no women to take but strangers. To the which I answer, if they had so objected, they had spoken untruth, and so would *Nehemiah* have replied, for there were Jewish women captives as well as men; and further I say, that this their marrying of strange women, was the cause of the destruction of many Jewish women, who being forsaken of their own people, must of necessity be married to Infidels, which could never return to *Jerusalem*. Again, these sons of *Elimelech* by their marriage, gained greater favor of the Moabites; but especially the hand of God was in it, that when they both should be dead, *Ruth* might be married to *Boaz*, and be made a mother of Christ.

Exod. 2.21
Neh. 9.1-3

  First therefore we note out of this, that as these Moabites were kind to the father in giving him residence, so they were loving to the sons in giving them wives: a notable example of humane courtesy, given unto us by these heathens, that we with the like favor should entertain strangers. But many covetous parents in these days, which would be accounted Christians, are so far from doing this unto strangers, that they will hardly do the like to their natural countrymen, rather imitating that ungodly *Laban*, who made merchandise of his daughters, than godly *Caleb* in bestowing them on *Othniel* be he never so poor, if they have deserved well of Church or commonwealth, rather desiring to advance their posterity in the glory of the world, than to discharge their

Gen. 31.15
Judg. 1.13

duties in the presence of God. They will say they aim at this, the fear of the Lord, when as if they had matched their children with Turks or Infidels they would not or could not be more profane than those, saving only these are outwardly obedient to a Christian prince, that they might with more liberty follow their licentious Atheism, when as peradventure the other would not so dissemble: so that goods, and not goodness, the world and not the word, earthly vanity, and not heavenly felicity, our parents aim at. But what shall we say to them that force their children not only to match against their minds, but to marry with public Papists and known Recusants, only for things of this life. Truly, I answer, that it is against these that the Lord speaketh, when he saith, You shall not take their daughters to your sons, nor give your daughters to their sons, but as they have married without the counsel of the Lord, in murdering the fruits of their own bodies, even so they shall prosper without the blessing of God, in confounding the souls of their own posterity: and as the children of the Jews which were born of strange women, were separated from the new founded Temple, even so these shall be excluded from the everlasting *Jerusalem*.

Deut. 7.3

And they tarryed there. This time of their abode in *Moab*, signifieth the great continuance of this misery. First, for the Jews at home, who endured famine: and secondly, for these abroad, which lived among Infidels ten years together. It is a fearful thing with us that we have but one year's famine, oh then we think that the Lord hath forgotten to be merciful. But we have heard already of famines of great continuance, that in *Joseph's* time was seven years together, that in *David's* time was three years and a half, and this misery lasted ten years together. Wherein many godly persons did patiently endure it. How is it then that for this little dearth among us, there are so great exclamations for corn and plenty, such horrible blasphemies against the Lord himself, saying: Shall this endure always? Was there ever any poor people thus afflicted? Is this the fruit of the Gospel? Are these the favors of God and his righteousness, in keeping his promise? with such like, too horrible to be suffered as if the Lord were not able to relieve us; or else were unjust in punishing our sins, how can that be, seeing he calleth for repentance and amendment, and then promiseth plenty and abundance? These saints endured some three, some seven, and other ten years' famine, and yet we say, was there ever such a people thus afflicted like to us with one year's dearth?

They were driven to wander abroad in their enemy's country for many years together; shall we then think it such a misery to go two or three miles for our corn? They adventured the loss of their lives, and we are afraid of the lessening or diminishing of our goods. And shall we yet say, there was never any people tormented like unto us? Yea, I add this, that even at this day there are people in the world, which scant in all their lives do eat any bread, but only the bark of trees, with some other unseasonable fish; others live on the roots of the earth, some on the fruits of trees. And what shall I say more, our wickedness is greater than our want, our sore is smaller than our sin, our transgressions have deserved to be punished with the scourge, and yet we are scarce corrected with the rod, our complaints are greater than our hurt, and our murmuring exceedeth our misery: therefore we have greater cause to tremble at that which hangeth over our heads, than to fear or cry for this which we already suffer, for it is hardly the beginning of sorrow.

So Mahlon and Chilion. Now when they were compassed about with the friends of their wives, which did promise security, then after a few years, spent in safety, the Lord called them away after their father. Where we see our former doctrine justified, that the end of one sorrow was the beginning of another. When they were most like to continue, then they gave over, as it were, in the arms of their wives, and the sight of their aged mother, to whom no doubt, this was the greatest grief of all other, that now being left destitute both of husband and children, she should without comfort live with the Moabites, and without joy return again unto her own Country, as a bird robbed of her young ones. Yet seeing this is our worldly lot still to endure misery, let us set both our shoulders under the burden, if it be too heavy, let us flee to the finisher of our faith with zealous and earnest prayers, desiring him either to ease or to remove his hand. But seeing we have spoken of this before, this shall suffice at this time to serve for a remembrance.

Then she arose. When her friends were departed, and her self left comfortless, yet the Lord remembered her, for even then came the rumor unto her, that the famine was ceased in Jewry, that the Lord had visited the sickness of his people, and restored the plenty of the earth again, and therefore it is time for her to be hasting home again, for here the holy Ghost setting down her return and the cause of the same, showeth that it was even then when her children were dead, for what should a godly woman live there, where were none that could strengthen her in the ways of the Lord, but rather provoke her to embrace infidelity? And again, even at that time when she was most comfortless for the loss of her children, came this rumor unto her of the restoring of her Country, so that now *Naomi*, thou art here in *Moab* a sorrowful pilgrim, go home to thy Country and be a joyful inhabitant: indeed thy children are dead, but thou shall have greater comfort of thy ancient acquaintance. What knowest thou, but now the Lord hath called thee to consolation, whereas of late, thou mightest think, he had wrought thy confusion. By which we first of all note how the Lord watcheth to relieve and comfort in due time, as saith Saint *Paul*, God comforted me by the coming of *Titus* lest I should be swallowed of sorrow:

and this is the property of his Majesty, like a nurse to stand by his children, and let them awake, but take them up as soon as they cry. He suffered *Peter* to sink, but not to perish, *Paul* to be imprisoned with *Silas*, and to be whipped, but even then the earth quaked, and gave comfort to the prisoners. Oh what Angel's pen or tongue can express this goodness that ever bringeth good tidings in the midst of sorrow? When my soul fainted within me (saith *Jonah*) I remembered the Lord, and my prayer came unto him in his holy Temple. My heart and my flesh do fail me, but the Lord is my portion forever. Consider this I beseech you, and believe verily, that you shall have some cause of comfort in the midst of sorrow, for if nothing else then these things must relieve us in all the sorrows of life (saith Saint *Augustine*) our love toward God, our godly devotion, our assured hope of mercy, and presence of the holy Ghost.

Jonah 2.7

Psal. 73.26

    By this we note, that the Lord deferreth to help till greatest necessity, even as he stayed the stroke of *Abraham* when he was at the very instant to cut off little *Isaac's* neck. So we read that when the king of *Assyria* had invaded the kingdom of *Hezekiah*, won his Cities, subdued his Country, conquered his people, and had not left him two thousand horsemen, and being destitute of all help, then the Lord raised up the king of *Ethiopia*, who called the Assyrians from the siege of *Jerusalem*. What shall I say of *Lazarus* raised from death? Of the deliverance of *Peter* out of the hands of *Herod*, the day before he should have been martyred? Of the shipwreck wherein *Paul* was, and yet not one of them were lost. And excellent is that of Christ, sleeping in the ship on a pillow, suffered his disciples to be so long tossed with the violence of the sea, till they cried out, Lord save, we perish, and then he awaked, rebuked the rage of the winds, and stilled the storms of the sea, and a peaceable calm followed. This is that preservative against desperation, which must stay our minds on the leisure of the

Gen 22.10,11

2 Kings 19.3

John 11.43

Acts 12.7,8
Acts 27.44

Matt. 8.25,26

Ruth Chapter 1. verses 1-6

Lord: we must not at the first look for our desires, but as *Abraham* and *Zacharias* were old before they had any children, and yet in the end the Lord promised and also performed, even so when we have least hope for obtaining of our desires, we most often receive them. For the Lord deferreth our requests for the trial of our faith and patience, that like as the *wheat corn groweth not, till it be dead,* even so his works do not answer our expectation, till they seem to us impossible: that as the most precious pearls are farthest brought, and longest in coming, when we have them we keep them more carefully: even so his excellent mercies, being with difficulty obtained should be esteemed more thankfully. Therefore be of good comfort, you that now sorrow, for you shall be comforted, you that now hunger for you shall be satisfied, you that now weep for you shall laugh; the Lord will shortly come, bear but a little and he will wipe away all tears from your eyes, and then oh how happy shall they be which have trusted in him.

1 Cor. 15.36

That the Lord had visited. This is the last part of this Scripture, being the reason that moved her to return into her Country. Oh it is as if the holy Ghost had said. The Lord looked upon the afflicted estate of his people, and supplied their want of food. To visit, in the Scriptures is taken two ways, first to punish, as when God saith in the second commandment, that he will visit the sin of the fathers upon the children, unto the third and fourth generation: secondly it signifieth sometimes to pardon or to show mercy, as that of *Zacharias.* The Lord hath visited and redeemed his people, that is, he hath showed mercy in redeeming his people. In this later sense it must be taken in this place. Now the word properly signifieth to go to see, and is referred to them that are sick, which by a metaphor is applied to sin, for sin is the sickness of the soul, and is very fitly applied to punishments sent of God, for when he scourgeth he cometh to see, as he said of *Sodom*: I will go down and

Exod. 20.5
Exod. 32.34

Luke 1.68

Hos. 4.9
Matt. 25.43

see whether it be altogether so, if not that I may know; for he cometh to see us in our miseries, as a physician to his patient, whom he hath first or before made sick with his potion or corrosive, and bringeth a wholesome or speedy remedy with him. Where we note the miserable estate of men in the sickness of sin, or under any of God his judgments, as dearth and famine, war or pestilence; that even as sick persons are not able to help or comfort themselves, or to take any pleasure in their wealth, though they possessed the whole world: so if we be oppressed in the punishment of our iniquities, we cannot or may not rest in ourselves but in the Lord our Physician and Watchman: for if the Lord shut who can open, if he wound who can heal, if he curse who can bless? he that hath the bond or writing must discharge the debt, and the Lord that stroke must bind us up again. Oh my dearly beloved brethren, now are the children come to the birth, and there is no strength to be delivered, for this is the day of tribulation. Now are we in the balance of the Lord either to visit our offences with his famine, or to scourge our sins with the rod of dearth, if either of both continue, what end can we look for but the pining of our bodies, and the consuming of our souls? Whither shall we go to escape the judgments of the Lord, we are already clogged with his irons and fast bolted, if we strive to shake them off, what do we else but rebel against the power of the highest? if they continue, we are but miserable prisoners and can look for nothing but the fearful day of execution. Let us turn to the Judge before that day, and send up our prayers as our dearest friends unto his son, that he may visit us with the forgiveness of our sins, that he may sue out our pardon, and be entreated for our transgressions, that we may obtain the release of our present misery, the removing of his judgments, the increase of the fruits of the earth, that he would visit us in giving our daily bread, to satisfy the poor with his goodness, and give us all the bread of this life, to banish

Isa. 37.3

Ruth Chapter 1. verses 1-6

our dearth, and the bread of life to escape damnation. And thus much for this time. Now let us give praise to God.

The Second Lecture

7   *Wherefore she departed out of the place where she was, and her two daughters in law with her, and they went on their way to return unto the land of Judah.*

8   *Then* Naomi *said unto her two daughters in law, Go, return each of you unto her own mother's house: the Lord show favor unto you as you have done with the dead, and with me.*

9   *The Lord grant that either of you may find rest in the house of her husband: and when she had kissed them, they lift up their voice and wept.*

10   *And they said unto her, surely we will return with thee unto thy people.*

11   *But* Naomi *said: turn again my daughters, for what cause will you go with me? are there any more sons in my womb that they may be your husbands?*

12   *Turn again my daughters: go your way; for I am too old to have an husband: if I should say I had hope, and if I had an husband this night, yea if I had borne sons.*

13   *Would ye tarry for them, till they were of age? would you be deferred for them from taking any husbands? nay my daughters, for it grieveth me much for your sakes, that the hand of the Lord is gone out against me.*

14   *Then they lift up their voice and wept again, and* Orpah *kissed her mother in law and departed, but* Ruth *abode with her still:*

In these words is expressed how *Naomi* departed out of *Moab*, to go into the land of Jewry. The words divide themselves into two parts: the first is the journey, in this seventh verse. The second part is the communication, in the next seven verses. The journey is described by the persons, which were *Naomi* and her two daughters in law.

The communication which they had by the way principally consisteth in the persuasion of *Naomi* to her daughters, that they should return back again: and first she speaketh in the eighth and ninth verses. Her speech containeth two parts, the first is the counsel she giveth to them, in these words, *Go return*. The second is her prayer for them, which is double, or consisting of two parts. The first is general, in these words, *The Lord show favor*, to the end of that verse. The second is special in the ninth verse, in these words, *The Lord grant you that you may find rest, etc.* Which being spoken, they lift up their voice and wept, being sorrowful for this news, and therefore they answer in the tenth verse that they will return with her to her people. In the next verse to the fourteenth, *Naomi* confirmeth her former counsel by weighty arguments, which are expressed in her questions, and they all are taken from their second marriages.

The first is in the eleventh verse: that she had no more sons to be their husbands, either already born; or which hereafter might be born, therefore their labor would be but lost if they went with her; seeing she could provide them no more husbands. This is amplified in the eleventh and twelfth verse.

The second reason is in the thirteenth verse, that although she had now children born, yet it would be too long to stay for them till they were of age: much more she having none born: and lest her daughters should think she cared not for them, she addeth in the thirteenth verse, that it grieved her more for their sakes, that is, the love she beareth to them, than for her own, but it is the hand of God, and therefore she is contented. Lastly in the fourteenth verse is declared the effect of this communication, what it wrought, for *Orpah* departed as a woman overcome by these worldly persuasions, but *Ruth* abideth still with her. Of these let us briefly speak in order as they lie, by the permission and assistance of the almighty.

And she arose. This journey of *Naomi* to her own people, as in the former verse we heard, was undertaken when she heard, that the Jews were delivered from their famine; so it is more commendable if we consider the objections, lets and hindrances, that may be made against it. First, the way was very long between *Moab* and *Bethlehem*, which might terrify an old woman: but if any say that it was no longer to return than it was to come down: I answer, when she came thither she had her husband and children to bear her company, but now she was to return alone, and therefore the journey would be the more tedious. Secondly, the consideration of her age might have hindered this travel, for her withered body would be wearied in the journey; and what knew she but that she might die in the journey, and that among strangers, who peradventure would have no regard of her age, honor, or honesty: again, no doubt, but she had some wealth in *Moab*, which of necessity she must be constrained to leave behind her, and forever to lose, with many other such grievous thoughts, which might encumber her troubled breast. But notwithstanding all these, she proceedeth on her intended journey, committing herself to the preservation of God in all places, who she knew would give her some comforts for the adversity she had endured.

Ruth Chapter 1. verses 7-15

Where first of all we note the duty of all the godly, if with *Naomi* they are far from the company of the faithful, or compelled to depart from them upon the like occasion, as famine, poverty, persecution and such like, that when occasion shall be given, they return with *Naomi* to the temple, to the people, to the ark, to the gospel of the Lord. For as God said to *Elijah*, when he was in mount *Horeb*, What doest thou here *Elijah*? even so he speaketh to all persecuted pilgrims, and poor true Christians which are at the gates and tables of carnal Atheists, the enemies of Christ, What do you here? there is corn and bread, in *Israel* again, the Church, your brethren, have now received maintenance: return to the place of sacrifice: they that worship must worship God at *Jerusalem*: the mountains of *Samaria* are no place of God his worship, but at *Shiloh* is his tabernacle and his dwelling in *Sion*. This we may read practiced of the ancient fathers long ago. When *Moses* had dwelt forty years in *Midian*, then the Lord bid him return to his poor brethren again. *David* being in great security with the king of *Gath*, yet the Lord would not suffer him there to dwell. And as the Israelites might not dwell with the Egyptians, but must go into the land of *Canaan*, so the Lord's people must abide but where he appointeth them. And as the *Shunammite* woman, after the seven years famine returneth to her wonted dwelling, even so must not we linger with recusant Papists, Atheists, swearers, blasphemers, and open despisers of God his ministers and ministry.

Secondly, we may note in this verse a godly example of holy obedience and commendable friendship, for here the daughters in law are going with their mother to the land of Jewry. Where, either for religion or love, which they bear to their mother in law, they forsake both Country and friends to go with her. Was it not sufficient for them to take strangers for their husbands, who being dead, and they at liberty, but they must go from their

1 Kings 19.9

John 4.22

Exod. 3.10
1 Sam. 27.9

1 Kings 8

own kindred, with a mother in law: was it not well for them to abide with her so long as she would abide with them, and was able to maintain them, but now when she had forsaken her dwelling and wealth, must they accompany her in her poverty. Surely it seemeth, that as *Paul* saith to the Corinthians, he sought not theirs but them, so these women desire rather the presence than the wealth of *Naomi*, O excellent obedience and godly friendship, worthy to be registered with eternal memory! They had not past ten years space to learn this point of Religion that it is true friendship to love at all times, whether it be in wealth or prosperity, in want or adversity. We have many old professors in Christianity, which have not profited thus much in twenty, thirty, or forty years profession. They say to their neighbors as *Joram's* messenger said to *Jehu*, Is it peace? so they ask, is it wealth? is it riches? is it honor? or is it favor of Prince or Gentleman that dwelleth near them? As if they should say, if thou be wealthy, thou shalt have my friendship, but if thou be poor, then as *Nabal* answered *David's* messenger, what is *David*? and what is the son of *Jesse*? so, what art thou? I care not for thy company, get thee from my presence, I can abide on such beggars. Is this the fruit of Religion, condemned of the heathens, abhorred of the brute beasts, hated of the wicked, and yet practiced of or among Christians? surely I had rather be a friendly Moabite than a thousand such carnal Israelites: yea, the very civil honest men among us will rise in judgment against us in this point: they will live without hypocrisy, we dissemble in all vain glory, our friendship is like the company of the Dolphin, if it be fair weather, she will never be from the ship, but if a storm come, she withdraweth her fellowship. Away with this most beastlike, yea rather unnatural smiling upon prosperity, but grim and strange countenances upon the afflicted, either love at all times, which is *Solomon's* friendship, or love at no time, which is *Satan's* amity.

Ruth Chapter 1. verses 7-15

Prov. 17.17

1 Kings 19.17

Prov. 17.17

Then said Naomi. The counsel that this godly *Naomi* giveth unto her daughters, is simply that they should return to their own parents, as if she should say unto them, Be advised my daughters, some will think you very unnatural, that you forsake your own mothers, to go with me your mother in law, and forsake your own Country to go unto a strange place: the journey is long and tedious, you are tender and weak, better return before we be far gone: to be wise too late, is to repent too soon, care not for me, the Lord will enable me to go as well alone as with your company. Where we first of all note, a most godly example of mother-like love and godly charity, for if *Naomi* had gone alone, it could not choose but be far more dangerous than with company, and none could receive any disadvantage by her counsel, beside herself, yet we see she careth not for her own commodity, so she might procure the welfare of her daughters. She might have friendly accepted their own proffers, and if any dangers had come, she might have said, she did not entreat them, it was their own up-seeking, yet she dealeth more plainly with them in telling them the danger, and as before, they desired more her company than her wealth, even so now she loveth their company well, but counselleth their safety better. This is the duty of all that fear God, as the Apostle saith, *Let every man seek another's and not their own good*; this was so dear unto the Lord himself, that he commanded by *Moses, that if their neighbor's cattle went astray*, they should bring them home again. Doth the Lord take care for oxen, and not much more for men? But oh where is the careful keeping of this commandment? now every man saith, every man for himself and God for us all: but rather, how shall the Lord be for us, when we are not for one another? Now this wicked world is full of deceitful bargains, now men's houses and lands are bought over the heads of their young and unthrifty sons: now men's farms and leases are forestalled by others, that they

1 Cor. 10.24

Deut. 22.1,4

themselves cannot enjoy them: such buying, and selling, cozening and deceiving, borrowing and lending upon usury, taking of fines, raising of rents, undoing of the poor, and thrusting the weakest to the wall, as if charity were forgotten, and the precept of the Lord had never been written, and finally, as though all were our own which we can get in our handling. Many give counsel like lawyers for their fees, but few like *Naomi*, for their conscience. They lick their own fingers, as the proverb goeth, but few will cast any salt on their neighbor's meat, if they can get advantages of their neighbors upon statutes, they sue the extremity, as if they were infidels. They will not say as *Abraham* to *Lot*; If thou take the right Gen. 13.9 hand, I will take the left: that is, my brother my neighbor take thou the choice, I wish not thy wrong, ask counsel, and let there be no occasion of strife between us: men will hardly give either coat or cloak in these days, by suffering injury, they will rather take both, and although they think it better to give alms than to take, yet they had rather take bribes and rewards than to give. Oh my beloved, let us at the length be ruled by the counsel of the Lord, and esteem better of others than of ourselves, Phil. 2.3 help as many as we can, but hinder none. Cursed are they that lay stumbling blocks before the blind, and give Lev. 19.14 evil counsel for their own advantage.

Secondly, by these words we may gather to whom widows belong, their husbands being dead, namely, to *their own mother's house*: that is, to their parents: if the parents of their husbands will not provide for them. Therefore is it that the Lord commanded, if the daughter of a priest were a widow, and returned to her Lev. 22.13 father's house, having no children, she might eat of the peace offerings of the children of *Israel*. And *Paul* giveth 1 Tim. 5.16 charge to the godly in his time, that if any of their kindred were a widow, of their own costs they should provide for her, and not charge the church. This is a profitable doctrine both for parents and children: for parents that they be careful to bestow their children in godly marriages, where they may be well provided for, neither must they then cast them off, but if need be receive them to their own families again: for children, seeing the Lord doth thus commend their welfare, and careth for their widowhood, as well as their virginity, that they cast not themselves away upon every one they can love, without the consent of their parents, whereby they impoverish their friends, undo themselves, and bring a woeful curse upon their innocent posterity. Thirdly and lastly, by this counsel of *Naomi* we gather, that if the father be dead, we owe the same duty to our mother which is alive, for she saith, to her own mother's house. And *Solomon* saith, it is foolishness or wickedness to despise one's mother. The Lord curseth him in the Law, that despiseth or curseth his mother as well as his father. In the fifth commandment he commandeth to honor the mother equally, or as well as the father. Many think they may be more bold with their mothers, because they are more tender over them, than with their fathers, but the godly must know, that upon pain of God's heavy curse, they must follow the counsel of their mothers with *Jacob*, as well as the advice of their fathers with *Esau*. And the Lord doth often clothe the weaker vessel with more honor, that thereby we might learn to continue our obedience to our parents.

The Lord show. In these words the general blessing or prayer is contained, which *Naomi* maketh for her two daughters, where she prayeth to God for his favor upon them as they showed favor to her, and to their dead husbands, as if she should say, I wish no more acceptable blessing upon you, than you have done to others.

Where we briefly note, that our duties which we discharge to parents or husbands, are as pledges before the Lord to do good unto us. This maketh him delight to pour his blessings upon us, when he seeth we dutifully walk in his presence, and it provoketh those to whom we offer this obedience, to pour out their prayers for us into the ears of the almighty: even so the neglect of our duties, the contempt of our parents, and the disobedience to our superiors procureth both the curse of God and them, not only in this life, but also in the life to come. This was ever observed like the *Talion* law, that goodness procureth goodness, and evil begetteth evil, like as birds breed birds, and fishes fishes: for he that soweth to the flesh, shall of the flesh reap corruption, but he that soweth to the spirit, shall of the spirit reap life everlasting. Be not deceived my beloved, such as you sow, such shall you reap. *Ahab* did spill the blood of *Naboth*, therefore the dogs did eat both his and *Jezebel's*, for such measure as we mete to other, shall be measured to us again: for receiving a Prophet, we shall have a Prophet's reward, for hurting a Prophet, we shall have the Lord's displeasure: *Phocas* the greatest benefactor to the Pope, slew his Master *Mauritius*: the like fell upon him by *Heraclius*, who burned him alive, and took away his Empire: so let all wicked men expect for cruelty, cruelty: for hatred, malice: for wrong, extortion: for earthly evil, spiritual misery. But let the righteous go on in goodness, for not only the loss of their houses, lands and revenues shall be recompensed, but even a cup of cold water shall be rewarded.

The Lord. These words are her special prayer for her daughter's marriage, and are thus in effect, I can pray for no greater worldly blessing upon you than this, that either of you being young women, may find quiet and loving husbands, and be made joyful mothers of many children.

Where we first of all note, that as parents are bound by the law of nature to provide marriages for their children, so they are willed by the law of God, to pray for their prosperous estate, both before and also after they be married. And truly this never sinketh into the heads of carnal parents, who are able to do more with their purses than with their prayers, who wish extremities to their children, minding only a wealthy, and not a quiet life. Oh how are we beholding to such ignorant parents, who only take care for us that we might be lifted higher, when they provide not for us against the stormy tempests of unquiet lives, and the dangerous downfalls of worldly confusion? Let them never think that their wishes are prayers, when they say, I would God my son were married to such a man's daughter, or my daughter to such a man's son. This is all they aim at, simple and bare wealthy marriages, never minding or praying for God his blessing upon them.

Secondly, by this prayer of *Naomi*, we note the duty of all husbands towards their wives, which is, that they should prepare rest for them: their minds being troubled, they should pacify them with counsel: their bodies diseased, they should comfort them with their love: their estate endangered, they should deliver them with carefulness, and finally, they should love their wives as their own souls.

Psal. 128.3

The Prophet *David* compareth a wife to a vine, which if it be not propped up with a stay by the hand of the gardener, what will it do but wallow on the ground and remain fruitless? Even so the best wives if they be not carefully maintained by the kindness of their husbands, their sorrowful lives will increase their curse, yea, and destroy the fruit of their own bodies.

Eph. 5.25

The Apostle wisheth husbands to love their wives, as Christ loved his Church, which is not only mindful to deliver it out of present dangers, but also hath redeemed it from the curse of eternal damnation: so the husbands' duties are to provide for the temporal welfare of their wives' bodies, and especially for the everlasting salvation of their souls: that they twain which in this life, have had corporal society, in the life to come might enjoy eternal felicity. Now this condemneth the carnal behavior of wretched husbands, who use their wives as their servants and not as themselves, who deal with them as men do with nuts, first, they reach and travail for them, and having gotten them, they take out the kernel but they tread the shell under their feet: so they having gotten the wealth, the beauty, the health and young years of their wives, despise their gray hairs, which are their greatest credit, as the shells wherein the kernel was, giving them over in their weakest days, wherein they want greatest comfort. Is this the rest you provide for your wives, to cause them to wear their bodies with weary travails, to consume their minds with daily grief, to procure their pains by bearing of children, and to lay the greatest burdens upon the smallest beasts, for so some most wretchedly term them. Oh look unto it, this measure will the Lord measure to you again, ye unnatural husbands which follow your pleasures, and pastimes abroad, and neglect your profits and sorrowful wives at home, to fly over the seas with unnecessary journeys, to frequent the company of suspected women, to follow the counsel of vain persons, spending their patrimonies, and bringing themselves, their wives, and posterity to woeful misery. Is this to dwell with your wives like men of knowledge? Is this to give honor unto them as the weaker vessels? Is 1 Pet. 3.7 this to account them the heirs of the same grace? and finally, is this to see their prayers be not interrupted? Nay rather, there are many thousand husbands which never either could or would pray with their wives, that think neither upon heaven nor hell, and have no knowledge of their duties towards God or their neighbors, (much less to their wives) than brute beasts, carnal infidels, profane Atheists, the murderers of themselves, and of their own posterity. Oh fearful danger that hangeth over your heads whom neither the laws of God can compel to learn their duties, or men instruct them to amend their lives. But you my beloved, who are guiltless in this point, are the blessed of the Lord, and forsake not your carefulness already begun, that you lose not your reward.

Ruth Chapter 1. verses 7-15

Thirdly, by this prayer we observe the duties of wives or women in families, namely, that they should be peaceable themselves, for if they seek peace they must ensue peace, and if their joy consist in the quietness of the family, they must be careful they break not the unity. If like *Ishmael*, their hands be against all, the hands of all will be against them, if they will be the loving turtles, they must not be the chattering pies, if they be the vines, their fruit must be grapes, and out of grapes cometh wine, and wine rejoiceth the heart of man, so women must rejoice their husbands and families. Some women will never be at rest till they bear rule, and will say their husbands love them not, except for their sakes they will displace their servants, fall out with their neighbors, envy their friends, and in all things follow their minds: such men give not peace, to their wives, but swords to slay themselves withal. The harkening overmuch to women's counsel, old *Adam* and we his posterity may forever lament, yet godly men may hear their godly wives, remembering alway themselves to be the head, and the choice to rest in them, either to like or dislike their counsel.

And they answered. This is the answer of these women to the counsel and blessing of their mother in law, wherein they refuse to return, and promise to go with her to her own people, as if they should say, we are rather bound unto thee than to our own mothers, and for thy sake whose godly conversation we know, are we drawn in love with the whole people: so that in these words they testify their loving affection to their mother, their desire to be with her among her people, and the cause undoubtedly to be her godly and wise conversation with them in the land of *Moab*: where we note the duty of all the faithful, which is, so to walk that others by their good example may be drawn to love the truth. For surely, these women liked well of the religion of *Naomi*, but much better of her conversation, as a thing they better understood than the other. For this point, the Apostle warneth that we walk in wisdom because of them that are without. And *Peter* saith to the dispersed Jews of his time, that they must have a good conversation among the Gentiles, insomuch as their enemies might have no occasion to speak against them. And our Savior saith, *Let your light so shine before men that they may see your good works, and glorify your father which is in heaven.* For as the unbelieving husband may be won by the godly behavior of the believing wife; so many infidels and carnal persons, are sooner drawn to the Lord by the works which they see, than by the words which they hear. Seeing, this is plain by the word of God, where shall I begin to complain of this our unhappy age, wherein are but few talkers of God his word, but much fewer walkers, when the Gospel of Christ is made the cloak of wickedness? Oh how grievously is the Church of God rent in sunder by daily disquietness, insomuch as there is no peace among us. Can the infidels and papists say of us, as old *Hamor* said of *Jacob* and his family? These men are men of peace, therefore let us be circumcised with them? What peace is there left in the Church of God? Truly we are like unto a tree, we agree all in the body of religion, but as the branches spread themselves an hundred ways, so in our indifferentest points of Religion there is little or no unity. There is no care had of giving offences unto the weak, there is no conscience to stay the slander of the Gospel, Oh how grievous is it, that many nowadays will defend their dissimulation, by saying, Take heed to our words, and not to our deeds: live as we say, and not as we do, making Christianity like the profession of Pharisees, which say and do not. Esteeming of Religion like the occupation of a Smith, wherein one is discharged by blowing, and another by beating: so these think, if they can blow out any good words, and be able to cry, the Gospel, the Gospel, the preachers, the preachers, and to say unto Christ, Thou hast prophesied in our streets, and

Col. 4.5

1 Pet. 1.12

Luke 8.16

Gen. 34.21

Matt. 23

Ruth Chapter 1. verses 7-15

we have eaten in thy presence, they are right good Chris-
Luke 13.26,27 tians. But the Lord shall say unto them, Depart from
me ye workers of iniquity, I know you not. Yet let us be
warned by the examples of the godly, the exhortations
of the Scripture, and the motions of God his spirit in
our hearts, that seeing Christ is our wisdom, let us walk
1 Cor. 1.30 in wisdom, or else we dwell not in Christ: seeing Christ
is our light, let us shine forth in holy conversation, and
John 13.30 seeing the world is our enemy, which daily lieth in wait
to discredit our profession, let us adorn the Gospel we
profess: either make the tree good, and the fruit good, or
the tree evil and the fruit evil, cast away this counterfeit
holiness, which is double iniquity, let us confess with the
mouth unto salvation, believe in the heart to justification, and practice in life unto sanctification, and let everyone that calleth on the name of the Lord, depart from
iniquity. Thus much for the Daughters' answer. Now to
the mother's reply in the next verse.

But Naomi. In this verse and in the two next following, *Naomi* confirmeth her counsel by forcible reasons, taken from their second marriages, and studying
more for their good than her own. The first reason is,
that she hath no more sons either born or unborn to be
their husbands: for by the law one brother being dead
without issue, the next was to marry his wife, and to
raise up seed to his brother. They knew she had no more
children already born, and she proveth that she is out of
hope to have any more, by her own age, she is too old to
marry and therefore to bear children, so that the force
of this reason is to persuade them to go back again, that
they might marry at home, for she knew not how to bestow them in her own country. In the which words thus
taking a reason from their marriage, she noteth the duty
of younger widows and women, which is to marry and
to bear more children, and in herself persuading them
unto it, she noteth the duty of godly parents, which is
to deal privately with them for their public commodity.

For the apostle *Paul* willeth the selfsame thing, that the younger widows marry and bring forth more children, as the most acceptable condition for their fruitful days, and a necessary duty for replenishing the Church. But these persons must not so marry for wantonness, as if they minded nothing but procreation of children, but they must join with it all Christian obedience to the advice of their husbands: secondly, they must be careful to bring up their children in the fear and nurture of the Lord. Thirdly, this must be the end of their marriage and childbirth, that they may the more devoutly give themselves to the worship of God, and by their children to increase the number of the faithful. For it is better to be barren than to bring forth children to the Devil, which they do that mind nothing less than their careful education, and Christian instruction; yea, it is more excellent to be a religious widow than a profane married wife. But some will say that second marriages are not lawful at all, because *Paul* willeth that such widows should not be chosen into the number of church servants: and the holy Ghost giveth such commendation of *Anna* because she never married, though she were left a widow very young: moreover, the counsel of *Paul* is that if they be loosed from husbands or wives, they should not seek to be joined unto them. Unto all which I answer with the same *Paul*, that a woman so soon as she is loosed from her husband, or so soon as her husband is dead, she is at liberty to marry with whom she will, only in the Lord. *Anna* is commended more for her Religion than her chastity. And *Paul* his counsel is to them that could forbear in those days of persecution.

But to come to *Naomi*, she saith, she is too old to marry, therefore it seemeth, though second marriages be good for young women, yet they are not lawful for the old. To this I answer, her meaning is not that it is simply unlawful for her to marry, but that it should not profit her in regard of child bearing: men desire young

1 Tim. 5.14

1 Tim. 5.9

Luke 2.36

1 Cor. 7.27

Rom. 7.2

Ruth Chapter 1. verses 7-15

Non certum

and fruitful women, not old and barren, and her purpose is to persuade her daughters, that she neither had, nor could have any more children for them, therefore in the next verse she addeth, *If I hoped, or If I were this night with an husband.* But in my judgment, I see no reasonable cause why old women (especially) should marry, howsoever others may be contrary minded, my reasons are these: First, I read it not practiced by anybody in the Scripture, I mean such old women as in their own consciences are persuaded they are past child bearing. Secondly, they break the greatest consideration in marriage: they undertake it for lust and not for children, for marriage was not ordained for the lust of the mind, but the necessity of the body, to withdraw it from sin. Now their withered bodies cannot accomplish the desire of their carnal minds. Thirdly, it bringeth great inconvenience with it: if they marry with a young man there is no equality, as anon shall be proved, if with old men like themselves, what comfort can they minister unto them? Lastly, such marriages are more for wealth than woman or necessity. Yet this is but my poor judgment, if any doubt of it let them examine my reasons, if they be weighty, let them receive them, if light, amend them. If any say they marry for comfort, as they can say nothing else, I demand why poor women have not this comfort as well as the rich. I see seldom any poor widows married, but the wealthy so soon as either honesty or modesty will suffer them. Again, comfort is no sufficient cause for marriage, because it may be had without marriage, but children cannot. It is the duty of married folks with their mutual love to comfort one another, but not a cause that ought to constrain to marriage. The *Eunuch* wanteth comfort, yet who thinketh such a person fit for marriage: a continent person, which as Christ saith hath made himself chaste for the Kingdom of God, wanteth comfort, yet he should sin grievously if he married for comfort: let lawful things be joined with expedient, and

I think old women will never marry.

Yea if I had. This is the second reason where-with she persuadeth her daughters to turn back again, namely, grant she had sons new born, yet it were too long for them to tarry till they were grown up, and fit for marriage, yea, then they would be past children, also, they should lose the season of their youth, and so should reap no harvest of their days: there would be no agreement in years between them, when they should be as a withered stub, and the young men as green olives. Where we note, that by the judgment of this godly *Naomi*, there must be an agreement in years between the parties that shall be married, for she saith, would we be deferred for them, from taking any husbands? nay my daughters: by the which words she signifieth that it would be no fit marriage that one should be so old and the other so young. The Lord created *Adam* and *Eve* in one day, not only that marriage should not be deferred too long, but also because their age should be alike, but if any be the elder, let it be the man. In the planting or gardens, they get the youngest imps, for the continuance and equality of the fruit: they will not dig up an old tree, and plant him in an orchard of tender imps, even so must it be in marriage, for the matrimony of old men and young women, is like *Joseph's* party-colored coat, which caused jealousy in his brethren: for, as, that was a sign of love in his father, so this is a token of fondness in a husband. But most unseemly is the marriage of young men and old women, which a godly preacher in our days com-pared to the grafting of a young head upon an old pair of shoulders: and I may compare it to the mixture of oil and water, the which are quite against the nature of all medicines. And even the brute beasts and the birds, as we read of the Turtles, the Harts, and the Elephants, condemn herein the folly of mankind, which from their youth choose their mate, and being dead refuse another, fearing inequality of age and nature. Both these kind

Master H. Smith.

Ruth Chapter 1. verses 7-15

of matches are neither begun in the Lord, continued in nature, or satisfy the desire of both parties, but break out into impatient jealousy or filthy adultery, thinking every day a year till the eldest party be dead. Oh unseemly and unfriendly behavior towards those to whom they have bound themselves to love and live together, being the only cause of the breach of fidelity, cursed discord mutual envy, and everlasting misery.

 Secondly, by this we note, that it is the duty of parents in time to provide for their children, if they be willing to it, some godly and fit marriage. So did *Abraham* for *Isaac* his son, so did *Isaac* and *Rebecca* for *Jacob* their son, so did *Jethro* for his daughter *Zipporah*. The neglect of this duty in parents, is the cause that so many children match contrary to their minds, even to their own undoing. And then they cry out town and country, My son or my daughter hath married against my mind, when as themselves are in the only fault: then they punish them by keeping away their portion: so, as before by their negligence they sought their dishonesty, now by their willfulness, they bring them to perpetual beggary. I defend not the rash and headlong marriages against parents' consents, especially where godly parents are: and surely I fear there are but few in England that ever married so, but they procured the curse on themselves, and have often (though too late) repented their willful and ungodly marriage. But yet beloved; be warned, if you desire the discharge of your own consciences, or the safeguard of your children, deal like parents with them, and they will perform like children to you: the Lord punisheth your negligence with their disobedience: you sinned first, and they followed your steps, forgive them their offence, and receive them to favor again, and the Lord will likewise pardon your transgression, and bless your posterity with more dutiful obedience to you.

 But this. Now when she had persuaded her daughters to return, lest they should think she careth

Gen. 24.3

Exod. 2.21

not for them, and was willing to be rid of their company, as those that were troublesome and burdenous unto her, she addeth this clause in the end of this verse. Wherein she testifieth her care for them, and her patience to the Lord. Her care for them when she saith, It grieveth me much more for your sake than for mine own: the death of my husband and loss of my children grieve me, but not so much as this, that now either I must depart from you, or else with your company endanger your safety. I could not but sorrow for the dead, yet I am more grieved for you poor destitute widows: I have lost their company for a while, till I meet them again in God his kingdom, but now we depart, I to the Lord's people, and you to Infidels, and we shall be separated forever. Would God that I could so promise you prosperity with me, that so you might receive the peace of your souls. Thus and such like she uttereth in these words for her own excuse, and their comfort.

Where we are first given to understand, how hardly true friendship is separated, yea though some parties are endangered thereby. *Naomi* would have her daughters depart, they weep at it, and she is sorrowful: insomuch as either party striveth who shall receive the worst. The mother counseleth their good, and the daughters promise hers: she would have them return, and live at rest in the arms of some loving husband, but they had rather travel than she should go alone. And this telleth us that true friendship is not to receive good of other, but to do good unto other. Choose thy friend, that when he is in heaviness thou mayest comfort him, when he is hungry thou mayest feed him, when he is cast down, thou mayest raise him up: and finally, when he wanteth make thou a supply. This is godly friendship, like *Jonathan's* and *David's*. If any choose friends for other respects, their friendship is carnal and not spiritual, momentary and not everlasting, like the standing pools which dry up in summer, not like the running streams which endure continually.

Secondly, by this we note that one misery cometh not alone, for wars cause death, dearth, envy, and robberies: sickness bringeth pain to the parties, and sorrow to their friends: even so death doth not only bring sorrow for the dead, but grief for the living, as *Naomi* saith, it grieves me much more for your sakes. There is none that die but some shall want them, many friends comfortless, many children harborless, many servants masterless, and many creditors moneyless by the death of men. I will say nothing, that the godly may and ought to mourn for their friends that are dead, as *Abraham* for *Sara*, *Jacob* for *Rachel*, the *Jebusites* for *Saul*, *Mary* and *Martha* for *Lazarus*: and the Apostle willeth us to *mourn*, but with this clause, *not as men without hope*. Therefore the use of this doctrine is, with patient and brotherly love to bear with the weakness of them, which seem in our conceits to weep more for their husbands and wives, children and friends, than we think needful. It is their weakness, and what know we, if the like burden were on our backs that we should not be pressed down under it like them? Let us therefore consider with ourselves least we also be tempted, and help them with brotherly kindness, not increase it with daily murmurings: that which is today their sin, tomorrow may be our wickedness.

1 Thess. 4.13

But the hand. In those words she gathereth patience for the remedy of her own grief, and showeth howsoever she is afflicted, yet she is not ignorant, that as the showers come from the clouds, so her afflictions from the Lord: his hand that wrought her felicity, hath also brought her to misery, her ease is her patience, her weakness is her sorrow, her comfort, that God with whom is mercy hath wounded her heart.

The hand of the Lord is taken in the Scriptures many ways, but generally it signifieth the means whereby he accomplisheth his counsel, and is referred either

to his mercy and favor; as when it is said, the hand of
the Lord was with *John Baptist*, or else to his judgments,
punishment, or chastisement: so the hand of the Lord
was against the Israelites, *when they had forsaken him* Judg. 2.19
and served Baalim. So when the Ark of God was in the
house of *Dagon* the god or idol of the *Philistines*, the
Lord overthrew their god, cut of his hands and head, and
smote the Priests with hemorrhoids, then they confessed
the hand of God to be sore against them: so in this place
it is taken for his chastisement or correction upon *Nao-* 1 Sam. 5.7
mi. Out of the which we note many profitable doctrines.

First, that all our afflictions come from the Lord,
that he might chastise his own and confound the ungodly. Read but the 34th and 36th Chapter of *Job*; most excellently entreating of this matter, wherein is showed that
neither the godly escape, nor the wicked go scot-free.
This is the confession of *Moses*, to terrify the Israelites, Deut. 31.18
of *Joshua* to keep them in obedience, and of *David* a man Josh. 24.20
more exercised in trouble than all the world beside. This Psal. 119.71
must we account with ourselves in all our miseries, we
are robbed by thieves, spoiled by murderers, stroke by
brute beasts, reproached by slanderers, evil entreated by
the world, hurt by our enemies, sustain the loss of our
goods, the danger of our health, and are oppressed with
sickness: surely, in all these things say, The Lord gave,
and the Lord hath taken away, even as it hath pleased
the Lord, so cometh things to pass. But men will say, we
know it well enough already, and we confess it. And do
you know and confess, and will you not practice? A man
being sick, at the beginning never thinketh on the Lord,
but posteth to the Physician for counsel, without crav-
ing the forgiveness of his sins, the cause of his sickness:
yet you say, God hath sent it and laid upon us, as if the
Lord sendeth sickness to help the Physician to money;
for with him you agree for his pains and cunning, but
with the Lord you agree not for your own pains which
you endure. But you will say, we find ease by medicines,

Ruth Chapter 1. verses 7-15

and our sickness is abated. I answer, so the Lord suffereth witches and conjurers, to tell them that come unto
them, the things they desire, yet you will not say, they
are guiltless. I speak nothing against the excellent and
commendable profession of Physic, but rather for the
commendation of it, seeing God so accepteth it, as that
thereby he seemeth to salve up the sins of many, doing
away their pains, and also to give them longer time of
repentance. But this I wish both in this and in all other
miseries of mankind: that first we purge our consciences
from notorious crimes, and then the Lord will stay his
hand from striking our hearts from wavering, our goods
from wasting, our bodies from pining, and our souls
from everlasting dying.

    Secondly, by this we note, whence it cometh,
that the godly are so patient in all their tribulations;
even from this consideration, that the Lord's hand af-
flicteth them. This is worthy to be noted, in the example
of *David*, when *Shimei* cursed him: *Abishai* standing by,
wisheth *David* to punish him: but *David* answereth him,
what have I to do with you ye sons of Zeruiah? he curseth, because the Lord hath bidden him to curse me: as
if he had said, I may punish the Lord as well as *Shimei*.
The very like did *Job* answer his wife, when she would
have him curse God and die. Thou speakest like a foolish woman, what? shall we receive good at the hands
of God and not evil? as if he had said, we are bound to
receive evil at the hand of God, as well as good, and if
we receive the one with blessing, let us not curse him
for the other. This was it that made the *Apostles to rejoice,* that they were accounted worthy to suffer for the
name of Christ: and this must sink into our ignorant
and rebellious hearts, that we may learn at the first to
humble ourselves, lest as we now suffer for sin, so anon
we be punished for impatience. The patient abiding of
the righteous, availeth much in the sight of the Lord:
men think they be forgotten, if they be a little afflicted,

*Mitigat
uim doloris
considerata
equitas fevi-
entis.*
2 Sam. 16.10-
12

Job 2.10

Acts 5.41

Lecture 2

and cry out like desperate persons, Lord, Lord, but they never pray for patience, but all for deliverance. Oh how excellent is this example of *Naomi*, which being in many miseries in a strange country, having buried husbands and sons, being now to depart from her acquaintance, to take a tedious journey into her own country, poor, weary and desolate, yet all her words are these: The hand of the Lord is gone out against me: as if she had said, he that gave them took them, and he that took them, left me patience. Thus must we stay our minds on the work of the Lord, as the *Ark was stayed by the Priests in the midst of the river Jordan*, which made the waters to fly back, till all the children of *Israel* were passed through: even so the floods of great troubles shall not overthrow us, if we stay our minds on the hand of the Lord, and safely escape the dangerous destruction of worldly affliction.

Josh. 3.16,17

Then they lift. Now cometh the effect of this communication, wherein is showed how sorrowfully these daughters took it, and yet diversely minded, for *Orpah* notwithstanding her gentle proffers to her mother in law, her bitter tears and pitiful lamenting, yet she taketh her leave with a sweet kiss, and returneth back to her idolatrous friends. *Naomi* used no persuasions but worldly reasons taken from marriage, to persuade them both: she seeth her sister remain constant, and she that even now for the love of people, and mother in law would go as far as the farthest, now for the cogitation of a heathen husband, forsaketh both God, people, mother and sister. Who would have thought that *Orpah* which bid her friends farewell, her country adieu, her kindred forsaken, and idolatry abhorred, would thus cowardly (as I may term it) fly back again in hope of a husband. But yet we see she doeth, and out of her example we may note many things.

First, that the world and carnal reasons are fearful hindrances unto us in Religion. We see this woman, how doth she fall away from God, his people, all the

Matt. 22.5

Church that she knew, her mother and sister? We know, how *many being sent for to the great man's supper; which is the Lord, they excused their absence, one for his farm, another for his oxen, another for his wife*, as *Orpah* doeth

Jam. 4.4

for her husband: What shall I say? The love of the world is the hatred of God: and *John* saith, *Love not the world,*

1 John 2.15

nor the things of the world, for he that loveth the world, the love of the Father is not in him. And Christ saith,

Luke 14.26

Whosoever cometh to me and hateth not father and mother, and wife and children, is not worthy of me. Where are now our Naturals, that would be professors, but their friends will not let them, they would be Christians, but their wives will not agree to them, this year they will be worldlings, and the next year when they have overcome their business, if they have any leisure they will hear the word preached. Oh dangerous delays of subtle Satan, studying by the world, to draw men from God: they lie like sluggards; in winter it is too cold, in summer it is too hot to work: so they in their youth, will be religious when they are old, being in age, when they be rich, being rich, they wax harder and harder, and so continue till the day of their damnation.

Secondly, by this we may gather how far an hypocrite or an infidel may go in Religion. *Orpah* forsaketh her own people, for the love of God his people, she weepeth and cryeth, when it is but mentioned unto her that she would depart, she traveleth on the way towards the country of God his people; and in this her journey, for a few worldly reasons, she turneth back again, though as it may seem with a bitter heart. Even so hypocrites may forsake the world and their friends, join themselves to God and his people, travel and profit in Religion towards the heavenly *Jerusalem*, be ready to weep with them that weep, and lament with them that lament: and in any good action, set his foot as far forth as the best: yet some occasion given, either for profit or pleasure; fear or danger, suddenly turneth sail, and cometh to the

world again. Even so saith our Savior of the seed, that
is sown in the second and third ground, it taketh root, it   Mark 4.16,17
springeth, and groweth up, but suddenly the heat of persecution ariseth, or offence taken at the doctrine, which   John 6.66
is taught them, or the cares of this life and deceitfulness
of riches choke them. By this we learn what to think
of our soft hearted Christians, many among us that will
diligently hear, and wring out tears from their moistened
brain, at the hearing of God his judgments thundered
and threatened by the Preacher: yet, being gone, will
make no conscience of oaths, carding, dicing, tabling,
gaming for their neighbor's money, going abroad on the
sabbath day to feasts, and being sharply reproved for it,
then farewell Religion and profession also.

      Thirdly, by this we gather what exceeding kind-
ness an heathen, an atheist, or an infidel, may show to
them that fear God: *Orpah* for the love of godly *Naomi*,
goeth with her on the way, weepeth and kisseth at their
departure, so great love did she bear to her mother in law,
that had it not been for one thing, she had gone through
with her to her own people. In like manner we read about
the year of Christ, 745. when the Mahometans did fear-
fully and cruelly punish all Christians. For one *Abbas* a
prince of that faction forbad the Christians to preach, to
build Churches, or to look upon the Cross. And another
called *Habdallas*, forbad all Christians to learn to write
or read any kind of books and learning. Then the Christians of *Antioch* requesteth of *Marnes* their Mahometan
Prince, that they by his license might have a Bishop, who
granted unto them that worldly *Theophylact*, giving express charge, that no man should molest or trouble the
Bishop or the Christians: and yet this kindness he af-
forded them out of his pity, that could not find in his
heart to become a Christian and turn to the Lord. So we
may see many among us speak well of Religion, yet they
will not go so far as *Bethlehem* for it, that is, they will
wish they had a Preacher, yet they will hardly, either on

the Sabbath day or weekday, stir one foot from their own place, to hear a Sermon, so cold is their devotion: but if they give a poor man a meal of meat, or lend him a little money at his need, or receive a Preacher for a night, then he is the only man in the Country. But oh Lord, open their eyes, that they may see their courtesy is but light, in regard of their duty: if for their brethren they would die, it were but their duty, how little is it then that they give them meat? But they would know of us what is the way to be saved; I answer, so would the young man in the Gospel, yet when Christ told him, he would not do it, but went away sorrowing: even so these men may outwardly and inwardly in some measure profess kindness and humility to be instructed, but alas their profession is far from true feeling of Christian religion.

Matt. 19.22

Lastly, by this verse we note that as *Orpah* and her companions are carnally minded, so *Ruth* and her fellows are spiritually minded, though one be overthrown with worldly reasons, yet the other remaineth invincible in her first pretended purpose. So that here is an image of a congregation, where all hear, and yet there is a difference of hearing in one and the same Company: one part with profit, another with disprofit, one to their health, another to their sickness, to some the savor of life unto life, to other, the savor of death unto death. Yet blessed be God, that hath no earth so barren, but it bringeth forth some fruit, no people so rude, but there are some sanctified persons among them, which will not be drawn away till death: no battle so cruel, but some escape with life. If the Pharisees will not believe in Christ, yet the poor people that know not the law will receive him for the Messiah. Among the mockers at *Athens*, *Paul* received some fruit of his labors, and the Gospel was never preached in any country, but it gained some. This teacheth us to follow the example of *Ruth* and we shall have the reward of *Ruth*: stick to the Lord, and to the faithful, with purpose of heart, let not the vain glitter-

Acts 17.34

ing pleasure, of pleasant pastime or profit, draw us from the hope of our everlasting blessedness. The time is but short we have to spend, the labor easy if we willingly endure it, the profit everlasting if we continue to the end. This is the victory that overcometh the world, even our faith: for to him that believeth are all things possible: Let us therefore hear the word with diligence, that our faith may be strengthened, believe with assurance, that our souls may be justified, and stand fast in the trial of this world, that body and soul may be crowned: for blessed are they that endure to the end. And thus much of this conference or communication, and the effect thereof. Now let us give thanks to God for that which hath been spoken. ^{1 John 5.4}

The end of the Second Lecture

Ruth Chapter 1. verses 7-15

The Third Lecture

Ruth Chapter 1. verses 15-17

15 *And* Naomi *said, behold, thy sister in law is gone back to her people and to her gods, return thou after thy sister in law.*

16 *And Ruth answered, entreat me not to leave thee, nor to depart from thee, for whither thou goest I will go, and where thou dwellest I will dwell, thy people shall be my people, and thy God my God.*

17 *Where thou diest will I die, and there will I be buried, the Lord do so unto me and more also, if ought but death depart thee and me.*

In these words the holy Ghost declareth unto us, the conference had between *Naomi* and *Ruth*; after the departure of *Orpah*, wherein *Naomi* ceaseth not thoroughly to try and examine the mind of *Ruth*, for what cause she would go with her; the words contain in them two parts. The first is the persuasion of *Naomi* in the 15th verse, to make *Ruth* to return by the example of her sister. The second is the answer of *Ruth*, in the two next verses, consisting of two parts; the first is the petition she maketh to her mother in these words, *Entreat me not to leave thee, etc.* which she amplifieth by the resolution of her mind in the next words. First, that for her life she would dwell with her, and go with her. Secondly, for her profession, *her people and God should be*

Naomi's. Thirdly, for her death, that she would die and be buried with her. The last part of this answer of *Ruth*, is the confirmation of it by an oath in these words; *the Lord do so unto me, and more also, if ought but death depart thee and me.*

Behold thy sister is returned: Now *Naomi* goeth forward to deal with *Ruth* alone, for the Castle may seem almost won, where one half of the soldiers are overcome; the unity between these two sisters being broken, and *Orpah* being departed, what was poor *Ruth* able to do alone? surely, this was a greater discouragement unto her than any she had yet, namely; that her sister being departed, she should lay before her her sister's example to draw her likewise to fall. And truly thus the spirit of God dealeth most times, with those that labor to come unto him, setting some in the way like the Disciples which forbad young children to come unto Christ, and as the press of people kept the poor man diseased of the palsy from coming to our Savior: even so many scandals, stumbling blocks, lets, interruptions and hindrances come between the godly and Christ, as did between *Naomi* and *Ruth*.

Mark 10.13

Mark 2.4

But here we note, that the examples of our kindred, and especially of those that seemed anything in Religion, are dangerous arguments to draw us from Christ. We see in this place *Naomi* taketh example of one ungodly sister to draw away the other: which when our Savior foresaw, he gave this commandment, that for his sake we must forsake both father and mother, brother and sister, wife and children, or else we are not worthy of him. And in another place, one desiring of him but a little space to bury his father, he said unto him, *Let the dead bury their dead.* This is a very profitable doctrine for these days, wherein men are thus discouraged from Religion, for fear of their friends, for now Satan stirreth up one brother against another, to hinder them from hearing the saving word of God, now

Matt. 10.34

Luke 9.60

they cry out against us, Are you wiser than your forefathers? Hath not all thy friends before thee believed
on this wise? And wilt thou be singular? And surely
beloved, we know it is the greatest argument, that popish atheists have, their ancestors, fathers and mothers,
their masters and mistresses, have misliked this preaching, and these new doctrines, wherein many repose their
greatest felicity, and God send us (say they) to live no
worse than they did, and to die no more blessed than
they. But would you so rather be followers of your popish and ignorant predecessors, than of the doctrine of
Christ and his Apostles revealed in his word: this is to
build your selves upon another foundation, which when
the fire cometh, will utterly consume it. But they say,
are all our predecessors damned which did as we do?
to whom I may well answer, How do you know that all
your fathers were of your mind? but we are not in God   Acts 17.30
his place, to judge and arraign them: but say with the
Apostle, The time of this ignorance did not God regard,
but now he admonisheth all men everywhere to repent,
because he hath appointed a day to judge the world in
righteousness. So that if God seem not to regard it, why
should we stand upon it? And seeing now the trumpet
of the Gospel is sounded by the Lord's Ministers, let us
not with *Mary* lament over the graves of the dead, but
leaving them at their rest, trudge and travel to the mount
of the Lord, that of him we may freely receive that which
many kings and prophets could never obtain. Though
Moses went not into the land of *Canaan*, yet he saw it,
so it may be the Lord let our predecessors see the light
of the Gospel, though they could not enjoy it. *But as Pe-*   Matt. 17.6
ter and John were with Christ when he was transfigured,
and saw his kingdom, yet could not enjoy the continual
presence of his glory, but being warned of Christ, told it
to no man: so many godly in time of darkness not only
saw but embraced the truth, which it may be is forgotten
of their graceless posterity. Let the parents eat the sour

Ruth Chapter 1. verses 15-17

grapes, shall the children's teeth be set on edge? if they made cakes to the host of heaven, shall we worship the sun and the moon? what discredit is it to a blind father that hath a son well sighted? no more is it to idolaters, whose children are the appointed heirs of the land of *Canaan. Let us abide with him that hath the words of eternal life*, and as the wealth of our parents is dear unto us, yet many thousand times more dear is the health of our souls.

John 6.68

Secondly by this we note, that to stick by our friends and to go with them from the Lord, is to commit idolatry, for *Naomi* saith, *Thy sister is gone to her people, and to her Gods*: as if she had said, indeed for kindred's sake she is gone back, but it is unto idols and false gods. Yea and more also, unto Devils: this is a worthy lesson for our naturals to learn, who will forsake Gospel, church, prayer and preaching; some for the love of their wives to keep them company at home, when God calleth for them in one congregation or other, some their idolatrous friends which are notable recusants, yet because they should think well of them, they will falsify their faith to the Lord and be unjust in his work, that they may please them with their present company: some are hindered by their profit, some by unlawful gaming, and many by bare idleness. Thus men make gods, some of their people, some of their wives, some of their popish friends, some of their profit, some of their pleasures, and some of their idleness, and few or none are to be found, that are both able and willing to follow Christ when he calleth them, as little *Zacchaeus* did, but every one hath some excuse to keep them from the Lord's Supper, who shall never taste of his heavenly pleasures, seeing they mind earthly things, making their glory their shame, their belly their God, let their end be damnation. But oh my beloved, let us be warned by the dangers of others, when *Peter* rebuked Christ and bid him favor himself, Christ rebuked him and called him Satan: even so when

Luke 19.5,6

Matt. 16.23

our dearest friends would have us be slack in preaching, and favor our bodies, come to the church seldom and make no toil of it, agree with the most in religion, or rather in worldliness, and so shall we have favor, aspire to the greatest promotions, for there is greatest profit, and finally take pleasure in unlawful things, let us say, come behind us Satan. For it is not our friend, but our enemy Satan, that thus allureth us with the bait of pleasure, ease, and profit, that we might hang on the hook of perpetual perdition. Then seeing we have espied his policy, discovered his deceit, and tried the discommodities that ensue his obedience, let us innocent children once burned, dread the fire, and as *Jacob* said by his own sons *Simeon* and *Levi*, My soul come not into their habitation, so let us say to our dearest friends when their counsel and a good conscience cannot stand together, better break the league of friendship between us, than suffer the shipwreck of a precious and peaceable conscience. The wisest *Solomon* by hearkening to his wives, 1 Kings 11.2 disobeyed the Lord, and it cost him ten tribes of his kingdom: if such green pieces be destroyed, what shall become of the rotten and sear [*withered*]: therefore if angels from heaven must not be heard, much less devils from hell drawing us away from following the truth by the mouth of our dearest and nearest friends, though it were by your wives that lie in your bosoms. Therefore let us take unto us the whole armor of God, that we may stand fast in the day of battle: better never run, except we obtain the price, better never to have known God or his Gospel, than now to fall away from him again.

    But Ruth *said, entreat me not.* This is the first part of the answer of *Ruth*, to the argument of her mother, and it is her petition with the reason of it: wherein she protesteth that it is better unto her, not to be entreated to depart, or once to have it motioned, or mentioned to go from her, for her resolution is, that neither the troubles or travails of life could separate her, neither the sorrows

of death or desolation of the grave should deprive her
of *Naomi's* company, for she saith, *Where thou diest will
I die, and there will I be buried.* Out of which I observe
these things. First, how the godly behave themselves in
all trials and temptations, namely, that the very thoughts
of departing from God and yielding to sin, are very gall
and bitterness unto them, insomuch as they say with
Ruth, entreat me not to leave thee, that is, never speak
word to move me from hearing God his word, to overthrow my faith, to turn me to disobedience, to perish
my conscience, to hinder my course, or to subvert my
profession. A notable example hereof is in *Elisha*, who
was entreated by *Elijah* as here *Ruth* is by *Naomi*. First,
he *bid him tarry at Gilgal till he went to Bethel*; but *Elisha* said, as the Lord liveth, and as thy soul liveth, I will
not leave thee, nor depart from thee: then they went to
Bethel together, and bid him tarry there, for the Lord
sendeth him to *Jericho*: but *Elisha* answered, as the Lord
liveth and as thy soul liveth, I will not leave thee nor
depart from thee; then they went to *Jericho*, and *Elijah*
bid him tarry there till he went to *Jericho*, and *Elijah* bid
him tarry there till he went to meet the Lord at *Jordan*.
Elisha answered as he did before: for *Elisha* did foresee,
that if he went not with *Elijah*, he should have no benefit
by his service: so if we abide not the objections of our
friends, the reproaches of our enemies, the enticements
of the world, and the persuasions of our own fathers and
mothers that are against us in religion, we shall lose all
that we have done before, yea though they should say as
Rabshakeh said to the men of *Hezekiah*. The Lord hath
sent us to speak unto you. But many will say, if profane
worldlings should discourage us in religion, and those
that are open contemners should persuade us from it,
then we could abide it, but it goeth nigh us when our
own wives or husbands, fathers or mothers, brethren
and sisters, companions and acquaintance shall try us
so narrowly. But mark dearly beloved, thou art not

2 Kings 2.1-7

Isa. 36.10

Lecture 3

alone, *Ruth* was thus handled by *Naomi* her dear mother in law, for whose sake she had departed from kindred and country, yet she trieth, molesteth, and vexeth her; yet by the saving grace of God's assisting spirit, in the end she acquiteth herself, like a woman of strength in the Lord's quarrel: for the Lord for our farther trial doth not only prove us in the least, but in the greatest afflictions. The Israelites cared but little for the Philistines, had they not had giants among them, so the Lord will bring crosses like armed men to dismay us, that our valor and courage may be known, *Job* had first one herd taken away and then another, in the end his children crushed to death, and then he was strangely visited in his own body, but having only one comfort in all the world left, his wife, she bid him curse God and die. But some say, we would willingly be professors, but the preachers themselves tell us how we must be mortified; and they call us in their sermons wretches, and cursed creatures, these hard words hinder us, if they spoke fair unto us and cried mercy, mercy, we would with more diligence frequent their exercise. I answer, *if they speak in God's name, whose ambassadors they are,* cannot you bear it for his sake: they are not common persons in that place, but supply Christ's room: *now Christ called his disciples a faithless generation,* he called *Peter* Satan, and a poor woman he called dog, when she came unto him. How did he deal with king *Herod,* and with the Pharisees, every man knoweth, and are you better than these? *Paul called the Galatians foolish,* was it not to make them wise, that thereby he might draw them to the truth, they had forsaken? even so the ministers of Christ must handle this rough world, setting it out by the titles, that by the name they may guess of the nature. If the rich man promise peace to his soul in the multitude of his possessions, shall not the Lord call him fool for his labor? If all the world follow the prince that reigneth in the air, shall not we say that they be without God, and so without sal-

2 Cor. 5.20

Matt. 8.26

Matt. 15.26

Gal. 3.1

Luke 12.20

Ruth Chapter 1. verses 15-17

vation? Doth not the Lord chasten us in this world that
we should not be condemned in the world to come? Are
not servants contented to bear hard words at the hands
of their masters, because they receive wages of them?
even so suffer God his ministers to speak the worst they
can of you, yet I assure you, there is no faithful preacher
that will speak, so basely of the notablest wicked person
that is, but he speaketh and thinketh a thousand times
more basely of himself. Bear with them therefore, you
are children, and infants in Religion, not able to speak,
they speak for you to the Lord in as humble manner as
may be: knowing that the Lord resisteth the proud, and
giveth grace to the humble and meek: the prodigal son
by speaking most vilely of himself, purchased his father's
favor. Even so these hard speeches of our selves, and
other penitent sinners, are as faithful messengers to rec-
oncile us unto God.

1 Pet. 5.5

Luke 15.18,19

      Secondly, by this we note, how we must be en-
abled to encounter or resist the examples of others, that
are laid against us to draw us from God: even as *Ruth*
doth in this place. *Naomi* telleth her, *Orpah* is turned
away, and therefore she must also. *Ruth* answereth,
Where thou dwellest I will dwell: as if she had said; if
thou turn back, I will turn back also, but I know thy constancy is such as thou wilt never yield, therefore all the
examples of my slippery sister, and fearful fall-aways in
the world shall never move me: it is thy constancy that
I look upon and nothing else, which is as a safe ship for
me to sail in through the waves of my unsteadfast mind:
so that by this you perceive, how she opposeth the stead-
fastness of her mother, against the backsliding of her sister, depending upon the surest hold, not upon a broken
staff. Even so must we against the examples of ungodly
ruffians set the examples of sober minded. Match the
world and Christ together, what shall the world get, if it
say, be ignorant, the other saith if the Gospel be hid it is
to them that be lost: if it say follow the ways of thy own

heart, the other saith, for this thou shalt come to judgment: if the world say be covetous, and enrich thy self by
gaming, cozening, carding, dicing, buying, and selling,
the other saith, such shall not inherit God's kingdom:
if the world say, seek honor, the church saith, it is vanity: if it say, esteem best of thy self, the other saith, think
better of another: if it wish thee prosperity, the church
saith, rather suffer adversity with God's children than to
enjoy the pleasures of sin for a season. So the flesh lusteth against the spirit, and the spirit against the flesh: if
thou be tempted to infidelity, remember *Abraham* that
believed in hope; under hope, and beyond hope: if to incontinency, remember *Joseph* the mirror of chastity: if to
impatiency, think upon *Job*, if to unjust dealing, remember *Jacob*: if to idleness, think on the Pismire [*ant*]: if to
drunkenness, remember what *David* did with the water
of the well of *Bethlehem*. This is usual in the Scripture
to exhort by examples. *Peter* wisheth godly women to
look upon *Sarah* her obedience, *James* willeth the poor
in his days to take the prophets for an example of patience. *Paul* exhorteth the Corinthians to liberality, by
the example of the Macedonians: even so on the contrary, threatenings are denounced by the example of others, as we may often read in the Gospel. The Lord saith,
the Queen of *Sheba* shall rise in judgment against the
nation of the Jews which came to hear the wisdom of
Solomon, likewise he provoketh them by the example of
the Publicans and harlots, telling them, they shall be preferred in the kingdom of God, and I think there is none
so simple but they know they ought rather to follow *the
wise, than the foolish virgins.* But some will say, now the
world is altogether corrupted, and the most part is the
worst part, therefore they must needs follow their manners and be defiled. To whom I answer, if thou were in
a little bark upon the greatest sea, and sawest a thousand
mighty waves about thee, like huge mountains, would-
est thou forsake thy little bark which is alone, and leap

1 Pet. 3.6
Jam. 5.10

1 Cor. 10.6-8

Matt. 25.1

Ruth Chapter 1. verses 15-17

into the midst among the waves, because they are many? so thou shouldest work thy own destruction: even so, wilt thou forsake the manners, life, and company of a few godly persons, with whom is safety, to wallow in the millions of worldly men, with whom is no peace, but is like the raging sea that cannot rest? shalt not thou be tossed with them, I will not say troubled, but everlastingly confounded? I grant we should live by precept, and not by example, but seeing we must needs see the Gospel, before we believe it, let us look on the lives of the purest, and fewest among us, and join ourselves to them, as *Noah* to his ark, that the water floods of everlasting destruction overwhelm us not in eternal damnation: Prov. 28.4 For (saith *Solomon*) *he that forsaketh the law praiseth the wicked, but he that keepeth it resisteth them.*

Thy God. By these words it may seem that *Ruth* is not so well grounded in the knowledge of God as she ought to be, in that she dependeth upon her mother, in saying, thy God is my God, as if she had said: if thou worship the true God, so will I, if thou be an idolater, so will I, if thou turn backward, so will I, if thou go forward, so will I. But I take it far otherwise, that these words proceed from a heart fully grounded upon the truth: as if she had said, I know *Naomi*, thou wilt never worship any Gods but the true God, thou art constant in that which thy self hast taught me, I remain steadfast in that which I learned of thee, and therefore I can never forsake thee. The which interpretation is confirmed by the words that follow, *Thy people, my people*: who were *Naomi's* people but the Jews which always worshipped the true God? so that if *Naomi* could change her birth, parentage, people, and country, then also in the mind of *Ruth* she could change her God, and as she was persuaded, she knew her people, so she knew her God, and as she thought, she could not change her people, so she conceived she would never alter her worship: so that these words proceed of a steadfast persuasion in the knowledge of God, and an assured hope of her mother's continuance. Even as when the king of *Babel* calleth the almighty by the name of the God of *Shadrach, Meshach*, and *Abednego*, was persuaded he was the true God, by the miraculous delivery of those his servants from the fiery furnace. And as the *King of Media called him by the name of Daniel's God*, because he had delivered him from the hungry Lions: even so *Ruth* called the true God by the name of *Naomi's* God, because she was instructed by her. But some will say, is it not lawful for us to depend upon our fathers or elder friends in religion or to believe as the church or as catholic men believe? I answer, if the question be made of the necessary points to salvation, as the knowledge of the Trinity, the work of our redemption with such like, it is by no means lawful for us to depend upon men, though they be the chiefest in knowledge, and the greatest in authority in all the world, if they teach it never so truly yet we must have recourse to the word of God. For *Paul* wished the Corinthians that they should be followers of him, as he was of God, as if he had said, where I agree with God and his word, consent with me, where I disagree, dissent from me. We know what commendation the Lord giveth *the Jews of Berea*, which sought the Scriptures daily, whither those things were so or not, which were taught by *Paul* and *Silas*: we know how *Paul withstood Peter to his face*, who was a pillar of the church and a more ancient Apostle than himself, yet he was faulty: and to conclude, we must receive the Gospel as from God, the only author of it, not from man, least we make the preaching of the Cross of none effect: it is far surer to send us to the fountains of the written word of God, than to the brains of the best learned in the world. Therefore the conclusion is, that we must not in the foundation of Religion depend upon men or angels, though we were never so truly taught by them, but must refer our faith, and the credit thereof to the only written word of God.

Dan. 3.29

Dan. 6.26

1 Cor. 11.1

Acts 17.11

Gal. 2.18

Ruth Chapter 1. verses 15-17

But some will say? had *Ruth* this word of God,
or did *Naomi* carry it with her into the land of *Moab*.
I answer, that it is very likely they had, for the Jews at
this day have the old Testament with them in all nations:
secondly, if they had not, yet the Lord by his spirit did
persuade the heart of *Ruth* of the truth of those things
which *Naomi* had taught her, so did he persuade his
church when there was no word written, for the space
of above two thousand years: so doth he at this day keep
his church among infidels, where is neither preaching,
word, nor sacraments, yet not one of them is lost. But
if any say, let us then forsake the written word of God,
and attend to these revelations or private instructions of
the holy Ghost, I answer, so the Jews when they came
into the land of *Canaan*, might have eat no meat till the
Lord rained down more manna upon them: surely then
they had all starved many thousand years ago: even so if
we look for such extraordinary illuminations, and forsake the present food of our souls, God his written word
preached among us, the other being ceased, we shall
justly be condemned as the murderers and slaughter-
slaves of our own destruction. Let us therefore take heed
to God, not to men, ground our faith upon his word, not
on human gifts, attend to the voice of Christ speaking by
his ministers to the ears of the body, not waiting for extraordinary illuminations: if we want this means, labor
for it as a pearl worth all our merchants' substance, yea a
treasure greater than all the world. But of lighter points
of Religion, if we receive anything of men, who in one
point have diverse judgments, let us learn to examine the
reasons of all, and being proved by prayer and peace of
conscience lean to the best: neither doubting to depend
upon men or the credit of the truth, but to the word.
Where we note many things: what great care ought parents, magistrates, ministers and preachers, to have over
their children, people and subjects, for their instruction,
seeing as *Ruth* had truly learned of her mother in law,

that did she constantly defend, namely, the worship of
the only one God. If *Naomi* had perverted her from one
heathenism to another, it is very likely she would have
abode by it, but being instructed in the truth, and sealed   Eph. 1.13
by the holy Spirit of promise, she doth carefully maintain it, giving us thereby to understand how inestimable
is the benefit of good education, and first, training up in
Religion.

And ought not this to be dear unto us, that watch
over the souls of our people and children, who by us being rightly grounded in the foundation of Christian Religion may happily grow up, like to glorious olives for the
church and commonwealth. We read when *Laban* swore   Gen. 31.53
by his false gods, then *Jacob* swore by the fear of his father *Isaac*; so excellent was the instruction given him of
his father, that in the presence of idolatrous *Laban*, for
fear nor favor would he alter his religion: yea it seemed
to be fastened in his flesh, that having been twenty years
among the idolatrous Syrians, yet he had not changed
the manner of his oath, the which he learned of his father. Oh where are these *Isaacs* in our days, which teach
their children any religion? indeed men are too careful
for their children's temporal wealth, they put them to
schools and universities, to be students at the law, and
men of occupations, (which are good) but ask them why
they do so, they will answer, that they might have some-
thing to live by hereafter: never a word I warrant you of
the salvation of their souls, but for that, they will hope
in God they say: and thus they compass sea and land   Gen. 24.42
for trifles, but the never fading health they least think
upon. In times past servants prayed to the God of their
masters, but in these days if they should do so, they must
pray either to pride, covetousness, or ignorance: masters
and servants can swear by the name of God liberally, but
pray sparingly, insomuch as if the life of God consisted
in their prayers, they would surely murder him, they so
seldom call upon him. Oh that this hellish behavior of

Ruth Chapter 1. verses 15-17

masters and servants, could be reduced to the line of
God his word; but now they deal with their servants as
the Egyptians did with the Israelites, they look for their
tasks and worldly business, but they never exhort them
to sacrifice to the Lord: nay, they hinder them, and call
them idle persons, if there be any forwardness of servants and children that ways; truly now is like servant,
like master; like maid, like mistress, like father, like
son, like mother, like daughter, such is the seed, such
is the harvest, they go from cradles to graves, and from
graves to damnation, their whole care is for pleasure and
wealth, and therefore they have no part or portion but
in this present life. Yet let the children of *Abraham* do
like *Abraham*, teach their sons, daughters and servants,
the covenant of the Lord, that all their seed and posterity may be blessed, both with the temporal and everlasting promise, for godliness hath the promise of this life
and of the life to come. Secondly, by this we note, the
fault of ungodly flatterers; which will outwardly for show
or favor be godly with the good, and wicked with the
profane, they will in good company temper their speech
like good men, they will trudge and travel to sermons
and godly exercises, because it pleaseth some gentleman
or other, and will say to them, thy God, my God, your
preacher, my preacher, your profession shall be my profession, whom you love, I love, whom you hate, I abhor:
of this sort are many ignorant persons, one misliketh our
religion, because some popish friend of his mislikes it,
some speak against our government, because one or other which gape for the church livings speaketh against it:
and to say the truth, it is very lamentable to see, how all
religion of many is turned into man-pleasing, but these
tame beasts will one day come to the slaughter as well as
wild, when it shall be manifested, that the surest and safest way in Religion, is to depend on God, and not men.

Where thou diest. Having promised her life to
be spent in her mother's company, she proceedeth to

Gen. 18.19

1 Tim. 4.8

her death, showing unto her such perfect friendship as neither the travails of life or sorrows of death, could ever abrogate, and she addeth, that even in that place where *Naomi* should be buried, would *Ruth* be interred: for we know the ancient custom was to be buried with the fathers or predecessors, whereof undoubtedly the cause was, the hope of the resurrection, that as they were buried, so they should rise together, to be made partakers of eternal woes, or everlasting joys. And by this we observe, the love which we owe unto our fathers and friends must be of such continuance, that it reach unto the grave: not only to be here the inheritors of their lands, but also being dead, to give our bodies to their sepulchers, and the measure of it must be so perfect, that we must be the companions of life and death. And truly, such as is the love of children to their natural parents, such must be the peoples to their spiritual fathers in Christ. *The Galatians to pleasure Paul would have pulled* Gal. 4.15 *out their own eyes*, but men in these days are so far from this liberality, towards the small number of preaching ministers, that they will hardly give any penny towards their maintenance: they had rather have their gold than the Gospel of Christ, their paltry pigs than preaching: they cry out chargeable, chargeable is the ministry, when they themselves which should pay the tenths, yield not the twentieth of their increase, such suing for their right, such trying of customs, such overbearing the weak, and finally they would be religious, but the ministers must be as beggars among them. Who seeth not in many places where they cry out for preachers, and promise largely in their behalf, yet when the Lord hath sent them, they almost stink in their presence. I speak plainly I confess, and yet but the truth: and moreover, they are not only poorly provided for, but every base person, peasant, and pot-companion, are suffered to crow over them, and cry out against them. Thus Christ was before, and yet like us, contemned of the bravest and reviled of the basest:

Ruth Chapter 1. verses 15-17

the world I see is no changeling, although many hundred ages have passed since, yet the manners thereof remain, it agreeth in nothing save only to persecute Christ: and seeing we are sent forth as silly Lambs among ten thousand Wolves, and as men born out of due time, although our calling be despised, our labor unprofitable, and we made laughing stocks, yet our pains will be rewarded, our offences pardoned, we crowned, and they everlastingly confounded.

So let God. Last of all, that she might be no more molested by her mother in law, she confirmeth the resolution of her mind by an oath, in these words, So let God do unto me, and more also if ought but death do separate thee and me, which is a usual manner of swearing in the Scripture, as we read of *David* how he swore

1 Sam. 25.22   he would be revenged of the churlish *Nabal*, for the uncourteous message he returned him by his servants, and is used by all the godly in the old Testament, and indeed it doth most notably describe the nature of an oath, for it is thus much in effect, I pray God confound me if I speak not this with purpose of heart: out of the which we note many things most profitable. First, that in every oath we curse our own souls, if we publish not the truth, or perform not that which we promise: as if every time we swear we should say, The Lord confound me body and soul with Satan and his angels, if this be not so. Oh that our oath-mongers and common swearers in our days, would remember or understand this, that whereas in their days they have sworn many millions of times, so many curses and damnations they have wished to themselves, the very consideration whereof would make them as guilty in their own consciences as ever *Cain* was for killing a man, or *Judas* for betraying the Lord of glory: they have with their arrows of blasphemy shot through and bored the Lord to the very nearest place of his life, for every trifle. And truly as the common Inn is known by his sign, and the Black-Moor by his skin, even so is an

Atheist and carnal man by his oath. We shall talk with honest worldly men, who at every word or sentence, will break forth into most horrible swearing upon no occasion: if they be rebuked they wax much worse. *We* *read of an Egyptian Israelite that blasphemed*, and was by God his own commandment stoned to death. How if this law were put in practice among us? where would the gallant companions, which will swear by all the colors of the moon, become? would not they cry out to the hills to cover them, and to the rocks to fall upon them? was it not strange, that *among six hundred thousand men* *which were able to bear arms, with old men, women and* *children almost innumerable there should be found but* *one man that had blasphemed, or taken God his dreadful* *name in vain and he must be stoned?* But among us, if so many chosen men were taken, my life for it, there shall not be found among every hundred, ten persons which are not common blasphemers.

Oh Lord, how doth thy mercy stay the heavens from pouring down stones upon us; as they did upon the Canaanites. There is not now a child in the streets, if he be able to speak, but he murmureth an oath, only excepted some few which have godly parents: there is not a woman either maid or wife, some few excepted, which doth not daily increase their curse by their continual blasphemies: may we not now say, Lord what is man that thou visitest him, or the son of man that thou so regardest him. Truly the most follow the counsel of *Job's* wife, they curse God and die. A godly martyr required to curse Christ, and he should live, answered, seventy years have I served him, and yet he never did me any hurt, why then should I curse him? And I pray you, what hurt hath the Lord done unto you, that you thus blaspheme his honor, curse your own souls, rebel against his laws and swear many hundred times oftener than you eat or drink: surely the disease of leprosy was contagious, and whosoever had it was excluded from the congrega-

Lev. 24.23

Numb. 1.46

Judg. 10.11

Ruth Chapter 1. verses 15-17

tion, how much more ought this poison of swearing and swearers to be cut off from the society of God and men? And surely now help O ye Gods of the earth, I mean you magistrates and men of authority, this knot will never be unloosed, except you draw out your swords and strike it asunder: though you would give them all your possessions, and steal away their swearing as *Rachel* stole her father's idols, yet they will swear by false Gods still as *Laban* did; that is, they must either die, or the wrath of God must be poured down upon us forever, for his curse shall never depart from the house of the swearer. And if you help not to cure this evil, the Lord shall curse both you and them with everlasting plagues. He crieth and saith, whom shall I send? the ministers have said they will go; yea, they have told *Jacob* his sin and *Israel* his transgression, and *England* his swearing also, but they are come again with *Jeremiah*, unto you O princes, publish you the decree, that whosoever sweareth by the name of God rashly, he should be cut off from the people, and his house sowed with salt, never to be built again.

Isa. 9.3

Secondly, by this we observe, that it is not lawful to swear but only by the name of God, for *Ruth* saith so, *And so let God do unto me, and more also.* She calleth not heaven and earth to record, or any other thing, save only he which is able to punish, or else to pardon, and knoweth the secrets of every man's heart. Whereby we are taught, that it is sacrilege in God his sight to swear by our faith or truth, our honor or honesty, bread or drink, or anything else. Many think they avoid swearing very cleanly, if they swear by any of these, not knowing that he that sweareth by the gold, sweareth by the Temple, and he that sweareth by the Temple, sweareth by him that sitteth thereon: even so he that sweareth by his faith, sweareth by Christ (for faith is no faith without Christ) and he that sweareth by the Son, sweareth by the Father and the holy Ghost. Therefore dearly beloved, let us frame our tongues to honor, not to dishonor God, to glorify, not to defame his name. For if he that toucheth his Saints, toucheth the apple of his eye, what doth he which thrusteth at his name, which is dearer unto him than heaven and earth? Surely the Lord will not hold him guiltless, but as he hath not pitied the Lord in tearing him with oaths, no more shall the Lord show any mercy to his soul from punishing it in hell.

Lastly, by these words of *Ruth* we observe, that an oath must be the last thing we produce in the testimony of any truth. She denieth her mother once, and the second time, when her sister went away, but now the third time, after solemn protestation made, she addeth an oath, as the last refuge and end of all controversy. Against this do all the former offend, which will not tarry till the last, but even at the first rap out their oaths, as fast as a brawling dog his barking, swearing through custom to truth and falsehood, making no difference between weighty matters and idle toys, especially in gaming, playing, hunting, chiding, and such like, they spit out their poison against God himself, neither sparing the wounds, blood, heart, death, and nails of the Lord, renting him worse being in heaven, than the Jews did upon the cross. But let *Ruth* and her companions teach ten thousand of them, with what reverence they must use the holy name of God: she had not been past ten years with a godly woman, but she had learned her Religion, both of faith and manners, for in this she uttereth both: but we have a great many both men and women, which have had twenty and thirty apiece, not with one, but with a whole church of godly persons, and yet they have got neither faith nor manners from them, they can easily give them leave to practice Religion, but themselves wallow in pleasure. But be not deceived, God is not mocked, when he beginneth he will make an end, and consume your viperous tongues and beastly hearts, as the fountain of this mischief in the fire of hell. We are as importunate on you as the blind men of *Jericho*, the

Ruth Chapter 1. verses 15-17

more we are rebuked, the more we cry unto you, let not our Country be cursed, our Prince removed, our God blasphemed, his Gospel translated from us, and our souls and bodies everlastingly plagued. *To God let us give praise.*

The end of the Third Lecture

The Fourth Lecture

Ruth Chapter 1. verses 18-22

18 *When she saw that she was steadfastly minded to go with her, she left speaking unto her.*
19 *So they went forth both until they came to* Bethlehem, *and when they came to* Bethlehem, *it was noised of them throughout all the city, and they said, Is not this* Naomi?
20 *And she answered, Call me not* Naomi, *but call me* Mara, *for the Almighty hath given me much bitterness.*
21 *I went out full, and the Lord hath caused me to return empty, Why call you me* Naomi, *seeing the Lord hath humbled me, and the Almighty hath brought me unto adversity.*
22 *So* Naomi *returned, and* Ruth *the Moabitess, her daughter in law, with her, which returned out of the country of* Moab: *and they came to* Bethlehem *in the beginning of barley harvest.*

aving heard the conference between *Naomi* and *Ruth*, now the holy Ghost describeth the issue of this journey, to the end of this Chapter: wherein *Naomi* ceaseth to vex her daughter, or dissuade her to proceed in her purpose, but willingly taketh her with her, and both of them travel to *Bethlehem*, whither they come in a most fit and acceptable time, neither hindered in their journey, nor forgotten of their friends, but kindly received to their great comfort.

These words contain in them two parts, the first their consent to travel and journey unto *Bethlehem*, the second is their entertainment there. The first part is expressed in the eighteen and nineteen verses: and hath two members, first *Naomi* rested satisfied with the answer of *Ruth,* and vexed her no more, verse eighteen: secondly, their prosperous journey to the city *Bethlehem,* verse nineteen. In the end of this verse is set down the entertainment they found there, which is this, the citizens came flocking to see her, calling and welcoming her by name in these words, *Is not this Naomi?* unto the which salutation she herself answereth in the two next verses, first acknowledging her name, but confessing herself unworthy of it, in these words, *Call me not* Naomi, *but call me* Mara: secondly, she addeth the cause of her speech, in these words: for the Lord hath given me much bitterness: this is amplified in the next verse by an allegory taken from a vessel. In these words, *I went out full*: finally, she setteth down the use she maketh of her affliction, showing unto them, that she could not glory in all the vain titles of the world: first because the Lord had humbled her, secondly, because he had brought her into adversity: in the last verse is set down the time when these pilgrims came from *Moab* to *Bethlehem*, which was the beginning of barley harvest.

When she saw. As *Naomi* in the beginning dealt very wisely, in the trial of her daughters before they were too far gone, so in the end she dealeth very godly with *Ruth*, in that she yieldeth to her answer and petition, giving over to molest her with any more objections. This friendly and worthy meekness, is very commendable in all the godly, for without this they can never in charity and compassion try and examine their brethren. When our Savior Christ, had dealt with the Canaanitish woman about the like cause, seeing that silence would not answer her, nor denial satisfy her, nor the opprobrious

word of dog dismay her, then he yielded to her desire,
cured her daughter, and proclaimed her faith to be won- Matt. 15.22
derful: by which we gather that it is an ungodly thing, to
try any in religion or in any good motion beyond their
strength, for it is no doubt, but *Naomi* if she would, could
have multiplied more objections against this enterprise
of *Ruth*, but her mind was to try her, not to trouble her,
to confirm her, not to confound her, and to show unto
her what must be her resolution, if she go unto the Lord's
people, she can hope for no earthly felicity, she must
never repent and turn back again, she must bury both
country and kindred in the grave of forgetfulness, that
the thoughts or desire of their fruition must never hinder the course of her religion. Whereby all the godly are
by *Naomi* admonished, to be careful whom they receive
into their company, and how gently they must entreat
them when they find their fidelity: the Ravens will not
feed their own birds, or young ones so long as they be
naked, till their feathers come out, and they know them
to be their own, which jealousy of souls must teach us,
that if we see not the evident tokens of godliness, we
must not receive, yea our own kinsmen into the secret
of our hearts, to communicate unto them the sweet fellowship we have with Christ, for many daily creep into
the church to espy our liberty, but as *John* saith, if any
come unto you, and bring not this doctrine, receive 2 John 1.10
them not to house, nor bid them good speed. But in
this it is strange to see how far many godly persons are
deceived, which believe every light word of hypocritical
persons, esteeming them good Christians, giving them
the right hand of fellowship, and opening the treasures
of the Lord to these mockers of spiritual things, casting
the children's crumbs to dogs, and their precious pearls
before these filthy swine, which tread both Christ and
his Gospel under the feet of their hearts, and rent, revile, persecute, and seek the destruction of the truly religious: would God we were all *Naomis* in this point, to

Ruth Chapter 1. verses 18-22

1 John 4.1
John 2.24

try their spirits whether they be of God, seeing so many false spirits are gone out into the world; *for we must not commit ourselves to everyone that will outwardly say as we believe, but first see the fruits and afterwards judge of the tree.*

We know how many in the Gospel our Savior Christ refused, which offered themselves unto him, for none can come to him but those whom his father draweth. And against this especially do all the flattering *Michas* and please-man preachers of *England* offend, which as the prophet saith, sow pillows under the elbows of the people, that is, they give them rest in their singular sins, if they can say Lord, Lord, they tell them they are good Christians, if they come once a week to the church, their devotion is sufficient, if they spend all their days in ignorance and vanity, yet a few words at the later end will recover them. Oh, how fearful and lamentable is the condition of such pastors and people, where they are thus flattered in their sins, and stroked in their iniquities, they hear the Gospel, feed on the sacraments, dwell safely in the house of God, and eat of the fat of the lands; that their judgment might be without excuse, their damnation the greater, and themselves the prepared oxen for the Lord's slaughter-house; they cry, peace, peace, mercy, mercy, speak of plenty, not penury, of feasting, not famines, of pleasures, not sufferings, of mirth, not mourning, of new wine, not God his word; nay they bid the most covetous cormorants, encroaching usurers, prodigal ruffians, beastly drunkards, filthy adulterers, cursed blasphemers, common swearers, dumb ministers, and profane and carnal Atheists, to hope for salvation, whereas the Apostle saith, not one of these shall inherit the kingdom of God. Is not this to cast children's bread to dogs, and to make the most holy Gospel a cloak, nay rather a patent or charter to work all manner of licentiousness? surely, if *Naomi* would not promise anything to her dear daughter *Ruth*, but rather discourage her from following the Lord in the trial of her faith, you are as far wide from any hope of saving health, as heaven from the earth, or light from darkness: therefore to conclude, as the gold is not known but by the touchstone, so is not any Christian, till he be thoroughly tried in religion, and as the goldsmith will not accept it (though it seem never so fair) till he have tried it, so must not we loose the bands of sins, till they be repented, or bind the breaches of iniquity, till they be satisfied, nor account any a Christian till we have thoroughly tried him.

Other there are which will never be satisfied in their brethren, every day troubling them with vain and unprofitable questions, never giving them over, till they have wearied them with their wranglings, seeking to deface in them that little knowledge which they have, and discourage them from the profession of Christian Religion. But most abominable is the dealing of many with their neighbors, both Christian men and women, who forsaking the cursed pastime of carnal companions, espying the insufficiency of dumb and unpreaching ministers, burning in love for the pure preaching of God his word, and seeking that where it is to be found, absent themselves from their assemblies now and then, they present them to the courts as wicked recusants, where I warrant you, they find as much favor as *Paul did before Felix:* thus we are many times unjustly vexed for good consciences, turmoiled about for hearing of sermons, almost as much as any Papist for abhorring our Religion: and this it is that feareth many, causeth other to fall back before troubles come, and dismayeth many weak souls, when they see their poor brethren in this peaceable time, under the government of so godly and gracious a prince, so tormented as is incredible; the experience of this is too too common in every corner of our Country, where there is any diligent preacher or profitable hearer. Let us therefore my brethren, with *Naomi,* cease to vex the godly minded *Ruths,* both men and women: our

Acts 24.26

Ruth Chapter 1. verses 18-22

damnation shall be the greater, if we draw and drive men from God, the laws require it not, the magistrates like it not, our profession forbiddeth it, and accursed are those godless Judges which pronounce any sentence against these innocent persons. Therefore say with the Prophet, Come let us ascend to the mountain of the Lord, even to

Micah 4.2

the hill of the God of *Jacob*, for he shall teach us his ways, and we will walk in his paths.

So they went forth. Now are these two good women both going, and also come to *Bethlehem*, and undoubtedly their tedious journey was eased by their mutual conference: but what things happened to them by the way the Scripture mentioneth not, only their entertainment is here set down, how their coming being noised about the city, they came unto them, and saluted their old acquaintance *Naomi* by name. For this ques-

Gen. 18.14,17

tion, *Is not this Naomi?* after the manner of the Hebrews is a usual manner of affirmation, as we may see in these

Judg. 6.31
2 Sam. 3.8

places of Scripture. Where first of all we see the wonderful mercy of God toward *Naomi*, which in so many years absent suffered not her memory utterly to perish, but at her first arriving, did publish her name, and comfort her sorrows. Thus God hath many blessings in store for the relieving of his poor afflicted saints, and surely he

Gen. 45.28
Psal. 30.6

is careful that the candle of the righteous be not put out forever. But as in one day (after many years sorrow for *Joseph* and famine for bread) *Jacob* received tidings of the welfare of his son, and provision for his family, even so the Lord compasseth about the faithful with songs of deliverance, that though heaviness endure for a night, yet joy cometh in the morning. Let us therefore with the loss, and laying down of our own lives confess the good-

Dan. 4.33,37

ness of the Lord, for as he drave the King of *Babylon* for seven years from the throne of majesty, to the wilderness of wild beasts, so he called him again and restored to him his scepter and seat, established his kingdom all the days of his life. Therefore fear not, fear not my beloved,

Lecture 4

have we now famine? we shall have plenty again: do we
carry forth our seed weeping? we shall come again with
plentiful sheaves. Have we sowed in tears? we shall reap
in joy. Have we been strangers in other lands? we are
come home with *Naomi* to the City of God his people:
and finally, those that fear the Lord shall be as *mount
Sion,* which can never be moved: for as there is a time to
mourn, so there is a time to rejoice, and as the wicked   Psal. 125.1
shall have measure for measure, so the godly shall receive reward for reward.

Secondly, by these words we observe the fruit
of charity, or duty of neighbors and acquaintance: for as
these citizens of *Bethlehem* came to see and to comfort
Naomi, so must every one bear some part of his brother's
or sister's sorrow, in relieving their troubled minds by
their presence and speeches. We read that *Mary* went to   Luke 1.39
her cousin *Elizabeth,* being with child, that they might   John 11.33
commune and comfort themselves in the promises of   Acts 9.39
the Lord. We read how the Jews accompanied *Mary*
and *Martha* weeping for *Lazarus,* and the same also we
read was done at the death of *Dorcas.* What shall I say
of the *four men* which brought the sick of the palsy unto   Mark 2.4
Christ: and most excellent is the fellowship of the saints
in the primitive church, which are said to continue and
abide together with one accord in prayer and breaking
of bread; so that their spiritual comfort of praying, and
temporal refreshing of corporal food, were private to any,
but also for their comfort, as a young child is wrapped
in his swaddling clothes, so was the infancy of Christ's
church maintained by the company of their faithful fellowship. Oh that we could love and live thus together in
the bond of unity and Christian concord, that as we are
members of one body, so we should not be so strange
one to another, as if the eye had never seen the foot, or
the head never known the legs: such is the scornfulness
of our age, wherein men are ashamed of Christ in his
members, if they be a little fallen into decay, how hardly

Ruth Chapter 1. verses 18-22

will they comfort them, as these *Ephrathites* do *Naomi*, a poor widow now, though once a noble woman. They will rather curse them with *Shimei*, than bless them with *Ziba*, but let the faithful like feeling members of their brethren's afflictions look upon the *Naomis* in our days, some are poor and friendless, other sick and harborless, some sorrowful, some hungry, and many destitute, let us gather to us these members of Christ, our company will more refresh them than our contribution, our talk more than our alms, our feeling and fellow prayers, more than the distribution of our money, let us lay hold on that, and yet forget not this, for as God hath given both to us, so he looketh we should give both to other.

Thirdly, by this we observe, how the world is wont to comfort one another, for these Bethlemites say unto her, *Is not this Naomi?* that is, they comfort her with the consideration of her name, which in Hebrew signifieth beautiful or pleasant, as if they had said unto her, Although thou art old, yet thou art beautiful, for thou remainest *Naomi* still, thy name is a prophet unto thee, to forewarn thee of thy welfare, and if thou be now like the stubble after the crop, yet thou shalt shortly be as the green herb or pleasant plant, comfort thy self, *Jacob* always prevailed with God, because his name was always *Israel*: the Dove shall be chaste, because it is a Dove: the eye shall be bright, because it is the eye, and *Naomi* shall be blessed, because she is *Naomi*. Thus worldly persons wish worldly things, and the best they desire most, is outward prosperity. Neither is this simply unlawful, for such as is the sore, such must be the salve, and where the wound is, the medicine must be ministered: if in the world they be oppressed, in the same they may not only wish, but pray for release, yet always remember, that friends and parties must so desire and request it, as may be most for the glory of God. Therefore this is our duty, that in praying for earthly benefits, we aim at God his will, but in desiring spiritual blessings, we must

regard our salvations. And more also, we must not so
ravish the minds of the worldly afflicted, as if they had
no other hope, but this temporal welfare: but so promise
the blessings of God, as they may have a spiritual signifi-
cation, for worldly misery is abated but with everlasting
felicity.

 And Naomi *said.* In these words *Naomi* answereth to the comforts of her friends, and telleth them
she rather deserveth to be called *Mara* than *Naomi*, that
is, bitter than beautiful: whereby she teacheth us how
vain are outward and worldly titles: for which cause
James wisheth us not to be called many masters, know-   Jam. 3.1
ing we shall receive the greater damnation, as if he had
said, worldly honor bringeth death, but desire or love of
carnal comforts cause damnation. When the ark of God
was taken by the Philistines, and the sons of *Eli* both
slain, the wife of *Phinehas* the son of *Eli* died after her   1 Sam. 4.21
travail, and named her son *Ichabod*: which is by interpretation, Where is the glory? although there a man-child
was born, yet the woman forgat not her sorrow, because
the ark of God was taken by the heathen, for if she were
the daughter to the chiefest in *Israel*, as she was, and wife
to the third, yet what glory had she of her place, when
her husband was justly slain, and her people overcome,
therefore she called her son (no glory) for neither dignity
of place, highness of birth, fruitfulness of children, or the
dominion over a whole country, may minister any comfort to them whom the Lord hath humbled. *Rachel* that
bid *Jacob* give her children or else she should die, at the
birth of her second child died, and yet had children, she
supposed if she were made fruitful, and had many chil-   Gen. 30.7
dren, she could not choose but live in felicity; but having
the first, she called him *Joseph,* because God would add
more, yet at the second, she called him *Benoni,* which is   Gen. 35.18
the son of her sorrow, because she died in travail, so that
she which accounted bearing of children her chiefest
joy, by that which she loved, came her greatest sorrow.

Ruth Chapter 1. verses 18-22

Thus *Naomi*, which was once as beautiful and pleasant in prosperity as any, yet now in adversity who more bitter than she, yea the very remembrance of her name increaseth her grief. Were she the daughter of a prince, yet now being a beggar, it is a greater discomfort unto her, than if she had been born poor, for man's nature is like a pleasant plant, which prospereth when it groweth higher and higher, but decayeth if it fall lower and lower: if *Naomi* had been a Lady, yet having lost her husband, children and wealth, the cogitation of her wonted welfare, increaseth her disquietness, even as *Phinehas* his wife and *Rachel* at the birth of their children. Why then do men thus highly esteem of worldly vainglory? Cannot one measure of honor afford one mite of comfort to a distressed person? Do not men because they are proper, wax proud, and because they are learned, ambitious, what then is the fruit of worldly titles? is pride the reward of proportion? loftiness of worship? scornfulness of riches? and ambition of learning? surely these things in the day of trouble can minister no medicine to make ease, if godliness be not with them. What was *Achan* the better for his gold, when he was stoned to death? *Absalom* for his beauty, when he was hanged? *Haman* for his honor, when he was mounted upon his own gallows? the sorcerers of *Egypt* for their knowledge, when darkness was over the land? or *Herod* for the people's voice, when they cried a God and not man, and the worms fell upon him and consumed him? Trust not therefore in princes, much less in the titles of princes, in the strength of an horse, much less in the wealth of man: say not, I shall be the better because I am a gentleman, a doctor, or a nobleman, for when *Solomon* had considered all these things, he said all is vanity and vexation of spirit.

Eccles. 1.17, 18

    For the almighty hath. This is the reason wherefore she denieth her name, or rather changeth it, showing that her first name had nothing in it, which did express the relation between herself and it, but her second

name doth most significantly declare her bitter affliction.
Where we first of all observe the cause which moved the
fathers to give such names to their children, which to
signify or put them in mind of their duty, or some other
event. So God called the first man *Adam* which is as
much as man or earthly, because he was made of the
earth, or the red earth: so *Adam* called his wife *Chavvah*
(which we call *Hevah* [*Eve*], by reason of the Hebrew let-
ters) because she should be the mother of all living: the
like may be said of *Noah, Seth, Abraham, Isaac, Israel,
Samuel, John Baptist* and many others, who being named
either by the Lord himself or by other, were so called, to
put them in mind of their duties, or to note the thankfulness of their parents. The which is also lawful for godly
parents now to imitate, in giving such names to their
children, as may be notes to all the world of their profession. But some cannot brook this liberty, accounting it
newness and preciseness in them that use it, as though
it were a deadly sin, one jot to depart from the custom
of the multitude. But this curiosity is well confuted by
the name of *John Baptist*: ancestors must not always be
followed, those which are new creatures in Jesus Christ,
may also have new names. But in this the world be-
wray [*betray*] their palpable ignorance, for they like the
old names which were very plain in their own tongues,
wherein they were given, but English names they cannot abide, belike [*perhaps*] for very fear, lest their names
should be witnesses of condemnation against their licentiousness. Again, they account it a glory proper to a few
persons, to be called by the worldly surnames of some of
their great ancestors, but they will not bear these names
of rejoicing, thanksgiving, repentance, godliness, mercy,
constancy, and such like, they will as easily admit them,
as a deaf Adder the voice of the charmer. But let the
godly in this use Christian wisdom and ancient liberty,
for that which was lawful in this point in the first age, the
Jews commonwealth, and the primitive church, with the

Gen. 1.27
Gen. 3.20

Luke 1.59,60

Ruth Chapter 1. verses 18-22

practice of all ages since, is also lawful for them to give holy and significant names to their children, for I would have all (if it were possible) to have no other names but such as they understand: if they be called by the names of the ancient fathers, kings, or prophets, which we read of in the Scriptures, it is also needful that they understand the lives and the dispositions of those persons, that as they have them for the evidence of their names, so they might look upon them, as the examples of their faith and manners.

Secondly, by this we note, what God his children think of their suffering, which *Naomi* setteth out by this word *Bitterness*, for bitterness of all other tastes doth most dull the sense, and corrupt the stomach, so that they account their afflictions, as sharp to them as to any, and may as lawfully complain of them unto the Lord. This I speak for instruction of them that are ignorant, and the comfort of the afflicted. First for instruction, because some think they are not truly religious, except they feel their miseries no more than a stone, when they are afflicted, and this maketh them so to waver and doubt of themselves, that in their greatest plagues, they can hardly receive any comfort, being always troubled with this, that if they were faithful they should delight more in their tribulations. Yet beloved, mark a little, *Naomi* calleth it in this place, bitterness, as if she had called the enemy to her health, for when *Peter* would express the danger of *Simon Magus*, because he offered money for the gift of the holy Ghost, he telleth him he is in the very gall of bitterness, by that metaphor or allegory, declaring the loathsomeness of sin to his soul, as bitterness to the body. *David* saith that his affliction was his death, as if he had said, even as a man striveth to be delivered in the pangs of death, so he from his tribulation. *Job* that mirror of patience, did so delight in his sufferings, that in one place he seemeth to accuse God himself, to add to his transgressions, that is, to make his sins seem

Acts 8.23

Psal. 31.10

Lecture 4

greater than they were, and how doth he desire to plead
with God about his affliction, and cursed the day and
hour of his birth. Our Savior would never have warned   John 16.18-22
us that in the world we should have sorrow and lam-
entation, had he not known that the smart of our sufferings would thrust forth abundance of tears, through
the vehemency of the pains, and presently he addeth a
secret comparison between a woman in travail, and a
Christian in persecution, so that as the one hath most
vehement sorrows and pitiful lamentations, so also may
the other: infinite testimonies might be brought for the
proof of this, to teach us that God his children are made
of flesh as well as of spirit, and the flesh is weak, though
the spirit be willing: therefore we may fear and cry under the burden of our pains, that our afflictions are bitter
unto us, and that the hand of the Lord is grievous upon
us. Again, for the comfort of the godly I speak this, that
if any have grievously complained of their sufferings, let
them impute it to the sharpness of their pains, and the
weakness of their natures: we see this *Naomi* calleth bitterness unto her, such as she would not willingly take
except it were for the physic of her soul, and now almost
ten years' space this grief hath grown upon her, so that
it may seem of all others she was most grieved, for now
she uttereth her mind as freshly, as if the potion were yet
undigested in the stomach. Be comforted therefore my
sorrowful brethren and sisters, you see you are not alone
in this misery, for *David, Job, Naomi, Anna, Nehemiah,*
and many other are as far indebted to the Lord in this
point, as ever was any: strive to suppress it by prayer, and
quench it by singing of *Psalms*: neither let us judge but
charitably of those which in this case are troubled, be it
for the loss of their children, the death of their husbands,
the decay of their wealth, or the lack and want of their
health. If they seem impatient and weaker than ourselves, let us bear part of their burdens upon our Christian comforts, that they with us, and we with them, like

Ruth Chapter 1. verses 18-22

feeling members of the same infirmities, may sustain our crosses by our mutual supplications, and obtain our deliverance by the blood of Christ.

I went out full. In these words she amplifieth her former complaint by this comparison of a full vessel and an empty, showing that as the fullest vessel is the soundest, and the emptiest good for nothing, so it fareth with her when she looketh upon her former life, when she went forth she had plenty, but now she returneth in want; then she was sound, but now broken, then joyful, but now sorrowful: why should she be called pleasant or beautiful, or by her old name, seeing God hath humbled her, whereas in times past he upheld her in prosperity, but now he hath cast her down into adversity. Where we first of all observe the nature of worldly prosperity, which today is like a full vessel, but tomorrow like an empty, now it is green, anon it is withered, now it groweth, anon it is cut down, now like *Nebuchadnezzar* sitting upon his throne, with his counselors and courtiers of estate about him, but anon both Court and Country drive him to the company of wild beasts: for as a little breach emptieth the barrel so a little trouble bringeth worldly welfare to wallow in the mire: like a bladder, so is worldy prosperity, a puff doth make it swell, but a prick doth make it fall again. Therefore we read of none, either King or Country which had such a prosperous estate, but it had one enemy or other to work his woe: if we consider the 1 Kings 10.17 reign of *Solomon*, where gold was innumerable and silver as plentiful as stones, yet it wanted not his miseries, the people were punished by payments to their prince, the King was threatened with the loss of ten parts of his 1 Kings 11.14 Kingdom, and God stirred *Hadad* the Edomite against him, where ended their peace. Where is then the royalty of *Solomon*? was it not cast down in one day, his riches consumed, his buildings burned, his children captivated, his wisdom turned to idolatry, his prosperity decayed, and all his honor overturned. Oh that worldlings would

Lecture 4

consider their fickle estate, and be admonished of their immanent dangers: the Lord putteth them into his balance, and finding them too light, casteth them out. *Jeremiah* saith, they are but fatted sheep, kept for the day of slaughter, now in the pasture, and presently it the fire, they are but advanced to be cast down again, as the vessel is filled to be emptied in due time, the ears which are now full of corn in the field, anon shall lay without on the dunghill. *Babylon* the Queen of the world, which ruled as yet, was trodden down and made a servant. *Tyrus* that crowned men with her wealth, was consumed by water: for the Lord of hosts decreeth all this, to stain the pride of glory, and to bring to contempt all that be mighty upon the earth. Weep, weep O daughters of honor, the days will come when the tender shall not be regarded, for your wealth shall not always endure, the crown abideth not from generation to generation, your houses shall be overturned, your names forgotten, your children impoverished, your glory defaced your inheritance changed, your welfare poured on the earth like water, and your worship shall be never repaired. This have God his dearest children felt, and the greenest trees have been scorched with the fire of God his wrath, for he is not delighted in worldly bravery, but hath buried great treasure in the sea which shall never be found, to keep mankind from the end of his purpose: for this is their honor, they get nothing but with much travail, and in one hour, lose labor, life, and wealth.

Secondly, that which in our text is, *the Lord hath humbled me*, in the Hebrew is, *The Lord hath testified or witnessed against me*, for by his judgments he humbleth us, as it were producing witnesses to accuse us of our iniquities, as we see in common judgments all things pass by evidence, if they be ancient, and by witness if they be late, so the Lord when he hath a quarrel against us, he first proveth us guilty by witness of our sins, and then punisheth us for committing transgressions. For this

Jer. 12.3

Isa. 23.9

Deut. 31.5-26

Ruth Chapter 1. verses 18-22

cause *Moses* commandeth the book of the Law to be laid up in the side of the Ark of the Covenant, for a witness against the people: so the Lord speaketh by *David*, Hear O my people, and I will speak, hear O Israel, and I will testify unto thee, for I am thy God: and after this he reporteth his witness against them, first that their sacrifices were corrupted, that their Religion was all outward, they spake well but did ill. And thus God witnesseth the sins of commonwealths by the changing of their Prince, the sins of public persons, by casting them out of their office, the sins of private persons, sometimes by imprisonment, sometimes by scourging or poverty, and sometimes by sickness, alluding to trials of judgment where the noble is condemned for treason, as well as the meaner person for stealing. And this my beloved, hath the Lord testified against us, our peace hath been threatened by war, our Prince by treason, our banqueting by famine, our excess by penury, our pride by poverty, our people's contempt of preaching by pestilence, and still the Lord hideth our sin from this witness that we might repent for all. Then we must needs set down with ourselves, that our actions are noted, our profaning of sabbaths registered, our contempts against God his ministers described, the times of our drunkenness, idleness and wantonness numbered, our own consciences examined, the witnesses produced, we arraigned, and now, even now before God his judgment seat in danger to be everlastingly condemned, for as *Naomi* saith, the Lord emptieth us of his graces, and testifieth against us: who shall plead for us when the judge knoweth our guiltiness, surely, surely, there is no hope of pardon, but to the penitent, and patience must be prayed for, that our sufferings may be eased.

So she returned with Ruth *the Moabitess with her.* This verse is the conclusion of this first Chapter, where is described the time of *Naomi's* return unto *Bethlehem* from the country of *Moab*, which was the beginning of barley harvest, that the report she heard in *Moab*, (how

Psal. 50.7

Prov. 28.1

Esther 7.9
Isa. 22.19

God had visited his people and given them bread) might at her first arrival be found true: wherein is noted the blessing of God unto her, that she came in the beginning of harvest, the pleasantest and profitablest time of all the year. This barley harvest was in the latter part of the first month, and the beginning of the second among the Jews, which with us are called *March* and *April*, for the warmness of those countries is such, that their harvest is ripe much sooner than in ours.

By the which also we note, that she had a prosperous success in her journey, that even in those dangerous days, she came safely to *Bethlehem*: all those doubts which in the beginning we showed you, might have hindered her journey, she well overpassed: for no doubt in so rare a matter, if any let had been offered, the holy Ghost would not have omitted it. So that this teacheth us with *Naomi*, that as she was not hindered in her travel from *Moab* to God his people, even so must not we be stayed from the profession of true Religion. She was an old woman, yet she would go so tedious a journey to the company of the faithful, therefore let no man think that age excuseth them from the true worship of God, or sincere profession of Religion. She had little company to encourage her, only poor *Ruth* her daughter in law waited upon her, therefore it must not hinder or discourage us that so few follow Religion, for Christ's flock is a little flock, like the first fruits of the harvest field, which is but a handful to many cartloads. *Naomi* adventured her body and forsook her goods, to come to the house of the Lord. Oh how cold are our days, when men need neither of both, yea they will hardly go any farther for knowledge than the vilest Atheist in the world. And to conclude, many dangers hung over her head, yet by the providence of God she escaped all, even so my brethren admit no delays, invent no excuses, receive no hindrances, imagine no suspicions, and abstain from all stays which may let you from coming to the mountain of

Ruth Chapter 1. verses 18-22

the Lord, the company of the faithful, for blessed are the people, whose God is Jehovah, and it is better to abide but one day in the courts of the Lord, than a thousand years in the palaces of the wicked. Now let us give praise to the Lord.

The end of the Fourth Lecture.

The Fifth Lecture

Ruth Chapter 2. verses 1-7

1 *Now* Naomi's *husband had a kinsman, a man of great wealth, of the family of* Elimelech, *whose name was* Boaz.

2 *And when* Ruth *the Moabitish said unto her mother in law, Let me go, I pray thee, into the field, to gather ears after him, in whose eyes I shall find favor, and she said, Go my daughter.*

3 *And she went and came to gather in the field, after the reapers: and she met with the possession of a field pertaining to* Boaz, *who was of the family of* Elimelech.

4 *And behold, when* Boaz *came from* Bethlehem, *he said to the reapers, The Lord be with you, and they said, The Lord bless thee.*

5 *And* Boaz *said to his servant which was appointed over the reapers, Whose is this maid?*

6 *And the servant which was appointed over the reapers, answered and said, This is the Moabitish maid, which came with* Naomi *from the country of* Moab.

7 *Which came and said, Let me gather, I pray you, among the sheaves, after the reapers, and so she came, and stayed here from morning until now, only she tarried a little at her house.*

In the former Chapter we heard by our general division, that the occasion of this history was therein contained: but now in these three Chapters following, is declared the means whereby this marriage was accomplished, whereof the first is described in this second Chapter, which is the acquaintance of *Boaz* and *Ruth*, and the circumstances thereof, as shall appear in the special treatise of every particular thing. The occasion of this acquaintance is the gleaning of *Ruth*, in the field of *Boaz*. These seven verses contain two parts, the first and principal part is of *Boaz*, and the second of *Ruth*. The first part is contained in the 1,4,5,6,7 verses wherein *Boaz* is described, verse 1. to be *Naomi's* kinsman by her husband. Secondly, to be a man of great wealth: in the other verse is set down his diligence, which came to the field to visit his workmen, and view the company. His actions after he came to the field, are, first the salutation of the reapers, verse 4., and they do the like to him: secondly, his question, he asketh his servant who *Ruth* was, verse 5. To which question the servant answereth, first, telling his master that it was *Ruth* the Moabitess, the companion of *Naomi*, verse 6. Secondly, he excuseth her gathering, because she asked leave, and tarried there but only that morning, verse 7.

The second part which respecteth *Ruth*, is contained, verses 2,3. Wherein, first is her petition, she asketh leave of her mother to go and gather ears, where she should find favor, and her mother granteth, verse 2. Secondly, her chance, and good hap [*happening*], the place where she gathereth is described, which was the field or possession of *Boaz*, her husband's kinsman. Of these parts let us briefly speak, as the spirit of God shall give utterance, and the time permit.

Now Naomi's husband. In this verse is contained the description of *Boaz*, upon whom the whole history following dependeth. This *Boaz* was the son of *Salmon*, who was son to *Nahshon*, the Prince of the host of *Judah*: the mother of *Boaz* was *Rahab* the harlot (which received the spies of *Israel* into her house at *Jericho*) as we see in *Mathew*, and is commended for her faith, by the author of the Epistle to the Hebrews. So that every way we see this dignity commended unto us: if we look for birth, his grandfather was the chief of the princely tribe of *Judah*: if for authority, he was, saith this Scripture, of great power: if for wealth, his inheritance must needs be great, who was derived of such noble ancestors, and the reaping of his corn lasted to the end of all harvest, and the chief of all, his religion is excellently commended unto us in the text and history following. So that we have not to deal here with mean and base personages, being all of a kindred, howsoever some are sooner come to decay than other: but out of this we learn many profitable lessons.

1 Chron. 2.10

Josh. 2.4,5

Matt. 1.4
Heb. 11.31

Chapter 2.23

First, that seeing *Boaz* and *Elimelech* are said to be kinsmen, as those which are descended from the same predecessors or ancestry, we are admonished of the frailty and vanity of worldly dignity, that howsoever parents provide for the maintenance of posterity, yet the Lord must dispose the decay of their children. Here we see poor *Naomi* hath a wealthy and an honorable kinsman, yet she a destitute and a desolate widow. Her husband and she were no mean persons, but undoubtedly both descended of noble families: the years were but few since the death of *Joshua*, under whom the inheritance of every tribe, was given by lot, and all the Jews and Israelites wealthy possessors: yet see this godly *Naomi* is fain to live off the gleanings of her daughter, which neither her parents, nor her husband did ever think upon. Behold therefore as in a glass, the perfect image of temporal felicity, the father a king, the children beg-

Ruth Chapter 2. verses 1-7

gars, the father honorable, the son not worshipful, the predecessors the chiefest in authority, but the successors the meanest in calling: this made the fathers think that the world was like the sea, here a mighty wave, and there a great downfall, some thought it to be like ice, where a man can never stand sure, but the one will be breaking, or he be sliding, some like to trees, whereof the tallest are soonest overturned, but all agree in this that worldly felicity is miserable vanity: for our present wealth is like a pleasant summer, which must needs come to an end, though all the world should strive to the contrary: it was accounted to King *David*, for a special blessing of God unto him, and none other, that she should not be without a son to sit on his seat, if his posterity would observe his commandments: yet we see in *Joseph* and *Mary* the mother of Christ, being both of his offspring, how they could not obtain in his own city, a chamber to lie in, but were fain to lodge in a stable, so that this is not only to the wicked, but happeneth to the dearest saints of God. *Adam* continued not still in paradise, but was cast out that his felicity might be heavenly, and not earthly: even so the posterity of the righteous are brought into poverty, that they set not their minds upon temporal glory. Therefore the Lord doth here correct us, with pinching poverty, that there we should not with the world, be condemned for delighting in vanity.

2 Sam. 7.12

Luke 2.7

Then by this we learn humility in our wealth and worship, honor and dignity: set not up your homes so high, saith *David, and if riches increase set not your hearts upon them*, for the Lord resisteth the proud, and giveth grace to the humble and meek. We read of stately Kings and Emperors which have been cast from throne to the footstool, of wealthy persons, which in one hour have been utterly undone, but of children whose parents were honorable and rich, many thousands brought to perpetual slavery. If you fear not your own estates, yet care for your posterity, and make much of them whom

Psal. 62.10

now you see cast down, the poor, the destitute, the despised, the miserable: for if *Jonathan*, in his honor, make
of *David* in his humility, when *David* cometh to his kingdom, he will advance his offspring to his own table: even
so if you make much of them that are poor, now, when
you shall be humbled in your posterity, the Lord shall
provide for your issue by these that have been favored by
you. The wheel of the world runneth round, sometime
that which was lowest is highest, and that which was
highest is made low again. So be you assured, the Lord
advanceth daily out of the dust, to sit with princes, therefore make you friends of the unrighteous Mammon, that
when you shall have need, they may receive you into
their everlasting habitations. Distribute liberally, give
plentifully, live peaceably, walk humbly, for the wealth
of the world doth not alway last, neither the crown from
generation to generation.

    Secondly, by this we gather, that the godly may
safely enjoy great possessions, and of the blessing of God
be exceeding rich men: but some will say, indeed they
may be wealthy, but with the hazard of their souls, for
Christ saith, How hardly shall they which have riches,
enter into the kingdom of God: it is easier for a camel
to go through the eye of a needle than for a rich man to
enter into the Kingdom of heaven. Then if the danger of
it be so great, the poorest condition is the safest welfare.
I grant you, but Christ speaketh of carnal wealthy, which
make their goods their God, as after he saith, those that
put their trust in their riches. Of this sort the world was
never fuller: as on the contrary, of the other there was,
never fewer, you shall have them in all places which speak
against the Gospel, because it is an enemy to their livings
and offices, promotions and honors, like *Demetrius* for
Diana, a heathen Devil: you shall have other that will
offer largely to the Gospel, like the young man that came
to Christ, but when it toucheth a little greater cost, then
farewell Religion. But this is the fault of the men, not of

Luke 18.24,25

Ruth Chapter 2. verses 1-7

their wealth, and yet I am persuaded that there are many wealthy *Abrahams*, which will give of the tenths of their possessions, to the heavenly *Melchizedek,* Jesus Christ, many *Lots* that will harbor the angels of God, and rather wish violence to their own daughters than to the righteous: and finally, like to this *Boaz* in riches and religion, of whom we daily pray the Lord increase the number.

Thirdly, we see in this *Boaz* an excellent example of the reward of religion and faith: for we have heard that he was the son of *Rahab*, which received the spies of *Joshua*, who afterward was married to *Salmon* the son of *Nahshon*, by whom came this godly and wealthy *Boaz*. In this then we see true the saying of the Apostle, that godliness hath the promises of this life and of the life to come: for in herself she was blessed with an honorable marriage, in her posterity with a godly and a wealthy son. This my beloved is a notable encouragement to Religion, for Christ saith that whosoever shall for him forsake father or mother, wife or children, shall receive many times so much in this world, but eternal salvation in the life to come. This answereth and stoppeth the mouths of the enemies which call the professors bankrupts, impoverished, and decayed persons, yea, as base as beggars in this world, which by their Religion undo themselves and their posterity. But on the contrary, we affirm that Religion bringeth no discommodity, even in worldly things; the reason is, because it teacheth us to use our riches aright. If a man had mountains of money, and knew not how to employ it, what profit could he receive thereby? even so surely, without Christ and his Gospel, I mean the true knowledge thereof, there is no lawful use of these worldly benefits, and except every one learn to apply them by the word of God, he possesseth his wealth, as a thief doth the purse of a true man, and in the presence of God is no better than a violent robber, which taketh away the money from the lawful possessors, which have proved and learned the way to

Luke 18.30

use it, and as they have it without his knowledge, even so they shall use it without his blessing. Therefore be not discouraged my dear brethren, come forward in religion, it is the Devil that telleth you, you must make bread of stones, that is, you must rely upon the world, and follow the custom thereof: there is greater plenty and store in the garners of God his word, than in all the cornfields of the world. He which could feed *five thousand people*, with five barley loaves and two fishes, hath he not enough for the maintenance of thy family? He which fed the host of *Israel* almost forty years with angel's food, are not the heavens his for evermore? when almost all the world was in a famine, did he not provide for his servant *Elijah*, first commanding the ravens to bring him bread and meat, morning and evening to the brook *Cherith*, and that being dried up, sustained him with a widow and her son, by a handful of meal and a little oil for a long season. Did not our gracious father multiply the oil of a poor prophet's widow into many vessels, which before could not fill one? And what shall I say more? I have never seen the righteous forsaken, or their children left destitute. John 6.13 1 Kings 17.4,9 2 Kings 4.5,6

And Ruth. After the holy Ghost had set down the description of *Boaz*, as the necessary occasion to understand that which followeth, in the next place he expresseth this of *Ruth*. Wherein he showeth us the carefulness of *Ruth*, for her mother and herself being in a strange place, would not in hunger harbor at home, but rather adventure her peril in an honest labor, by going abroad to glean in the fields, therefore to her mother she cometh and asketh leave, which being granted, forth she goeth, the providence of the Lord directing her journey, she cometh to the harvest field of *Boaz* her kinsman. Verses 2,3

Where first of all we gather, what manner of life they lead after they came to *Bethlehem*, namely, a very poor, base, and despised estate, not half so good to see to, as that which they lead and lived among the Moabites, insomuch as one may now say unto me, you told us even now, the golden rewards and precious commodity of true Religion, which it bringeth to all them that faithfully receive it but you see these two godly women, as armed examples against yourself, they lived wealthily in *Moab*, but poorly in *Judah*; with the wicked they found gentle liberality, but with the godly they endure woeful poverty. What cold entertainment do they find at *Bethlehem*, even in the Church of God, for whose sake one forsook her country, the other her wealth, and both of them their welfare? so that the profession of Religion loseth our friends, denieth our country, disquieteth our peace, engendereth our trouble, consumeth our wealth, and decayeth our substance. Is this the profit of your profession, which promiseth mountains of security, and payeth multitude of miseries? How shall we be encouraged to Religion, when at the first entry we shall pay so great an income, and depart from a fine worth all our substance? To this I answer, that if the beginning be not so joyful as you or they wished, yet the end answered their expectation. I grant, you shall first find a little want, but in the end you shall possess a great gain. A man that hath a thousand pounds laid beside him, and layeth it out upon a bargain, whereof he shall receive no profit in many years, but the date expired, and the day of receipt come, he receiveth his own, and many thousand pounds for his gain, you will grant at the first he emptieth his coffers and bags, and leaveth himself bare and moneyless, yet you would account him a fool, if he would not upon sure bands of so great advantage adventure his own, and give forth his money: Even so it is in religion, it is a pearl for which we must sell both living and lands, and yet it is worth both, and many a thousand times more: if thou feel not the profit at the first, tarry a while, thou hast the promise and band of the Lord of hosts, he is able and willing to perform and pay at the time appointed, and if thou canst abide a little want of

Tumultuosa esse solent initia bonorum, exitus magis gratus & amotnus.

earthly commodities, shortly thou shalt see them rolling
upon thee in excellent abundance, and exceeding quantities.

And this teacheth us with what mind we must
embrace religion, not for any present commodity, or
temporal gain, but with denial of our lives and riches,
that they may serve us as ordinary expenses in our journey to everlasting salvation, the kingdom of heaven. For
they are much deceived, that receive the truth to increase their wealth, making Christianity a gainful trade,
for although it hath the promises, yet it hath not alway
the possession of things in this life, but as the right heirs
are many times put beside their inheritances, which
are possessed by unlawful owners, so the godly are the
right heirs of the whole world, although the wicked have
driven them out of possession, for the which the Apostle
said, that godliness hath the promises of this life, and
also of the life to come. Again, those promises that the
meek shall possess the earth, and their seed shall inherit
the land, and especially that the very same which are the
elected heirs of grace, are also the appointed inheritors
of this world. But this my beloved must establish our
minds, that as the seed which is cast into the ground,
seemeth for a long season to be lost, yet in the end it
groweth for the comfort of mankind, and the great profit
of the possessors, so although at the first the fruit of religion is peradventure but sharp in worldly affairs, yet
if we wait like the husbandman until harvest, our consciences shall be plentiful garners of heavenly corn, for
the present comfort of our lives, and the perpetual benefit of our souls. A man dresseth his vineyard all the year
long, and doth nothing but empty his purse, and weary
his body in the tillage and pruning and digging thereof,
yet there is but one vintage or time of gathering grapes,
even so we must willingly depart with our wealth, and
travail in diligence, for the preparing of our souls, to
bear fruit to the Lord; and the end will be most profit-

Ruth Chapter 2. verses 1-7

able, though the beginning seem most chargeable. The like may be said of the merchant, which cutteth the seas, of the goldsmith, that melteth his metal, and of every worldly trade which at the first begin with charges, but at the last acquit [*repay*] the cost, and satisfy the desire, and end with the increase of substance, which are but carnal and outward things, to put us in mind of inward and spiritual significations, for as in none of these we are discouraged by the costly entrance, so more accursed shall we be, if we forsake the well of the water of life, the running fountain of everlasting health, to rake in the puddles of transitory riches, for fear the one will give us too much ease, and for fear the other will withdraw our wealth, which is like the Gergesites' sin, which had rather possess their herds of swine, than enjoy the presence and preaching of Jesus Christ. Come not to Religion for hope of worldly abundance, for neither *Abraham*, or the *Israelites*, or *Rahab*, or *Ruth*, or *Zacchaeus*, or *Cornelius*, or any of the faithful had this intention. But the Lord for our farther strengthening, hath given two blessings, that if the temporal fail which are but conditional, yet the everlasting benefits shall never deceive: for although the leaves fall, yet bodies of the trees abide continually. Therefore let us stay our minds upon this double string, which is grounded upon the credit of him that giveth the promise, before whom heaven and earth shall decay, and the sun shall lose her light, rather than he frustrate the hope of the godly.

Secondly, here we note a most excellent example of obedience to parents, and avoiding of idleness. *Ruth* was lately come to *Bethlehem*, where it is likely she might long have tarried, before her mother would have entreated her to so base a labor as gathering of barley, but seeing herself employed in nothing, first, she cometh to her mother, and after asketh leave, as one desirous of some honest, though never so simple a calling. If she had departed, not acquainting her with it, being to labor for

Matt. 8

Gen. 12.1
Exod. 12.38
Josh. 6.17-25
Luke 19.8
Acts 10.1

their living, she might well be excused: but this seemeth much, that she must come unto her, not to tell her she would go to such a business, but to give her leave to glean in the fields, promising she would not go beyond her bounds, but only gather in that place, where the owner thereof should grant her license: unto which when the mother had granted, forth she goeth to the field of *Boaz*. Where we see what effect godliness worketh in the hearts of children, for *Ruth* offered her service, which her mother entreated not, she abhorred no labor, were it never so base, she was not ashamed of her poverty, even in a strange country: and all this must be imputed to her Religion. For as *Joseph* for the fear of God, bore with the wrath of his father, when he told him his vision of the sun and the moon, and the eleven stars bowing unto him, so did *Ruth* with the poor estate of her mother in law, which had nothing to live by: thus the Apostle teacheth children to obey their parents in all things, that is, not only to be willing to perform their commandments, but also to be alway contented with their estate, for this wretchedness of cursed children, is worthy to be condemned, wherein those which have wealthy parents, will please them, till they have gotten their riches, which are like the prodigal son in the Gospel: other because their parents are poor, will think they are bound unto them in nothing, because they have little or no wealth to leave behind them: both these kinds of children are here condemned by the example of *Ruth*, who did not only forsake her wealth to go with her mother, but also labor with her hands to maintain her living, yea to her stepmother, which is more commendable than if it were done to her natural parents.

Gen. 37.10

Eph. 6.1

The use of this doctrine is, to exhort and stir up parents, to be more careful to teach their children the fear of the Lord, than to leave them mountains of riches behind them, which if they will practice, would their countenances be so sorrowful as often they are?

Ruth Chapter 2. verses 1-7

would not their natural olives, I mean their children, anoint their faces with the oil of cheerfulness: if mothers either would or could do as *Naomi* did for *Ruth*, teach their children the fear of the Lord, their hearts should not be so heavy, for their ungracious life. But since parents had no care to instruct their children, children had no fear to disobey their parents. Will they in these days acquaint their fathers and mothers with their journeys and labors? or run not they headlong to their own utter undoing? they choose them masters and services without father's consent, they marry and are married against parents' good will: do they not take pleasure for profit, and pastime for godliness? thinking themselves to be born for wantonness, referring the care of their old age to their gray headed parents, and never considering till beggary catch their bodies, and damnation their souls. Surely, as the fruit is sour because it is not grafted, so their manners are wicked, because they want religion: this lieth then in the overloving parents, who make such dandlings of their babes, while they are young, that they care not for their fathers when they be old. They consider not, that Lions are tamed when they are young, that trees are bowed when they are twigs: And that *Solomon* saith, Instruct a child when he is young, the way of his life, and when he is old, he shall not depart from it. Their own ignorance is so palpable, that their children learn nothing but folly: they themselves so vain, that the other are wanton: they so obstinate, that their seed is rebellious: and finally, a wild vine bringeth forth nothing but wild grapes, and ignorant parents must have ungracious children. Therefore, seeing by nature you would have obedient and wise children, teach them the fear of the Lord, for that is the beginning of wisdom, and if you would have your names in your posterity long to endure, the praise of it continueth forever.

Thirdly, here we may note an example of Christian honesty, one of the fruits of Religion; for she tel-

Prov. 22.6

Prov. 1.7
Psal. 111.10

leth her mother, she would go gather where she could
get leave, as if the holy Ghost had said, the gleanings are
for the poor, yet poor men must not take them without
the consent and favor of the owners. The Lord everywhere exhorteth to give to the poor, but he never bid
the poor take where they found, unknowing to the possessor: but they must as *Ruth* here doeth, not take their
right, the very gift of the Lord, without the favor of man.
This condemneth the rashness of many, which think if
they be poor, that men are bound to give to them, and
small matters they may take freely, without the consent
of him that possesseth it: yet we see not only religion,
but also plain reason to gainsay it: for the least thing
a man hath is his own, as well as the greatest, and one
law condemneth the taking of a handful, and a bushel
of corn, though the offence be not so great. But some
say, it was permitted by the Lord, that a man might take
the ears of corn and rub them in his hand and eat them,
as the disciples did, without the consent and trespass of
the possessor: he might also take a bunch of grapes and
eat them, and likewise the fruit of the orchard, by the
same law, and therefore we may take without the consent
of him that possesseth it. I answer, if the question be
made of an apple, or an ear of corn, or a bunch of grapes,
as then it was permitted, so I think there is none that
will now stand in it: but then you must remember by the
same law, that no man might put a sickle into the corn
to reap down a handful, neither yet fill any little measure
with grapes or apples, without the consent of the owner.
But now men will take great measures and quantities,
and yet think not themselves satisfied, and being winked
at for once, yet will they proceed till they be forbidden,
and then will they uncharitably and ungodly report of
such men as will not suffer their goods to be spoiled by
them.

     Lastly, when her mother had granted, forth she
goeth, and cometh to the possession of *Boaz* her kins-

Marginal notes: Lev. 19.9 · Deut. 15.7 · 1 Cor. 9.7 · Deut. 23.24, 25

Ruth Chapter 2. verses 1-7

man: where we may behold the hand of the Lord favoring her diligence, and leading her to the appointed place, where among all other she might be, as she was, most gently entreated: for she, a silly stranger, knowing none beside her mother, not acquainted with people or country, was ignorant whither to go, but God which directeth the goings of all, ordered her footsteps to his possession, where first, she should find favor and feeding, that by this means the way for her marriage might be prepared. Where we see an excellent example of the providence of God, looking upon the poorest as well as the richest, and working all things in the world from the highest to the lowest. He which directeth the descending of the sparrows upon the ground, doth he not also consider the goings of the poor? It is no dishonor to him (as some would have it, that they might more freely give themselves to iniquity) to note every vile and loathsome thing in the world, or to look upon the base as well as the best: surely, if anything be uncomely, it is to the sinful, but to him which is always righteous, are all things pure. What parents do not love the basest parts of their children's bodies, which were born of themselves? yet greater is the love of God unto us, than the love of a mother to her own son; neither doth he, or can he but love the meanest work of his creation, as well as chiefest, and the silly fly as well as the stately king. Oh how doth this comfort us more than all the world beside, when we know the king of glory beholdeth our nakedness and poverty, and giveth his angels charge over us, that not the poorest *Lazarus* may be lost, but our bodies either eased with relief, or parted from life, our souls may ascend to the bosom of *Abraham*. Even he which directed the servant of *Abraham* to the city of *Nahor*, and brought *Rebecca* out to draw water, and moved her answer to his prayer, her courtesy to satisfy his expectation, did also lead *Ruth* to the fields of *Boaz*, and guideth all the faithful to the end of their desires, knowing the counsels of the heart,

Matt. 10.14

disposing the words of the mouth, feeding the hungry with good things, and sending the rich away empty, conducting us all for his mercy's sake to walk in his paths of righteousness.

But behold. After these things set down by the holy Ghost concerning *Ruth*, he returned to *Boaz* again, and this verse is the beginning of the second part of that which respecteth him, in the which is declared his coming from *Bethlehem*, his salutation to the reapers, and their answer to him again.

By the which we gather the duty of all masters of families and great persons in the world, which is, not only to be careful their business be performed by other, but also that themselves as the eyewitnesses of their servants' fidelity, should look over their labors. This we may see in *Boaz*, he cometh from the city to the harvest field: he had committed the care of the reapers to a trusty servant: yet not contented therewith, in his own person he cometh to the work. And surely, this diligence of Lords and Masters, causeth faithful laborers and servants; as the idleness and negligence of the one causeth the unfaithfulness and slackness of the other, for while the Masters follow their worldly pleasures, the servants omit their careful business. Therefore we may read in the building *of the first and second temple*, there were overseers of the work, beside the ordinary laborers: and oftentimes would king *Solomon* and *Nehemiah* come in their own persons to view the works. The like may we read of *Elisha's* host, which was abroad in the field with his reapers, when his little son fell sick, insomuch as this seemeth a point of necessity, that everyone, whom the Lord hath made a master of possessions, although he labor not, yet must he certify himself of his laborers' diligence, with his own eyesight, which condemneth many inferior masters, of negligent slothfulness, and idle negligence, in not regarding their worldly talents given them of God, but referring the disposition to their

The master's foot maketh the best land, and his eye the fattest horse.

1 Kings 5.16

2 Kings 4.18

Ruth Chapter 2. verses 1-7

stewards and servants, refuse in their own persons to deal with God his benefits, as too base things for their occupations, which is the cause that so many masters fall to be servants, and so many servants ascend to be masters: their wealth is quickly consumed, and these which would not be their own servants to keep themselves in labor and wealth, come to be other men's slaves in drudgery or beggary, either in themselves or their posterity, as the just judgment of God: for he that would not use his talent had it taken from him. Therefore seeing this ancient nobility were employed in their own business, let not the new and sudden upstart wealthy men among us, disdain at poor laboring persons, or think it any disgrace to do as their fathers did, faithfully to labor in the meanest vocation.

Secondly, after *Boaz* came to the field, he saluteth the reapers and saith, *The Lord be with you, and they answered. The Lord bless thee*: where we see the first thing he doth, he prayeth for the laborers, in this his godly salutation, for he wisheth the presence of God to be with them, which is his favor, for his presence signifieth his favor and blessing (as absence betokeneth his judgments and cursings). This we may see in the dedication of the Temple by *Solomon*, the glory of the Lord so filled it, that the priests were not able to sacrifice in it, and the angel saluteth *Mary* the mother of Christ with the selfsame words, *The Lord be with thee*: wherein he signified the wonderful favor of God unto her, which should be the mother of the *Messiah*. And on the contrary, the absence of the Lord is the heavy wrath of his majesty, as appeareth by that complaint of *David*, Will the Lord absent himself forever, or hath he forgotten to be merciful? and *Paul* saith that the wicked are separated with everlasting destruction from the glory and presence of God. By the which we learn how reverently we must use our salutations, lest when we wish the favor of the Lord to be present with others, his mercy through

1 Kings 8.11

Luke 1.28

Psal. 77.7

our unadvised prayer be absent from ourselves: for how
lamentable is it, to hear in many places, with one breath
prayers to be poured out for other, and bitter blasphemies against the majesty of God, with woeful curses to
the death of their souls? May we gather any comfort by
these salutations, when men in derision passing by other
shall use the salutation of *Boaz*, other wishing they know
not what, do as well by their ignorant greetings pray for
their own destruction, as their neighbor's prosperity?
such precious balms let them not come upon the heads
of the righteous, for this is as certain as the world shall
have an end, that all their supplications, either at morning, noon, or evening, are but mere customary speeches,
proceeding of the usage and manner of men, not of the
spirit or religion of the faithful. Yet let it not grieve us to
use this language of *Canaan*, the phrase of the Scripture,
in our civil and godly communication: and though, all
the world cry out, puritanism, puritanism, yet blessed
is he that is not offended at Christ. Let the Samaritans
worship in their mountains, but we will worship at *Jerusalem* in spirit and in truth: and let us use in despite of
the world, the weighty words of God's spirit, that they
may be our own mother speech, we the children of the
church, and the heirs of salvation.

But in this it is noted, to be the duty of all men to
salute them whom they meet, to pray for the success of
laborers and workmen, For well we must remember, that
except the Lord do build the house, the builders build
but in vain, and except the Lord do give the victory, what
though millions of horses be prepared of the battle? *surely it is in vain to rise early and to go late to bed and eat* Psal. 127.2
the bread of carefulness, to labor hard, and compass the
world by a thousand devises, except their own prayers,
and the prayers of the faithful, appear in the presence of
the Eternal for them. And this noteth the carnal con-
stitutions of many men's hearts among us, which rashly
enterprise their works without calling on the Lord, and

Ruth Chapter 2. verses 1-7

unprofitably end them to their own destruction. Oh how it grieveth God his Saints, daily to hear his name abused by swearing, even among them that husband the earth. They cry out on their servants morning and evening, abroad, abroad, to work to the field: but who saith, Come let us first fall down together and humble ourselves in the presence of God, and call for a blessing upon our labors, or say thus much, The Lord be with us: no, no, that will hinder their day's work, they hire their servants to labor, and not to pray. Therefore the prophet

Hag. 1.6

saith, You sow much, but you bring but little in, you eat, but you are not filled, you drink, and are not satisfied, you clothe yourselves, but you are not warmed, and he that receiveth wages, putteth it into a broken bag: therefore thus saith the Lord, Hearken unto my ways. This is the plague upon us that mind our wealth, and not the welfare of God his Church, therefore we labor like slaves, but others receive the benefit by us: we imagine the earth bringeth forth of itself, children are born by nature, the clouds must needs rain, and our fruits must needs increase: thus we make many Gods, while we ascribe the power of God to his creatures. But be not so rude as brute beasts, the dog will crave his meat at the hands of his master: more accursed are they which pray not for a blessing at the hands of God the father.

Thirdly, by this salutation of *Boaz*, we observe the duty of elder persons or superiors, which is first to salute or speak to their inferiors, as masters to servants, magistrates to subjects, and pastors to their people: yet against this, in outward behavior we have many and daily offences, for you shall have Gentlemen and Yeomen which will hardly speak to a poor man, being asked a question by him, much less when they meet him will they give any courteous or friendly greeting. But here we see *Boaz*, though honorable, yet humble, saluteth his poor and hired reapers, who condemneth ten thousand that are contrary minded, for proud and surly persons. Old *Eli* would speak to young *Samuel*, a little boy: though he were the high priest, yet he scorned not so gentle a child: what then shall become of this stately person, which being saluted, will not salute again, as if every word were gold that cometh from them, so sparing are they to speak to a poor or a simple man, whereas with their betters, their tongues are too big for their mouths, whom they weary with their unprofitable babblings. This kind of evil spirit will not be cast out till the heart be humbled, pride abated, sorrow for sin increased, and the whole man perfectly regenerated, for by thy words thou shalt be justified, and by thy words thou shalt be condemned, for an humble heart will show it with meekness, but a proud heart will look strangely.

Fourthly, as *Boaz* prayed for the reapers, so the reapers returned to him, and said, *The Lord bless thee.* Where we see a mutual salutation much commended, for as he saluted, so was he saluted, like to the Queen of *Sheba*, which gave princely gifts to king *Solomon*, and *Solomon* gave royal rewards to her again: so that inferiors are bound, by the same law with as kind affection to pray for other, as they themselves were first entreated: for this too much shamefastness [*shamefacedness*] in many is worthy blame, because it doth not only cover the countenance, but also cover the tongue, leaving them speechless, when they are to answer their superiors: but as these laboring reapers use *Boaz*, so also must we any of our betters: which is with reverence to speak our minds, and godliness to pray for their welfare: and therefore we must put on the spirit of meekness, and everyone esteem better of another than of ourselves. But some will say, there is no such necessity of salutation as you would make it, for *Elisha* sending his servant, commanded him to salute no man by the way, and if any saluted him, he should not answer them: likewise our Savior Christ sending his disciples to preach, willed them not to salute any by the way: therefore it is no such sign

2 Kings 4.29

Luke 10.4

of pride as you would make it.

To the which I answer, first, that *Elisha* sent his man in wonderful haste, which respected the life of the Shunammite's son, therefore he willeth him to admit no let or hindrance in his journey, but with all speed to go forward, insomuch as he should not do the common courtesy to strangers, either in salutation or in answer: Even so meaneth our Savior, that his disciples being hastily sent, as it were, to gather the harvest of the Lord, might admit no delay, either in necessary or unnecessary business. And this teacheth us that the labor of preaching excelleth all earthly duties, yea, that all other must serve to it as handmaids and servants, to further the course, and not hinder the proceedings. Therefore this must remain inviolable, as grounded on the law of God and men, that courteous and godly salutations are very commendable.

Then Boaz. Now in these three verses following ensueth the communication had with his servant, who *Ruth* was: unto which his servant telleth or answereth in the sixth and seventh verses. First, that it is *Ruth* which came with *Naomi* from the country of *Moab*: secondly, that she asked him leave to gather among the sheaves: thirdly, that she came but that morning, and had continued till that instant. Where we see the carefulness of *Boaz* in doing good, would know the persons, whether they were worthy or not: and the faithfulness of the servant, which so plainly declared the truth to his master. And this is the pure meaning of the words: other doctrines can none be drawn from hence, and therefore let us give praise to God for that which hath been spoken.

The end of the Fifth Lecture.

The Sixth Lecture

Ruth Chapter 2. verses 8-14

8 *Then said* Boaz *to* Ruth, *Hearest thou my daughter, go to none other field to gather, neither go from hence, but abide here by my maidens.*

9 *Let thine eyes be on the field that they do reap, and go after the maidens: Have I not charged the servants that they touch thee not? Moreover, when thou art thirsty, go unto the vessels and drink of that which the servants have drawn.*

10 *Then she fell on her face, and bowed herself to the ground, and said unto him, How have I found favor in thy eyes, that thou shouldest know me, since I am a stranger.*

11 *And* Boaz *answered and said unto her, All is told, and showed me that thou hast done unto thy mother in law, since the death of thy husband, and how thou hast left thy father and mother, and the land where thou wast born, and art come unto a people which thou knewest not in times past.*

12 *The Lord recompense thy work, and a full reward be given thee of the Lord God of Israel, under whose wings thou art come to trust.*

13 *Then she said, Let me find favor in thy sight, my Lord, for thou hast comforted me, and spoken to the heart of thy handmaid, yet I shall not be like to one of thy maids.*

14 *And* Boaz *said unto her, At meal time come thou hither, and eat of the bread, and dip thy morsel in the vinegar: and she sat beside the reapers: and he reached her parched corn, and she did eat, and was sufficed, and left.*

n these words the holy Ghost declareth the communication which *Boaz* had with *Ruth*, for so soon as he understood who she was, he turned his speech from the man to the woman. This conference, according to the number of the persons, hath two parts. The first is of *Boaz*, and the second of *Ruth*. The first part which respecteth *Boaz* is the singular courtesy he offereth to Ruth, verses 8,9,14. Wherein first he biddeth her to glean freely among his maidens, not only in that field, but also wheresoever the reapers bestow themselves: secondly, he commandeth his servants that they do her no injury, but give her drink when she is thirsty, and himself called her to meat, and gave her so liberally, that she being sufficed, left for her mother.

The other part which concerneth *Ruth*, is her manner of behavior to this courteous entertainment of *Boaz*, wherein first she boweth herself to the ground, verse tenth. Secondly, she confesseth the greatness of his kindness in the same verse, because she was a stranger, and her unworthiness of any benefit, verse thirteen, because she should be as one of his maidens. For this speech of *Ruth*, *Boaz* showeth the cause of all his courtesy, verse 11. because she had dealt so well with her mother in law, and had forsaken country and kindred to come to the people of God, therefore she deserved to be honorably entreated: secondly, he prayeth for her, verse 12, that the Lord would not frustrate his promise, deceive her hope, but recompense her labor, and shield her with his wings. Of these parts let us speak in order, as the spirit shall give utterance, and the time permit.

Then said Boaz. So soon as he understood who that woman was, whereof he had demanded his servant, he turneth his speech unto her, that so soon as might be, he might comfort her afflicted poverty, and testify any goodwill to a godly stranger: where first of all it is commendable, that he vouchsafeth to call so base a person by the name of daughter, for truly this loving word betrayeth the tender affection of a godly heart, forgetting his lofty degree, and calling an abject stranger by the name of daughter, which proveth that he longed to give unto her some comfort of kindness. This humble and most tender title of daughter and son, are very usual in the Scripture, for when the Lord would comfort the Church of the Jews against the blasphemies of *Sennacherib* and *Rabshakeh*, he calleth it a virgin the daughter of *Sion*, as if he had said, even as a father is careful for the wealth of his daughter, so do I watch for the welfare of my church: in like manner Christ our Savior comforted the women that wept at his death, by the name of the daughters of Jerusalem.

Isa. 37.22

Luke 23.28

  Out of the which we gather this profitable doctrine, that it is one property and duty of an humble mind, to speak kindly where it wisheth friendly, especially, when we talk to our brethren, and the professors of the same religion, our hearts must be as the sweet roses, and our words as soft as butter, to supple and refresh their troubled days. For we must not do as many have both in their writings and familiar speeches, comforted them with the vilest reproaches, taunting speeches, and uncharitablest titles they could invent, that the poison of asps may seem to lodge in their mouths, being by their words right devils, they speak so cursedly, but handle them if they be faulty with gentle words, for men in authority must punish with the sword of magistrates, not the words of slanderers: equals by admonition, not by reviling: inferiors by petition, not by exclamations. If we will have humble hearts, we must show them by gentle words, for out of the abundance of the heart the mouth speaketh: the faithful are compared to sheep, which are

Ruth Chapter 2. verses 8-14

meek and silent, but the reprobate to dogs, which are always barking and brawling. If we brand other with the mark of contempt, we burn ourselves with the iron of an ungodly tongue: many can be content to distribute their wealth liberally, but their scornful words disgrace their devotion, because they taste more of wormwood than of the rose: and this I have noted in many great persons, that their words are as kind to their dogs as to the poor. Oh how unlike are they to the Lord himself, which calleth us sons, to this godly *Boaz*, which calleth *Ruth* his daughter, to the apostle *Paul*, which called the meanest in the church of God a brother. Why do you forget yourselves to be the children of *Adam*? or rather will you not be their fellow heirs of grace, that thus reign over your brethren in disdainful speeches, as though heaven were not high enough for you both to abide in.

Go not hence. Now we are come to another courtesy of *Boaz*, which consisteth in his commandment he giveth to *Ruth*, first, that she should not go into any other field to gather: secondly, that she should join herself to his maidens: thirdly, that she should follow the reapers whether soever they go: that by this it seemeth the man was delighted to handle her gently. Was it not sufficient that he suffered her without denial or reproof, or if he gave her leave by name above many other (as no doubt but there were many in the field) but he must admit her into the company of his own maidens: or having given her that liberty, he must also bid her to follow his reapers, whethersoever they go? surely this was strange kindness to a strange woman, to be entreated more like a daughter than a *Moabitess*; nay, he addeth the second part of his commandment, telling her that he had charged his servants quietly to endure her presence, and give her for her necessity. Where we first of all note the heavenly example of godly liberality, how far it differeth from worldly pinch-pennies. They give in gentleness, the other in pride, they in cheerfulness, the other in murmuring, they in liberality, the other in covetousness: and look how many degrees the moon is above the earth, so many the gifts of the godly surpass the carnal: the reason of this is, because the one are persuaded to what end they give, but the other do think it to be cast into the sea. Exod. 36.6 We read of the Israelites, when the Tabernacle of the Lord was to be built, they offered so much, that *Moses* proclaimed they should offer no more: this heat of liberality is well cooled in this frozen age, for we have much ice, but little water: as the ice will afford no water till it be thawed, so men will give nothing to the church, poor, or Tabernacle of the Lord, till they be dead: now there is such striving to go foremost in godly contributions, that every one sitteth still, many pluck from the church, parsonages, and profits, tithes, and sanctified offerings, but few add one mite into the Lord's treasury. Let the poor be famished, the gospel unfurnished, the churches unbuilt, the people untaught, learning contemned, idle and ignorant persons advanced, and many poor souls condemned for want of the bread of life: yet they say still, come, let us search for more treasure, let us take to ourselves the houses of God in possession: yea, they spare not the very altars of the Lord, but think it a charge that the sacraments should be so often administered, at the cost of the parish. Oh most miserable and ungodly behavior of wicked worldlings, who, like the Lion's Den, suffer all to come in, but none to come out: like the adamant, which draweth all things, but casteth abroad nothing. Where is the wonted contribution, *which in the primitive church* we read? The Apostle commended the *Macedonians, that they gave beyond their power, willingly, not of constraint.* 1 Cor. 16.1 2 Cor. 8.23 Which answereth the carnal objection of many which say, they must give of their abundance, so if they have not abundance, they are exempted from giving. But the holy Ghost would exempt none, for every one of his ability is bound to give to church and poor, none must appear before the Lord empty, he which

Ruth Chapter 2. verses 8-14

had not a Lamb must offer a Dove, and she which had no
more, gave two mites into the Lord's treasury. The servant for his wages, the laborer for his hire, the craftsman
for his taking, the yeoman for his profits, the gentleman
for his office, the noble man for his revenues, must everyone give somewhat to the poor and religion: but some
take from the Church one hundred pounds a year, and
give scant an hundred shillings: some have more, and
some have less, and they prey upon us as the Eagles on
the altars, carrying with their commodities coals of fire,
which shall burn both their houses and progeny, because
they took it from the Lord.

Secondly, in this kindness of *Boaz* unto *Ruth*,
this is worthy to be noted, that he commandeth his servants to offer her no wrong: for to touch, is to injury in
many places of Scripture, as when the Lord speaketh by
the Prophet *David*, Touch not mine anointed, neither do
my Prophets any harm. That is, neither do you hurt my
Prophets, or anointed. And again, by the prophet *Zecha-
riah*, He that toucheth you, toucheth the apple of his eye,
that is, which hurteth you, harmeth the tenderest place
of all his own body: even so doth *Boaz* take it in this
place. For well knew that good man, that her simplicity would be quickly abused by the rigor of his servants,
and we know it hath been, and also is a common plague
to most of the godly, evil and discourteous servants, as
appeareth in the history of *Abraham* and *Lot*, and very
often the masters which are well affected in Religion, are
abused by their servants, in their friends. If they be worshipful, then the servants will churlishly entertain those
godly persons which resort to their masters' houses: if
they be higher, they will scorn them, if baser, they will
envy them: this mischief had godly *Joseph* noted, when
he commanded his servants to use his brethren so kindly: and *David* by a servant was whetted on to be revenged
upon *Saul*. Therefore Right Worshipful, and yet our
brethren in Christ, as you are careful in your own per-

Deut. 16
Lev. 12
Luke 21.2

Psal. 105.15

Zech. 2.8

Gen. 13.7

Gen. 42.25
1 Sam. 24.3-5

sons to do good to the godly: even so follow this *Boaz*, in commanding your servants to deal friendly also. I know you shall never choose all your servants of your own disposition, yet if you often warn them, you may chance to win them, for the beginning of Religion is the love of them that profess it, even as hunger in a sick person is a token of recovery. Then shall you cheerfully receive Christ into your houses, in his poor members, and joyfully assure your consciences, you have unfeignedly loved him, for he which hath given his Angels charge over us, willeth also that we should give our servants charge over our brethren: the unkindness which many poor souls have received at the hands of your churlish and stubborn servants, hath discomfited them more than all your liberality hath comforted them. What access could the little children have to Christ, when the disciples forbad them? even so, how shall we repair to your dwellings, when your own servants, so much as in them lieth, diswarn us of your houses, keep us from your presence, envy our meetings, and deride our profession: Mark 10.13

Wherefore she fell. This verse concerneth *Ruth*, and her answer to those words of *Boaz*, first her gesture is described, that she fell upon the earth, and bowed herself to the ground, that is, with all show of humility: secondly, she commendeth this his kind courtesy, because she was a stranger: so that by outward behavior, she gratifieth his gentleness, and exalteth his liberality toward her, by the consideration of her own person, which was a stranger, and therefore unworthy of so great kindness.

Out of the which we chiefly observe, first, that it is a duty of the poorer sort, not only to acknowledge their thankfulness by words, but also to testify it by outward submission: for *Abraham* himself used it even to the idolatrous Hethites, when they gave him leave to bury his dead, twice together. This noteth a greater thankfulness than all the words of the world: insomuch as it is accounted a special duty belonging to superiors, as we may Gen. 23.7,12

1 Kings 1.16

1 Kings 2.19
see in *Bathsheba* to her husband, when she came to tell him how *Adonijah* reigned, and likewise in King *Solomon* toward her, when she came to ask *Abishag*. Now, if these stately persons bowed themselves, but in courtesy, much more ought we of duty. Then is here condemned, the uncivil behavior of many stout persons, which are so far from bowing, that they will hardly thank their brethren for their liberalities, accounting it their duty, as they say, to give: as if also it were not their duty to be thankful. The known example of the ten lepers, doeth much commend this kind of thankful behavior, and also condemn the ungrateful affection. Other there be that are in such love, with this cap and knee, that it doth them more good to see the poor people bend unto them, than they rejoice that they have given for Christ's sake, insomuch as they give, that themselves, and not the Lord might be honored.

This lack of reverence in the one, and love of honor in the other, are both unlawful, because they both proceed from one root, which is the pride of our own hearts, and the conceit of our own persons.

Esther 3.2
But some will say, we do but as that godly *Mordecai* did, which refused to honor the wicked *Haman*, so we abstain from doing reverence to the proud and vainglorious, because we will not feed their disposition. Unto whom I answer, that there were many causes for which *Mordecai* refused to bend unto *Haman*, which they can never allege for themselves: the first, because Exod. 17.9
Deut. 25.17 he was a wicked Amalekite, of a nation whom the Lord commanded the Jews utterly to destroy, neither to spare man, woman or child, as appeareth in the history of *Saul*, who, because he transgressed this commandment of God in saving *Agag* their king, and certain oxen to 1 Sam. 15.9 sacrifice, it cost him his kingdom and displeasure of God. Because of this law of the Lord, *Mordecai* would do no honor to this child of destruction, and was blameless.

Secondly, it is thought that the honor which *Haman* obtained, was proper only to God, because he was advanced above all other: and such kind of reverence we must alway beware of, for *Shadrach, Meshach,* and *Abednego,* had rather die than fall down before the image of the King of *Babylon*: even so we must not give more to man than is his own, but unto *Caesar* the things which are *Caesar's,* and unto God the things which are God's. And if any for these causes defend their stately behavior, let them consider that the Lord bids us not to destroy, but rather to love our enemies. And although they require such worship as is due only to God, yet we must not refuse to give them that which belongeth to man. Other can be content to honor them whom they know to be godly, but the wicked they think unworthy of all reverence, because our Savior would do none to *Herod* or *Pilate, Paul* to the high Priest, when he called him painted wall.

Dan. 3.16-18

To whom I answer, that Christ (though he called *Herod* a fox, and would do no miracle before him, because he desired but to wonder, and not to glorify God by it.) Yet gave to *Herod* that duty which pertained unto him. Likewise unto *Pilate,* when he told him, his power came of the Lord: so *Paul* did reverence, not only the high Priest, but also *Felix, Festus,* and *Agrippa,* who were heathen men, though magistrates, and therefore were honorable by the law of God. So then this must remain for a grounded truth, that our betters must be honored as men, not worshipped as God: we must with *Abraham* bend, as well to the idolatrous *Hebron,* as with *Bathsheba* to godly *David*: if they receive more than they are worthy, it is not our default, but their danger, let us give to the profanest person his right, and ungodliest caitiff [*despicable person*], that which is his own.

Secondly, by this we note, that the godly in giving, must have no respect of persons, country or kindred, strangers or neighbors' children, as *Boaz* did here to *Ruth*, who by her own confession was a stranger, and therefore unworthy, but we showed you this in the first chapter, by the example of the *Moabites*, to *Elimelech* and his family, to be a thing incident by very natural men, and by them condemned that use it not, much more in them that have known the truth. The which *Abraham* did to the angels, whereupon the Apostle wisheth, to keep hospitality, for so some have received angels instead of men. The Lord commanded very sharply, that no violence be done to strangers, neither yet that any should oppress them.

Gen. 18.1-9
Heb. 13.2
Exod. 22.21
Luke 19.33

Whereby the ungodly usage of strangers, that many wish for among us, is too wicked, envying, that any should be permitted to come and sojourn among us, like free-born children: Yet herein we are to praise God, that these persons cannot bite, although they bark at poor harborless strangers, and also that he hath blessed our magistrates with more pitiful minds. And let these persons know and consider, that it is as easy to go out, as to come into *England*, that is, they may as soon be driven to other places out of their own country to be strangers there, as these are, repaired for succor hither. The uncertainty of worldly estate that hath brought great princes to extreme poverty, should bridle their churlish and ungodly affections, from offering one thought of injury to these poor harborless strangers. We know the parable of Christ, of a man that traveled from *Jericho* to *Jerusalem*, and fell among thieves: the kindness of that stranger, a Samaritan, should move us to do good to strangers, while the world standeth, seeing we are more helped by their presence, than by our own neighbors: but these kind persons that thus rail upon poor strangers, are such as are grieved against God and men, who in their hearts would have no man living in the land, besides themselves and their cursed posterity. But some will say, you make too much account of strangers, the Lord doth not make such reckoning of them, because, *forbidding usury to the*

Deut. 23.20

Jews, yet he permitted them to take usury of the strangers.
I answer, those strangers were the cursed Canaanites,
and none other, whom God had vowed to destruction:
to the intent the Jews might have them in all slavery. Of
them he permitted to take usury: for this is the bless- Deut. 28.12
ing of God upon that people, that they should be able to
lend to other, but stand in no need to borrow of other.
Therefore that being but a permission for the Jews only,
hath ceased in that commonwealth: but in Christ there
is no difference of Jew or Gentile, male or female, bond
or free, for all are his, and he the Lord's: so that now the
name of a stranger is quite ceased, but all are neighbors
and brethren forevermore.

 And Boaz answered. In this verse is contained
the reply of *Boaz* unto the speech of *Ruth,* wherein is
set down the true cause of his liberality unto her, first
in regard of her mother in law and his kinswoman,
with whom she had dealt so well in her own country:
secondly, in regard of herself, she had forsaken father
and mother, with country and kindred, to come among
strange people.

 Where we first observe a singular encouragement to obey our godly parents, for we see that our good
actions need not to be preached abroad by other for our
farther commendation, but at the time appointed they
will show themselves, as the life of trees by sending forth
leaves in the spring time of the year. *Ruth,* as we have
heard, dealt most lovingly with her mother in law in
Moab, yet you see that her kindness hath followed her
to *Bethlehem* in *Judah,* many miles distant the one from
the other. If it had been known there to a few only, it
had been sufficient: but being spread abroad; the chief
man in a city doth commend her for it, among a multitude in a harvest field: the place could not hide it were
it never so far off, the time not conceal it, be it never
so secret: the commendation of it be covered, because
she was a stranger, nor the credit of it be lost in another

Ruth Chapter 2. verses 8-14

country. Such is the nature of good things which we do
to other, that oblivion can never bury it. What needeth
this boasting of our alms deeds, like the blowing of a
trumpet? this bragging of our worthiness? some of their
manhood, some of their friendship, other of their riches,
and many of their labor: as if they slept not soundly till
all the world did ring of their commendation. This one
thing loseth all our reward, for it is better that the works
than the words should witness it. We may also by this
assure ourselves, that we have done nothing so secretly
to the flock of Christ, but it is known, and the name of
God praised for it: for as evil deeds remain to the grave,
so good works redound to perpetual memory.

Rev. 14.13

Secondly, by this we observe the excellency of
religion, for whose sake it is commendable to forget nature, and praise worthy to forsake our parents and people. Which, if we should do for any other cause whatsoever, we were accursed.

When the Lord would establish his covenant
with *Abraham*, he called him from father and country,
to show that for Religion's sake, it is a glory, and not only
to do thus, but also for to be scourged, yea, and to suffer
death.

Gen. 12.1
Acts 5.41

Why then is it so contumeliously upbraided, so
scornfully refused of many, and but of few received till
this day? Among all the world, only *Abraham's* posterity
had the covenant and promises, and now though men
be as the sand on the seashore, and the stars of heaven,
which cannot be numbered, yet shall but a remnant be
saved; none come unto it, but by the especial grace of
God, whereby he draweth them, as it were, against their
minds: few persons would resort to *Noah's* Ark, because
they scorned his preaching: even so few are religious,
because they account it a base work to hear the word of
God plainly opened, and sincerely expounded. Where is
then become this ancient zeal, that made men and wom-
en, as well noble as base, to be obedient to the calling of

Rom. 9.27

the Lord, for which cause they forsook both wealth, parentage, country, and kindred? but in these days men will forsake Christ and his Gospel, religion and preaching for the least of these. Once the Apostle said, he accounted all things as dung in regard of Christ, but now Christ is regarded as dung in comparison of the world. Once Christ said, whosoever loveth father or mother, wife or children, house or lands more than me, is not worthy of me, but now whosoever loveth Christ more than these, is not worthy to live.

Once it was said, first seek the Kingdom of God, and the righteousness thereof; and all other things shall be cast upon you: but now, first seek the world's riches and wealth, and Religion will follow too soon. Oh what miserable days are we fallen into, where ignorance advanceth itself like a smoke, and is not ashamed, the Gospel reviled by every Atheist, the ministers molested for every Papist, the sacraments profaned, the professors termed by slanderous titles, which for Christ's sake have lost their kindred, and adventured their lives. Surely, surely, some great plague is approaching, for the quenching of this burning heat of sin, when they shall say, here is a God that rewardeth the righteous, verily, there is a God that judgeth the world.

Thirdly, we observe out of this verse, that we must not without consideration give liberally to all, but with special favor do good to the godly: for you see *Boaz* telleth this second cause, of her forsaking both country and kindred, as if he were bound to do for such, as for his own children, thereby signifying, that if we have never so much to give, yet we can never give enough to the saints of God. This our Savior signifieth when he saith, There were many widows in *Israel* in the days of *Elijah*, yet to none was he sent but to *Zarephath*, a city of *Zidon*, to a woman a widow: as if he had said, as God with special kindness relieved her in the three years famine, even so must we with the like favor succor the godly laboring

Luke 4.26,27

Gal. 6.10

poor. Therefore, when *Paul* biddeth do good unto all, he addeth, especially to the household of faith.

This is profitable for our days, that we might also learn to whom we may give: for now our land is full of wandering and rogueing beggars, who as their life is most base, yet their manners are far worse: first, they work not at all, but are idle, and he that worketh not, must not eat, because he walketh inordinately: secondly, they are for the most part, utterly void of all fear of God, Atheists, ignorant persons, blasphemers, profaners of Sabbaths, disobedient to magistrates and masters, common whoremasters and whores, having almost every week new husbands and wives; thieves and such drones as suck away the alms from poor laboring persons. They will pray at every door for any simple relief, with their hats on their heads, most unreverently: but if any man appear before them, they will presently break off their prayers, and uncover their heads, esteeming more of the presence of a silly man or woman, than of the majesty of the eternal God: if they be not satisfied, they will curse more vehemently, than before they prayed earnestly. Those are the poor which get our alms: but for other, I hear of few, for I speak nothing but that which I have heard and seen with my own eyes. And to speak nothing of their changing of their voice, their counterfeiting sores, and their common drunkenness: I think I may every way conclude, they are the Caterpillars of our country, the Canaanites of our commonwealth, the ungodliest and unprofitablest members among us.

For whom I have two suits, the one to the magistrates, that so often as they find such persons, they would duly execute the law upon them, that the other may beware: and my other to the people, that they would be deaf at their cries, and shut up their compassions from them, and bestow it upon the poor laborers among us, to encourage them with patience to endure their travails, and to discourage the other from this kind of wicked life.

Whatsoever you give them is but seed cast into the sea, whereof shall never come any profit: but those that are of the house of the Lord let us wish them prosperity.

The Lord recompense. This is the second part of this reply of *Boaz*, which is his prayer for *Ruth*: wherein as we showed you, are delivered two things: first, that the Lord would give her some reward: secondly, he comforteth her, in that he telleth her, she is come to trust under the wings of God. Where first of all here seemeth some hold for popish merits, seeing he prayeth for a recompense, and perfect reward. Therefore it may be probably gathered, will they say, from hence, that works after faith merit grace: for here I cannot conceal the subtlety of our English Papists which they learned from the Romish Seminary, being asked whether works merit, they answer no, meaning those works which go before faith, whereas they every one do confidently believe that works after faith do merit eternal life. Thus they blind our eyes with the school distinction of works before faith, and after faith, that they might the better cover their sophistry, but we (praised be God for it) most confidently affirm, that no works either before or after faith, do concur in Rom. 14.23 the matter or cause of justification. As for works before Rom. 4.2 faith, we acknowledge they are sin; for whatsoever is not Gal. 2.6 of faith is sin; and for works after faith, we constantly be- Eph. 2.6 lieve with *Paul*, that our salvation cometh not by them. But let us come to this Scripture, and continue a little with our salvation-workers. We grant *Boaz* prayeth for a reward: What then? therefore works either merit, or he prayeth amiss: both which we deny, and will confirm by this Scripture. First, did *Boaz* think that *Ruth* had merited by this forsaking of her country? I answer no: why then doth he pray for her? if she had deserved it, God is not unjust, but he that commanded that the hire of a laborer should not be kept back one night, would not, or needed not to be entreated for that, which he must of necessity perform. By the which we see, that the prayer of *Boaz* the merit of *Ruth*, and the justice of God, cannot stand together.

Secondly, for what cause doth he pray for a recompense? Was it not because she had forsaken her own idolatrous people, to come to the Lord's commonwealth? yes verily it was so. Then was it of faith or of works? no work assuredly, but faith; for faith caused *Moses* when he was grown up, to forsake the court of *Pharaoh*, and to join himself with God his afflicted people: Faith caused *Abraham* to come into the land of promise, from his own idolatrous country: and this same faith caused *Ruth* to come from the Country of *Moab* to the people of the Jews, and therefore *Boaz* addeth, that she was come to trust under the wings of God, but confidence proceedeth of faith, and not of works. Therefore to conclude, *Boaz* prayeth for such a reward, as God had promised to all the faithful: for as the sun looketh upon the earth, and the earth looketh upon the sun again, so faith respecteth the promise of God, and the promise of God regardeth faith; because it is written, whosoever believeth in me hath everlasting life, but whosoever believeth not (though he purchase lands for Catholics, build Churches, ordain Chanteries, and got never so far on pilgrimage) yet is he condemned already.

But now they will renew their wonted outcry, saying, we preach for faith, we condemn works, we drive men to a wicked life, and tell them all is well, if they believe well: we condemn, say they, housekeeping, giving to the poor, with builders of Colleges and Churches, and founders of Hospitals, with all charitable actions. These are great thunderclaps, but yet without rain. I ask the resolutest Papist living, where ever he read any of these, in all the writings of the Protestants, once mentioned without singular commendation: for I am sure none of you that are resolute Papists, will come to the churches, to hear our preachers speak against them: yet you cry out, believe them not, they broach heresies, that

Heb. 11.2

Heb. 11.8

John 3.18

is brought unto you, by your pensioner hang-bys, and lukewarm professors, papistical Atheists, which come to our Churches to sleep, and there dream, who being come unto you, make you believe that their dreams, were the preachers sermons: and you that are apt to believe lies, believe liars. But to come to the purpose, you accuse us for condemning good works, when we attribute no merits unto them: this we deny, for the reason is like this: None will become a Papist, but he that hopeth to be Pope: so none will do good works but he that hopeth to be saved or crowned by them: If they grant the latter, then they must give the former: which I am assured many honest minded Papists would not be, though they might have as much as the Pope's father, the Devil offered Christ, which was all the world. Therefore as a Papist is not a Papist, because he would be a Pope, so good works must not be done, that men might be crowned by them. Every Catholic which believeth as the Church believeth, must not presently step into *Peter's* chair: no more, every one that doth a good work, must by that ascend up into heaven. Good works have another use than to justify. Because the eye cannot smell; shall it therefore be pulled out? no, it was created to see, and not to smell: because good works justify not, shall no man do them? God forbid, they were given to the faithful, for outward testimonies of faith, and of God his spirit, that by them they might assure themselves and others to be sanctified and elected: not that they should help, in their salvation. As the tree dieth without the bark, and fire is nothing without heat, so works without faith, and faith without works, is cursed and unprofitable.

Therefore we say, let everyone that calleth on the name of Christ, depart from iniquity, eschew evil, and do good, feed the hungry, clothe the naked, visit the sick and imprisoned, harbor the harborless, provide for children and widows, yea, and build Churches and Colleges, for the maintenance of God his worship and learning.

Ruth Chapter 2. verses 8-14

Rom. 5.1-3

Yet we say, we are justified by faith, we have peace with God through our Lord Jesus Christ, by whom we were brought to this grace, through which we stand, and glory under the hope of the glory of God: for all the works in the world cannot satisfy for one sin, because there is none other name under heaven, by which we may be saved, but only by the name of Christ.

Out of this, first we gather the goodness of God, which of his own promise and own mercy, accepteth that little obedience of faith, which we offer unto him. What can we do to the fulfilling of the law, if we kept all and yet fail in one, we had lost all our labor: but if we keep one point only, and faulted in the rest, it were like to a man that was bound to pay ten thousand pounds, and should offer a shilling: but we keep none, and yet he accepteth us in the death of his Son, that our righ-

Rom. 5.21

teousness might abound to everlasting life. Now, the use of the mercy of God is, that hereby we should be made more fearful and careful not to offend him: not as some imagine, that hereby is given the greater liberty to sin, because the Lord speaketh peace unto us in his beloved Christ: for this is, as the prophet speaketh, be-

Isa. 24.18

ing escaped out of a ditch to fall into a snare, and as a man which is drawn out of a river, should cast himself into the sea. But the regenerate must be more afraid to offend the mercy of God, than the unregenerate at his threatening judgments. They will not sin, because they love God; the other will abstain for fear of punishment: the promises of the Gospel terrify them more than all the terrors of the Law; for they find a sweeter comfort in the presence of the spirit, than to rest in all the gardens of pleasure, when they find access to the throne of grace, through the blood of Christ, and by him all their infirmities covered, their petitions granted, their sins remitted, and they at peace with God, like joyful men discharged from everlasting imprisonment, they walk in holiness and righteousness before him all the days of their life. Oh that these mercies would sink deeper into our hard hearts, that the force of the cogitation of the blood of Christ might both soften and mollify, purge and cleanse them from wavering and doubting, wantonness and presumption, and prepare our fallow grounds fit to receive the Lord's own seed, his everlasting word, which is able to save our souls.

Secondly, by this when he saith, under whose wings thou art come to trust: the dignity of the faithful is commended unto us, for they live under the wings of the Lord: which is a Metaphor or borrowed speech, comparing him to a hen, which covereth her chickens with her wings, showing unto us that then we are in safety, when we are covered with the wings of the Lord. This our Savior noted when he said, that he would have gathered the City of *Jerusalem*, as a hen gathereth her chickens. This dignity of the faithful, is by many such speeches manifested in the Scripture, wherein the Lord showeth us the care he hath for our safety, when he calleth us the apple of his eye. He showeth his love, when he calleth us his children, his brethren and spouse, to teach us our duties: he calleth us the branches of a vine, which are good for nothing but to bring forth grapes: even so are the godly pleased with nothing which they do, save only the worship of God. This consisteth in the holy fellowship which the faithful have with God, which *David* saith, bringeth life for evermore, with whom is a well of life, and the fullness of all joy. And in another place the Lord saith, Behold I stand at the door and knock, if any man open, I will come in, and sup with him, and he with me: and *John* saith, He that abideth in the doctrine of Christ, he hath both the father and the Son. Here is the comfort of the spirit that dwelleth in us, the assurance of faith which overcometh all the world, the evidence of our salvation, even the confession of the Gospel with the mouth, and the believing in the heart, the hearing of it when it is preached, and praying in the assemblies

Matt. 23.37

2 John 9

1 John 3.24

Ruth Chapter 2. verses 8-14

of the faithful; for wheresoever are two or three gathered together in my name, there am I in the midst of them, saith the Lord: for he dwelleth among his saints, the Ark is with his ministers, the covenant or tabernacle of presence with them that fear him for evermore. Oh, who will not be drawn to be the member of Christ's own body, the heavenly Temple for the holy Ghost to dwell in, the sincere professor of true Religion, that they may have both the Father and the Son. Who will not open to the Lord's knocking, that he may receive the King of glory for his guest? Finally, who would not forsake the shadow of all the trees in the world, to be covered under the wings of the Lord's presence? Where is more comfort to be found but one day, than a thousand years in all the thrones of majesty?

Thirdly, and lastly, by these words, as is noted the dignity of the faithful, so on the contrary it uttereth the desperate and comfortless estate of the wicked, namely, they are like uncovered birds also, but never are shielded with the wings of the Lord: they lie open and scattered, subject to all the souls of the air, every minute in danger to be torn in pieces by the hellish and infernal devils.

Therefore *David* saith, howsoever they be Nobles, and Princes of the earth, and have houses and possessions, after their own names, yet they stand but in slippery places, so soon as they move they fall. Our Savior saith, They are like a man having no wedding garment: so soon as the king espieth him, he is cast into utter darkness. *Paul* saith, they are strangers from the life of God, so that being living, yet they are but condemned persons, which every hour look for the tormentor, and then to be burned in everlasting fire? Oh fearful estate of all Atheists, Papists, Idolaters, Jews, Turks and Pagans, carnal men and hypocrites, despisers of the ministry and Gospel of Christ; who as in this world they are without God, so in the world to come, shall be separated from his presence with the Devil and his Angels. Look

Psal. 73.18,19

Matt. 23.13

Eph. 4.18

on your reckonings, your guilty consciences, which every day add thousands to your former iniquities. The greater your debt is, the sharper shall be your imprisonment. The oftener you are warned, the more shall be your stripes. As none were saved but those that entered into the Ark, so not one of you shall ever see the face of God (except at your condemnation) unless you become zealous professors, and hear our sermons, be partakers of our prayers, and as obedient to the voice of the Gospel in the mouth of his ministers, as if there were a law of present death, to be executed on you for every default.

I find favor. This is the second part of the speech of *Ruth*, wherein she thanketh *Boaz*, and excuseth herself. She thanketh in the first words when she saith: *I find favor in thine eyes, Oh my Lord, because thou hast comforted me, and hast spoken those things which are to the heart of thy handmaid.* For she confesseth his courtesy: and thankfulness, by the verdict of the learned in the humble confession of a benefit. She excuseth when she saith, *I shall not be as one of thy maidens.* As if she had said, I am unworthy of this courtesy, because I come to labor for myself, not for thee, as these thy maidens do. Out of the which we observe these things.

First, a holy example of commendable thankfulness, much accepted of God and men, as unthankfulness is abhorred by heaven and earth: we have examples hereof in many wicked persons, as *Laban* his discourtesy to *Jacob*, *Saul* unto *David*, and the wicked Ammonites to his ambassadors: To speak nothing of *Pharaoh's* butler unto *Joseph*, of *Nabal* unto *David*, and also the inhabitants of *Keilah*, which being famous in the Scripture for the enemies of God, so are they branded with this note of unthankfulness, as if it were an especial fruit of unrighteousness. And truly this is most worthy to be urged in our sinful age, for the children forget their duties to their natural parents, the people tread their preachers under their feet, for telling them the truth; we

Gen. 31.2
1 Sam. 19.10
2 Sam. 10.1
Gen. 40.23
1 Sam. 25.10
1 Sam. 23.12

Ruth Chapter 2. verses 8-14

always remember what we have given, but forget what we have received: whereas it is a token of the best nature to forget what we have done to other, but to remember what we have received. Surely, surely, unthankfulness towards God, and towards men, never reigned or raged more. Toward God, for the continuance of his Gospel, peace, plenty, and welfare of our country: toward men, in gauging the benefits that are daily bestowed, by casting in the teeth, as if they were deserved. The heavens abhorred this wickedness, and the heavens will reign down destruction upon these thankless persons, as they did upon *Sodom* and *Gomorrah* for the like offence.

Luke 17.27,28

Secondly, by this we gather, that the prayers of the righteous are more acceptable to the godly, than giving or taking of alms. For when *Boaz* promised *Ruth* this kindness, she thanked him, and no more: but now, when he prayed for her to the Lord, she protested that he comforted her, and that he had spoken those things which were to the heart of his handmaid (that is) which pleased her exceedingly well. As if she had said, I am bound unto thee my Lord for thy kindness, but thou hast comforted me more with thy prayer, than with that: So that here for herself, and for all the godly, she protesteth, that of two benefits, she was most of all comforted by his prayer: which noteth in her, a more hungering and thirsting after righteousness, than after all the maintenance of this present life: for whosoever drinketh of that water of worldly welfare, shall thirst again: but whosoever drinketh of the water of faithful prayer shall never thirst any more. This one consideration made the blind men of *Jericho* cry so importunately after Christ, saying, Jesus thou son of *David* have mercy on us. Some heavenly benefit they looked for, earthly he had none. And this teacheth us, that when we give, we should also pray for a blessing upon our benevolence: for *Solomon* compareth the giving of alms to the casting of corn into a moist or fruitful land, so as the husbandman prayeth

Verse 10

John 4.14

Eccles. 11.1

for a blessing upon his seed, even so he which giveth to the poor must pray for a benefit upon his benevolence. But if any gather by this my speech, that it is sufficient to pray, and not to give to the poor, I answer, This Scripture condemneth this folly, when it saith: If a brother or sis- James 2.15,16 ter be naked, and want meat, and thou say unto him, go warm thy self, and feed thy self, and yet give them nothing, this is a dead and damnable, not a living and saving faith: of these kind of people the world is full, which say, alas, God help you, God provide for you, God give you patience, but nothing cometh from them, save only fair words. To whom we may say as a beggar once did to a Popish Bishop, desiring a piece of money of him, were it never so little, but the Bishop said no, he would give him a pardon: to whom the beggar replied, I perceive if your pardon were worth anything I should not have it: even so, if the prayers of these people were anything worth, they would not give them, because they give nothing.

Lastly, by this verse, when *Ruth* excuseth herself, that she should not be as one of his maidens, she setteth down a true example of Christian simplicity: for it may be she thought that *Boaz* was deceived in her, that he might think she came to work for him, and not for herself: therefore she telleth him plainly that she should not be as one of his maidens, that is, as one of his hired servants. So that these words of *Ruth* tend to her own hindrance, if *Boaz* had been deceived in her, yet godliness will not conceal that, which maketh against itself, if the question be made of profit. Whereby we note, that encroaching for bargains, facing for promises, suing for counterfeit titles, and such like actions cannot agree with the simplicity of a godly minded Christian, whose conscience is his court, his religion his attorney, and the word of God his judge, to pronounce definitive sentence against his own cause, if it tend to the peril and damage of his neighbor, or discredit of his profession. Oh that we had more of this simplicity, and less of this subtlety,

whereby we deceive our own souls, betray the glorious
Gospel of Jesus Christ, confound the weak minds of our
wavering brethren, make shipwreck of pure consciences,
and cast ourselves headlong for the world into the fire of
hell.

But Boaz said. This last verse showeth unto us,
that *Boaz* was not deceived in *Ruth*, but shutting up the
communication, by calling her to meat, and dealeth to
her so abundantly, that she leaveth some. By the which
words there is noted two degrees of the kindness of this
man. First, that in his own person he calleth her to meat.
Secondly, that with his own hands he gave her abundantly. Where we see again and again commended unto
us the humility and liberality of this *Boaz*, he disdaineth
not to call so simple a guest to his table, knowing her to
be a faithful sister; for whose sake, if need were, he was
bound to lay down his life. Whereby we are instructed
to cast off the stateliness of our stomachs, standing upon
our pantofles [*raised overshoes*], scant vouchsafing to
look friendly on a poor man or woman, much less to
speak kindly to either of both. Again, his liberality, by
giving so plentifully unto her with his own hands, it appeareth he was none of these counterfeit givers, which
promise much and perform little, and for every carnal
companions tale-bearing, and whispering, withdraw
their promised and bounden liberality, from church and
poor, from minister and Religion. Oh how cold is this
devotion, which proceedeth from a sudden humor, and
soon endeth to God his dishonor: Better had it been for
those men, not to show any favor at all, than after they
have rashly begun, causeless to withdraw their benevolence from Christ. But I consider, there shall be some
that shall say at the latter end unto our Savior; we have
prophesied in thy name, we have eaten in thy presence,
and yet he shall say unto them, *depart from me ye workers of iniquity, I know you not*: then shall they be blessed,
which have wasted their wealth for Religion, consumed

their living on the faithful, and continued their liberality unto the end. Now let us give praise to God.

The end of the Sixth Lecture.

Ruth Chapter 2. verses 8-14

The Seventh Lecture

Ruth Chapter 2. verses 15-23

15 *And when she arose to glean,* Boaz *commanded his servants, saying: Let her gather among the sheaves, and do not rebuke her.*

16 *And let fall some of the sheaves for her, and let it lie, that she may gather it up, and rebuke her not.*

17 *And so she gleaned in the field till evening, and she threshed that which she had gathered, and it was about an ephah of barley.*

18 *And she took it up and went into the city, and her mother in law saw what she had gathered, and she took forth and gave unto her, of that which she had left, when she was sufficed.*

19 *Then her mother in law said unto her, where hast thou gleaned to day? and where wroughtest thou? Blessed be he that knew thee: and she showed her mother in law with whom she had wrought, and said, the man's name with whom I wrought to day, was* Boaz.

20 *And* Naomi *said unto her daughter in law: Blessed be he of the Lord, for he ceaseth not to do good, both to the living and to the dead. Again,* Naomi *said unto her, the man is near unto us, and of our affinity.*

21 *And* Ruth *the Moabitess said, He said also certainly unto me, that thou shalt be with my servants, until they have ended all the harvest which is mine.*

22 *And* Naomi *answered unto* Ruth *her daughter in law: It is best, my daughter, that thou go out with his maidens, that they meet thee not in another field.*

23 *Then she kept her by the maids of* Boaz, *unto the end of barley harvest, and wheat harvest, and dwelt with her mother in law.*

hese verses unto the end of this Chapter contain those things which *Boaz* and *Ruth* did, with *Naomi* also after that *Ruth* had dined. The words have two parts. The first between *Ruth* and *Boaz* in the field. The second between *Ruth* and her mother in law at home.

The first part is in verses 15-17. wherein is set down what *Ruth* did after dinner: *that she arose to gather ears*, which is declared by the time, verse 17. and the quantity in the same verse, *an ephah of barley*. Secondly, *Boaz* reneweth his commandment to his servants for *Ruth*, wherein he willeth them, first, that they suffer her to gather where she please: verse 15. Secondly, that they willingly let fall unto her out of the sheaves, and suffer her to take it up.

The other part of *Ruth* and *Naomi*, is contained verses 18-23. and declareth what these twain did after *Ruth* came from the field, and after her coming home, verse 18. bringing both her gleaned corn, and reserved victual. They twain commune of those things which *Boaz* had done to *Ruth*. First, *Naomi* asketh *Ruth*, where she had gleaned that day, verse 19. To which *Ruth* answereth, telling the name of the man, in whose possession she had gathered to be *Boaz*. verse 19. Secondly, his courtesy toward her, not only for that present, but also biddeth her to abide with his maids unto the end of his harvest. After this, *Naomi* first prayeth for the man, verse 20. alleging his kindness not only to them that are living, but also to those that are dead, and telling *Ruth* that the man was their kinsman. Secondly, she counselleth *Ruth*, verse 22. that she take his proffer, and abide with his maidens, for fear she be denied in another field: which *Ruth* performeth, verse 23, and keepeth with them to the end of barley harvest, and wheat harvest, and afterward with her mother. Of these parts let us briefly speak, as the Spirit shall assist, and the time permit.

Then she arose. After dinner, like one careful of her business, she repaireth to her former work, and here by the way this question may be made, whether *Ruth* gave any thanks to God, for her meat, seeing it is not mentioned: for this doubt must not be omitted, nor pass undissolved, lest our carnal companions in this age, which come and go to their meat like brute beasts, may seem to have the example of some godly persons, for the defense of their abominable unthankfulness. To which I answer: first, if any godly person have at any time, omitted his duty, we must not by his example be drawn to do the like; for we must live by the rule of the word of God, not by the examples of the faithful. Secondly, we must know that every thing or circumstance is not needful in every place of the Scripture to be declared particularly: for in this place we read not that *Ruth* gave any thanks to *Boaz* for her meat: yet we must not conclude that she gave none at all, and if she thanked a man, much more the eternal God, which framed his mind to show her that favor. Thirdly, she being with *Boaz*, it was his duty at his own table to pray, and to give thanks, which no doubt but he did, and she did with him. Therefore to the words, where we first note the true use of eating and drinking, the benefits of God, which is, that by them we may be enabled to follow our vocations: For here we see, *Ruth* after meat, returneth to her work again, as if the holy Ghost had flatly set down, that for this cause we must eat and drink, that by them we might work more freely, and labor more diligently. Therefore *Solomon* pronounceth a blessing upon a whole country, *whose princes and nobles eat for strength, and not for drunkenness*: and these are accounted two sins of Sodom, *idleness and fullness of bread*, that is, eating and no working.

Eccl. 10.17

Ezek. 16.53

Ruth Chapter 2. verses 15-23

This point can never be stood enough upon, that the belly-gods and unorderly persons of our age, might be persuaded therewith to leave their drinking and drunkenness, their eating and gluttony, and their plays and pastimes: for the meat is no sooner out of their mouths, but the renewing of their sport entereth into their hearts, how they may spend more time in idleness and vanity. And above all, this is profitable for serving-men to note, who wish nothing but liberty, and their own consciences know, that if they may choose, they will dwell with no masters, but where they may do little work; therefore came the old proverb, a young serving-man, an old beggar; because unthriftiness in youth is seldom worn out in age. This I speak not against that calling which no doubt but is good and lawful, but only to warn them and exhort them, to banish their untimely eating and drinking, and to put away idleness, with some lawful and profitable business. And let us all be *Ruths* in this point, as in other her conditions, that we may eat our bread in the sweat of our brows, and rise to labor, not to pastime: that we may remember our old curse, which came by reason of sin, and ease the contagion of our diseased natures, with the daily following our honest vocations.

Secondly, by this also may we urge (although the holy Ghost in this place speaketh not of it) the worship and observation of the Sabbath: for as men go from work to meat, and after from meat to work again: even so reason would, that as we sanctify the Sabbath in the forenoon, by preaching and hearing, the afternoon should be hallowed with the same exercise. But of all works, this the greatest is in smallest reputation; for men go from hearing to their meat; but from their meat, either to sleep, or to open profaning the Lord's day, with most execrable and accursed pleasure or negligence. They say, once a day is enough, yea, and too much also, except they did it better. Such clipping of God his service to satisfy our pleasures, will not stand with the least and the smallest point of Christianity. And this they may be assured of, that in the last day, their own diligence and weekly labors, in worldly business, shall stand up in judgment against them, to condemn their negligence in the travail of godliness: yea and till this slackness be amended, the time lost and past repented, they shall never come to the knowledge of God or his truth, themselves, or their own salvation: for he that sanctifieth the Sabbath, hath all Religion, but he that profaneth the Sabbath, hath none at all.

And Boaz. In these words *Boaz* reneweth his commandment to his servants concerning *Ruth*, which we showed you was uttered in the ninth verse: and now he willeth them, that though she gather among the sheaves, yet none should shame her: meaning, none should reprehend her; for reprehension to a godly and modest woman, is a matter of blushing or shame: And this to be noted, that his mind is, though she deserved blame, yet none of them should say, black be her eye, (as the proverb is) that is, once accuse her for any fault. Where we note the wonderful care that *Boaz* had of her, that the longer he looked on her, the better he liked her: her solitary behavior, her contented travail, her diligent order in going so orderly to her business again, were as orations or persuasions, to make him being godly, to approve and commend her above all the residue. Which teacheth us, that we should be haled on with the same cords of honesty, diligence, and Religion, to extend our liberality in large gifts and courteous speeches, to every poor person that wanteth our help: and that the rather, considering poverty is a curse of sin, wherein we are all as guilty as they: therefore like feeling members of our brothers' miseries, where we see the foresaid graces appear, there let our bounden benevolence excel, that they may be encouraged with our benefits, and we may be comforted with their prayers, and both conjoined in this life, and in the life to come.

Ruth Chapter 2. verses 15-23

Secondly, *Ruth* would not gather among the sheaves, because, no doubt, she was studious to avoid offence, for if she had so done, she must needs incur the suspicion; though not the reproof of misbehavior, coveting more than was her due; for the ears, and not the sheaves were appointed for the poor. Whereby we note that the poor must be careful above many things, they abuse not the liberty of the rich: although they may go without correction to the sheaves in the fields, or the heaps in the barn, yet they must not eat up more than beseemeth them to ask. Now it were without conscience to ask so much as the owners cannot give, without the shortening of their hands to other their poor brethren. And this condemneth the raking desire of them, which are never contented, and those ungodly robbers and thieves, which ask, and yet have no need: both which kind of people will to the uttermost crave, and have all a man's possessions, without any mercy, under pretense of poverty, yea, and will never accept the willing mind of them that are not able to give, but like the sea, gape for the water out of the little land-brooks. These are officers and bribers, extortioners and usurers, rackers of farms, raisers of rents, takers of fines, and defrauders of simple persons in bargaining, who all are condemned in the last commandment, as the coveters of other men's goods, and therefore guilty of eternal damnation.

And do you. These words are the second part of his commandment, whereby the former point is confirmed, that *Boaz* knew *Ruth* would not pick the sheaves, and therefore willeth to let fall on the ground plentifully, for her to avoid her further and more unprofitable labor, which he therefore doth, that he might testify his goods, to be not only his, but all theirs that fear the Lord: for no doubt but there were many that did glean in the field beside *Ruth*, with whom *Boaz* did not thus deal: showing unto us that there may be a difference in giving, and that we are not bound to give equally to all, but as the persons are, so must be the gift: the poorest must not have the greatest share, but the godliest, for poverty without godliness is like the apple of *Sodom*, which is as fair to look on, as any other, but being taken in the hand, resolveth to smoke and powder; so if ungodly poor folks be a little examined, they shall be found as the apple not worth the eating, so the other not worthy to be given to; although they cry like the horseleech's daughters, give, give; yet we must answer them with spare, spare. But *Boaz* doth in this place, as *Joseph* did to his brethren, he feasted all of them, but *Benjamin's* part was five times so big as the residue: afterward, he gave to everyone change of garments, but unto *Benjamin* he gave three hundred shekels and five change of garments: the reason of all this was, because he was *Rachel*, his own mother's son, but all the other were his father's children only; even so must we do good to all that are our father's children by creation, but to our mother's children, which is, the Church of Christ, the household of faith, whereof *Rachel* was a type: we must with special portions, for feeding their hunger, and clothing of their nakedness, compass their wants, with the supply of our benevolence, for which cause Saint *Paul* in his preaching was willed by the other Apostles, to have special and heedful care over the poor brethren; which if it were put in practice, we should be more able to do good unto the godly: and to deny the contrary minded. This one thing is above all other to be required, that everyone give where God may most of all be glorified, but the ungodly sort take their relief as the hungry hounds their feeding, if they be hindered, they will fly upon their own masters, in like sort the wicked will blaspheme God liberally, and not humbly thank or praise him, for anything they receive. What if they murmur against thee and say, my part is not so good as thine, you give him more than to me, and you care for none but for these precise fellows? Tell them again, it is lawful for thee to do with thy own as thou wilt: neither ought thy

Gen. 43.34

Gen. 45.22

Gal. 2.10

Ruth Chapter 2. verses 15-23

eye to be evil, because my hand is good: the unworthiest
in the world shall have the worthiest portion: they which
with them are last, with thee let be first, and the first with
them, be last with thee; for spiritual men must look for
spiritual hearts, to cast the seed of their alms into good
ground, where the fruit may be increased, the want of
the faithful may be relieved, the glory of Christ may be
magnified, thy own duty may be discharged, a good conscience satisfied, and thy soul forever comforted.

Secondly, by this we observe, that *Boaz* might
have admitted many hindrances, whereby he might have
been better advised before he gave such large liberty, either to *Ruth* or to his servants for her, as to gather among
the sheaves, or to let fall handfuls unto her. He might
have thought thus with himself, it was lately a dearth for
a long time together, it may be shortly the Lord will send
such another, and then all that I have will be too little for
myself and my family, and therefore I must be wise, and
give not so much, till I know what I shall lack, but all this
could not turn away the heart of *Boaz* from doing good
unto *Ruth*, for he esteemed more of one godly *Ruth*,
than of all the possessions he had: neither ought any of
the godly once to admit any such doubt in their mind,
as to be vexed in distrust of the mercy of God to come.
They must pray with *David, O Lord incline my heart to
thy testimonies, and not to covetousness.* The widow of
Zarephath might have so answered *Elijah*, that she had
but so little left, as would only suffice for one meal, and
give him nothing, yet she was obedient, and believed the
word of the prophet, and her store increased, that she
wanted no more.

The Church of the Macedonians might have
said, that they were poor saints as well as the residue,
therefore, as they asked nothing but were content with
their poverty, so none should charge them in giving to
other, but yet the Apostle *Paul* said, they supplied the
want of the Corinthians, and gave more than they were

Psal. 119.36

1 Kings 17

2 Cor. 8.2-4

able. And everlasting is the commendation which he
giveth of *Onesiphorus*, how often he refreshed him and
was not ashamed of his chains, but came to *Ephesus* and
visited him there, and followed him to Rome many hundred miles, that there also he might succor him with
his charity. Which teacheth us, when we have to deal
with the godly, as all these persons had, no cost must be
spared, covetousness not admitted, no fear of want sus-
pected, for he which is Lord overall, is also rich unto all. *2 Tim. 1.16-18*

Obadiah in a famine fed an hundred prophets,
yea and hid them in caves, from the wrath of *Jezebel*. *1 Kings 18.13*
What want did he sustain thereby? surely none, for distrust causeth want, and not liberality, for he which maketh thee to feed his saints now, will also provide another
to feed thee when thy store is wasted. Oh hearken to this
you possessors of the earth, upon whom in this time of
dearth the eyes of the poor do look up, as on the hands
of the Lord, whereby he filleth every living thing with
his plenteous goodness. Open your gates wider, that
more poor may come into your houses, to be refreshed
with bread: open your purses farther, that more benevolence may come out, to be cast into the fruitful land of
the famished poor, for after many days you shall find it
again: put on the bowels of compassion, and let not your
own brethren want, seeing you have enough. He that
willeth you to do this for his sake, will command heav-
en and earth, to restore his own debt, which you have
lent him: fear not that you shall want, for the Lord is the
owner of the earth, and this is sent upon us to try your
charity and compassion toward the poor for his sake: if
you now be liberal, *Paul* hath prayed for you that you
may find mercy in the day of the dissolution of all things,
and the Lord hath promised to the merciful mercy, at
that day when he lieth sick upon his death-bed. Make
you treasures therefore of this worldly wealth, and send
them by the hands of the poor into God his kingdom
before you: spare not the sheaves in the barn, the ears in

the field, nor the heaps in your garners: for he that spendeth for the members of Christ, shall receive the greater advantage. Remember you are the partakers of the same faith, which they had that sold their possessions to give to the saints, and to gain heaven: but you need not to sell any lands, only deliver your corn plentifully to the poor: which if you do not, they shall rise in judgment against you at the latter day, because they spared neither lands nor lives, and you will not give a little corn for the name of Christ.

And so she gathered. This is the last part of that which *Ruth* did in the field, showing her diligence she used in her labors, by working out the whole day until the evening, and gathering an ephah of barley: for by this appeareth, that she labored as faithfully for herself and her mother, as if she had been an hired servant, or her mother looking upon her. By the which is noted unto us, the diligence of children and servants, in the labors and business of their masters and parents, for they must not seek or covet to please them with eye-service, but their duties are required, as well in the time of their absence, as in their presence.

Be *Ruths*, my beloved, in this point, whosoever are bond or free, for they which are faithful in a little, shall be made great rulers, and they which have not been faithful in the earthly treasures, shall never be trusted with the heavenly. By this also they may learn, which think they may lawfully take their ease in their own business: but we see by this example of *Ruth*, that Religion bindeth us to be as diligent in our own, as in another man's travail, committed unto us upon trust, for as to him we are faithful, because we receive wages, so in our own we must be painful, lest the Lord arise against us for the misspending of our time: and we owe more duty to our heavenly Father, than to all the earthly masters of the world.

Again, the quantity of her gathering is here described, to be an ephah of barley: for the understanding whereof we must note that there were three kinds of measures among the Hebrews, which are mentioned in the Scripture: the first was a homer, which was the measure of Manna that the Lord allowed to every household when they were wandering in the wilderness, and contained of our English measure, six pints, and somewhat more; the second measure was a hin, which after our measure, contained ten pints, and somewhat more, the third was an ephah, which is this that measured the barley of *Ruth*, and it contained ten homers, which cometh to sixty pints, which being divided by eight, amounteth to the quantity of seven gallons and one pottle [*two quarts*], which is a bushel lacking one pottle, after our English measure. By the which we may observe, how largely the Lord provided for *Ruth* by the liberality of *Boaz*, for she gathered more in one day than otherwise she could in two or three: where the Lord himself showeth us how she took the courtesy of *Boaz*, and the servants scattered for her according to their master's commandment, that her hand might be quickly filled, her travail the more eased, her labor better rewarded, and finally mother and daughter be both more comfortably refreshed with their kinsman's kindness.

Lev. 19.36
Lev. 27.16
Exod. 16.16

And when she took up. The day being ended and *Ruth* wearied with her unwonted, and yet diligent travail, up she taketh her bundle of corn, and the scraps of meat she had reserved, and trudgeth to her mother, that she might understand of her good hap [*happening*], and they both together rejoice for the corn *Ruth* had gathered, and the good will which *Boaz* had offered. Out of the which we may first of all observe a heavenly and godly example of obedience and love toward her mother in law, for we see in this place, that she doth not only labor for her living, but refresheth her with that which was given her to satisfy her own hunger, while she was in the field in her diligent labor. Was it not sufficient

Ruth Chapter 2. verses 15-23

for *Ruth* that she left her people and country to come
with her mother in law, but she must also go for her, she
sitting at home, in a poor and contemptible manner to
glean in the field: or if she did that willingly, yet must
she save the meat from her own mouth, and put it into
Naomi's? Here we see she failed in nothing that might
either commend her love, declare her obedience, and
signify her care toward poor and old *Naomi,* her dear
and godly mother. And this teacheth us, that we must
be *Ruths* to our aged parents, we must labor abroad, and
they must tarry at home, we must set our nimble bones
to the heavy business, and their wearied bodies must rest
in the houses. It is ungodliness to say, that the old man
or woman, shall labor and care for our wretched riot,
and careless expenses, but rather let the young gallant
take his own parents upon his back, carry them from
their house of trouble to the harbor of peace. Let *Esau*
and *Jacob* hunt venison for *Isaac*, for he is old, and must

Gen. 27.3

tarry at home. Let *Jacob* and little *Joseph* tarry in their
tents, and the lusty youths, his sons and brethren lie in
the fields and keep their father's sheep, and rather than

Gen. 37.14

old *Jacob* should go, let young *Joseph* trudge to his brethren, though he be sold for his labor. Let *Ruth* go glean
for *Naomi*, and not *Naomi* for *Ruth*, for this is the first
commandment with promise. But oh the graceless generations of our ungodly age, where men are become so
tender over their disobedient brood, that in their labors
they will spare their wanton children, and wear their
crazed carcasses, they had rather put both feet into the
grave by their over-labors, than bring their untamed
steers, and unruly heifers, their sons and daughters, to
the yoke of diligent travail. And these graceless imps,
will look and laugh upon their parents, and say, it doth
their old bodies good: And doth it so? why, is it better
for a tired horse to run a race, than for a resty palfrey
[*riding horse*]? You are ready enough to catch that which
is good from your parents, why take ye not their labors,

Lecture 7

if they be so good for them? No, no, you are the heaviness of your parents: you should be olives to make them look cheerfully, but you are onions that make them weep bitterly. But yet let not *Ruth* and the godly exhort us in vain, for if we do the labor, we shall have their hire, if we honor our parents, with our actions and deeds, as we do with our words, then shall our days be multiplied in the land, or else our lives shall be shortened with untimely death, and our posterity rooted out by the just judgment of God.

      Secondly; by this example of *Ruth*, that she brought her mother of that which she had left: we learn this doctrine, if our friends give us liberally, and we have plenty, let us not consume all upon ourselves, but let us reserve some for other. *When our Savior* had twice feasted many thousands, still there was something left which he commanded to be taken up: showing us thereby, if God liberally pour out his benefits upon us, it is not that we should the more riotously lavish them out upon meat or pleasure: for it is a common answer in these days, if we reprove gamesters for their play, drunkards for their costs, and proud persons for indecent apparel, wherein everyone spendeth more than would suffice two or three poor persons, they will tell us they spend nothing but their own, and what have we to do with it? But we reply, that they spend more than is their own, for the earth is the Lord's, and all that therein is. They are but stewards of their goods, and not lords and masters, and therefore they shall give account for every penny misspent, when it shall not profit them to say, we wasted our wealth at dicing and gaming, we consumed our lands by eating and drinking, and spent thus much money in gay apparel, and other bravery.

      Secondly, God gave them those benefits, not so much for themselves, as for others: for as the Sun shineth not for itself, but for us, the earth bringeth forth fruit, not for itself but for us: so wealthy men, are not

Matt. 14.20
John 6.13

Ruth Chapter 2. verses 15-23

Esther 1.8

wealthy for themselves only, but for all the poor members of Christ, that they might liberally bestow upon others. The Heathen King *Ahasuerus*, making a feast to all his Empire; yet he gave this law, that none should be compelled to drink or to eat more than they needed or pleased: so abominable is gluttony, even in nature, that it hurteth man, spoileth beasts, and killeth the fruts of the earth; for the rankest corn is none of the best. Then here is temperance by this example commanded: for the physicians say, that it is most wholesome, to come and rise from meat with a hungry stomach, and the word of God saith, that we must eat for strength and nature, not for appetite and drunkenness. But oh that our fat Basanites would admit this as a wholesome and a godly doctrine, then would not their bellies and paunches [*potbellies*] grow so great as they are, not their hearts so hardened against the poor; for their dogs, should go empty, their abundance would be diminished, their gluttonies and drunkenness banished, their pleasures and delights expelled, and their pride and apparel be humbled, and their godly and needy brethren succored.

Thirdly, by this we note, that the poorest must strive to bestow somewhat unto their brethren that want: yea, though they spare it from their own necessities: but especially children to their parents, and one kinsman to another: for thus we see *Ruth* doth, she spared when she had enough, and that she gave to her mother that wanted. Which godly kindness putteth us in mind of the poor widow in the Gospel, that came and gave two mites into the Lord's treasury, and the Lord doth greatly commend her for it, above the rich offerings of the wealthy: as if a little thing that a poor man doth, were more accepted than the multitudes of rich men. Indeed to the world the largest gift maketh the greatest show, but to the Lord the little portions of a willing mind, if it be but a cup of cold water, is greater than the flesh pots of *Egypt*, and all the dainty fare of the King of Babylon's

Luke 21.2

court. For our Savior encourageth us by this means that
they which have little to give should not abstain, but certainly know that the Lord looketh on the heart, not on
the hand, on the mind, not on the gift, for that which in
the presence of the world is despised, in the sight of God
is best accepted. Therefore everyone must look to deal
some good by their living, be it never so small, for as
there is no herb, but it yieldeth some fruit, so there must
be no man but he must give somewhat, that so he might
fulfill the glory of the Gospel.

But her mother in law. Here in this verse *Naomi*
seeing the plenty of the gleaned corn, and reserved victual, like a godly woman falleth to prayer for a blessing
upon him that had given so liberally unto *Ruth*: which
is as a thanksgiving for the benefit received: and afterward she questioneth with *Ruth*, where she had gleaned
that day, and *Ruth* telleth her in the possession of *Boaz*.
Where we first of all note the duty of parents to their
children, and masters to their servants, which is, to call
them to a reckoning where and how they bestow their
time: therefore saith *Naomi*, where hast thou gathered
today, and where hast thou wrought. Condemning this
softness and suffering in such kind of parents, as are
afraid to speak to their children and servants, not for
their work, but for their misspending the Sabbath, the
idle journeys they make to taverns and plays, to feasting and dancing, should be examined by their governors, as *Naomi* doth *Ruth*. Where hast thou wrought
to day? Whose business was thou employed in? what
place did call thee from the service of God? and what
motion did cause thee to dishonor the Sabbath? No, no,
they can suffer them to violate the Lord's day in pleasure,
that they might drudge all the week after in their worldly
travails. Why doth not some man give recreation to his
servants of his own six? but they must rob the Lord of
the seventh also: How unequal is this, to put him out
that hath but one part, and to score him up that hath so

many? I am persuaded, that of all other tokens of irreligion among us, there is none greater than this, to suffer our children and servants to violate the Lord's own day, that they might the more willingly labor and travail for them on the weekdays. But yet let the authority of parents remain, that God hath given this power unto them, and let the duty of children and servants appear, that as *Ruth* giveth answer to *Naomi* from point to point, how and where she applied her time; even so they are bound upon pain of God his eternal curse, to give willing and gentle accounts to them, when they are demanded in such like matters.

Secondly, by this prayer of *Naomi, Blessed be he of the Lord that knew thee*, that is, which approved thee and showed thee favor, we note this to be our duty, to pray for our benefactors, seeing we cannot reward them, so doth *Naomi* in this place, and so doeth *Paul* for *Onesiphorus*, that the Lord would show mercy unto him in the day of his appearing: teaching us that our spiritual prayers are more necessary for them, than their temporal benefits are for us: and therefore let us learn to pray aright, seeing it is our duty to pray for our friends. These painted prayers of many which come from the lips, or from wicked hearts, are such as the prayers of rogueing beggars at every door for base relief, and also the commonest that are among many poor people in these days, are abomination in the eyes of the Lord, no benefit to them for whom they are uttered, and the poison of those that thus do use them. Therefore beloved, learn to account of them as they are; clouds carried about with every wind, wells and no water, great words, but no grace in them: stop your ears at these bread-prayers, and withdraw your hands from giving any relief to them that abuse this heavenly blessing.

2 Tim. 1.16

Then said Naomi. In this verse *Naomi* repeateth her prayer, and addeth a reason of the same, because he hath not ceased to do good toward the living, and toward the dead, that is, he did good to my husband and children when they were alive, and now to us their posterity, they being dead, for in doing good to us for their sakes, they do it to them: for either interpretation will stand. For we must not imagine, that this liberality doth any good to them that are dead, because they were in Moab, these in Judah, they were consumed in their graves, and unfit for any benevolence, as for their souls they needed no earthly beneficence: for that remaineth true forever which *Solomon* saith, the living know that they shall die, but the dead know nothing, nor yet have they any more part, seeing their remembrance is forgotten, the thing which they loved, and the thing which they hated, and the thing they desired is now perished with them; neither have they any more part of all the things that are done under the sun. By the which we may see the delusion of them which teach us to buy prayers and pardons for our friends that are dead, that their pains may be eased which now they endure: for if nothing can profit them that is done under the Sun, then neither our prayers nor purses can give them any relief. But by these words we learn, that if we do good to the children and widows of our deceased friends, it is all one, as if we did good to their own persons. Thus said *Naomi* in this place, and thus *David* did good to his friend *Jonathan* being dead, when he did kindly entreat *Mephibosheth* his son, being alive. The Lord himself protesteth in the Scriptures, that he did good to the Israelites and Jews, for *Abraham, Isaac,* and *Jacob's* sakes: and our Savior in the Gospel declareth, that the good we do to the least of his brethren, being on earth, we do it to him which reigneth in heaven; for this is a duty of true friendship, to make much of our friends when they are departed, to be a friend to their friends, and to be an enemy to their enemies, as the Lord promised *Abraham.* Therefore, let us cast away this counterfeit kindness, and perform this godly love, wherein others before us have walked, and as we were

Eccl. 9.5,6

2 Sam. 9.11

Matt. 25.40

Gen. 21.23

Ruth Chapter 2. verses 15-23

wont lovingly to receive the parents, being alive, so let us joyfully entertain the children now they are dead, for true friendship loveth at all times, and godly kindness must never be removed. As we wish that others should use us when we are gone, so let us use others now they are absent.

Prov. 17.17

Moreover Naomi said. In these words she giveth comfort unto *Ruth*, showing her, that his benevolence was not causeless, seeing he was near unto them, and of their affinity, being an appointed person to redeem their inheritance. For, in the Law of the Lord, he hath decreed for the poor of the Jews, that if any person had sold his inheritance, the next of his kindred might redeem it, and restore it to the family again, which coming into the mind of *Naomi*, she hopeth that by this means they should come to their inheritance again, seeing *Boaz*, who was one of the next of her kindred, had so courteously entreated the widow and heir.

Lev. 25.25
Deut. 25.5,6

Whereby we note the great care that the Lord hath over the poor, which by a law decreed, that they should not forever be deprived of their inheritance, for at the farthest they should come to it again at the year of Jubilee. And truly this Law being ceased, because the Jews commonwealth is overthrown, yet the Lord executeth the same in some measure amongst the Gentiles daily. For now we may see and hear, how he exalteth many from the dust, to walk and sit with princes: how he giveth great possessions unto them whose fathers had not one foot of land, and casteth many from their unlawful titles. And every day we hear of some cast down and humbled, and others lift up and exalted. Who doth this? but the hand of the Almighty that putteth down *Haman* and raiseth up *Mordecai*: refuseth *Saul* and chooseth *David*: removeth *Abiathar*, and establisheth *Zadok*: banisheth *Shebna*, and advanceth *Eliakim*: and finally, that in few ages changeth all things. Therefore promotion cometh neither from the East, nor from the West, nor from

Esther 7.10;
8.1
1 Sam. 16.14
Isa. 22.20

the wilderness, but from the throne of the Lord of hosts, which openeth, and no man shutteth, humbleth, and no man setteth up, exalteth, and no man casteth down, and ruleth the course of all mankind by his unchangeable decree. Let not then the mightiest be proud for their honor and dignity, for the Lord destroyed the Anakims' great princes and giants before the family of *Caleb*: much more will he do those that are lifted up by their wealth, that should rather cast them down: and let us do good to these poor brethren among us, for they shall be lifted up unto riches, when the greatest and wealthiest among us shall be cast down into poverty. But of this matter we shall have more occasion to speak in the fourth chapter.

    But Ruth said. In this verse *Ruth* maketh relation of those things which *Boaz* had said unto her, and praying for a blessing upon him, because he vouchsafed to take her into the company of his maidens, and gave her leave to gather to the end of harvest. So that in this place, by these words of *Ruth*, we have an example of perfect thankfulness, omitting nothing that might serve to commend the kindness of *Boaz*: and also of womanlike and godly modesty, that concealeth the cause of all this courtesy, which was her own commendation, as already we have showed you. So that it is no part or point of godliness, to do as our evil conditioned and ingrateful persons do, which omit that which serveth most for to commend their benefactors, and to lay all the praise upon their own deserts. But *Solomon* willed that another man's, and not our own mouth should praise us: and most ungodly is it, when men will not in so ample manner confess the benefits they have received of other, but by all means extenuate them, which maketh men unwilling to do any good, because they can have no thanks for their labor. And this it is that caused covetousness and bribery, extortion and usury, to enter upon their bodies and wealth, that would not gratify with kind and deserved reports. So that now men will please themselves with money and rewards, that would have been satisfied with thankful words: which is a just judgment upon the world, that would not be contented to recompense kindness for kindness; are now plagued with covetousness for kindness.

Wherefore Naomi. This is the last part of this conference or dialogue, wherein *Naomi* counseleth *Ruth* to follow and take the proffer of *Boaz*, and abide with his maidens, to avoid all dangers, if the reapers deny her in another field. Where we first of all note, that if we acquaint our parents and friends, with our actions and enterprises, it might go far better with us in the things of this life, for their aged counsel which they have bought with much experience may stay our unsteady minds with their approved advice: *Ruth* in this place, declaring the courtesy of *Boaz*, hath it confirmed with the counsel of *Naomi*, and grounded upon a reason which she knew not, nor feared not. For she thought, that in every place she should have found the like entertainment, and the reapers that then were, would so continue to the end of harvest, but *Naomi* knew they were often changed, and so in the end it might fall out otherwise, than *Boaz* appointed, or *Ruth* expected. And this (me thinketh) doth show unto us what manner persons parents ought to be, for if children want counsel, they should be advised by their parents: if comfort, it should be ministered by parents, if necessaries, they should be provided by parents: if instruction, they should be guided by parents: and finally, if correction, they should be ordered by parents: which is not only to be wished, but is required by the Lord, that they bring them up in the fear and nurture of the Lord. And if this were duly weighed, and reverently considered, as *Elisha's* cloak parted the waters of *Jordan*, so this would part asunder, and break off many thousand marriages in our days, where parents are not able to counsel, nor willing to be counseled, which if they would, they had not been married. This I speak,

Eph. 6.2

not to the discredit of marriage, but only to exhort, as
from the Lord, that those which either are, or intend to
be married, would look and travail first for wisdom, and
then for wives, first for virtue, and then for husbands,
wherein, if they follow my advice, I assure them their
marriages will be much merrier, and their posterity
much happier.

Secondly, by this we gather, that it is a dangerous or indecent thing, for women to travel or work
alone without any company, for the weakest are soonest oppressed, and women are quickly conquered. We
know *Dinah* traveling alone was taken and ravished by
Shechem: and *Abigail* when she went to pacify the wrath   Gen. 34.1
of *David*, took servants with her, as in this place *Naomi*
counselleth *Ruth*, to abide in the company of the servants of *Boaz*, accounting it an indecent and unseemly
thing for women and maidens to be seen alone. And
truly, if servants in our days had many times more company, there would be less dishonesty among them; for
we know and see to our grief, that the daily and usual fa-
miliarity of a few, hath bred some disease in our church,
and distemper in our commonwealth. This I speak, that
even in these days of peace, men would be more careful
over daughters and servants, and not to employ them so
commonly as they do, in journeys and travail and solitary business, but for more assurance keep them with
company, which may be their defense against all dangers, if any happen, and the avoiding of dishonesty, if any
be so lightly disposed.

Thirdly, by this we note, what company were
best for both kind of youths, either young men or maidens, when *Naomi* saith, *It is good for thee to go forth with
his maidens*: that is, thou art a woman, and abide among
his women and maidens; for all companions are neither
fit nor lawful, maidens among men, and men among
maidens, is for many causes disallowed. First, because
there is no such equality in the sex, that they might keep

together: for if they labor, it is not alike, and if they sport, their pleasures are contrary, and if they dally, it is flat iniquity. In consideration whereof, in old time the wives had one tent to dwell in, and the husbands another: as we may see in *Abraham*, in *Sara*, in *Jacob* and his wives; and like this it is that *Miriam, and the women of Israel* praised God by themselves after their deliverance out of Egypt, and *Moses* and *Aaron* her brethren, with all the men of Israel by themselves. And also we know how the virgins of Israel went up every year into the wilderness to lament and talk with the daughter of *Jephthah*. Whereby we are taught, that not only for fear of danger, but also for modesty and conscience sake, we must avoid this mingled companies of men and women, except in necessary occasions, as prayer privately and publicly, communication of godly pretended marriages, and such like business. Whereby also we see at once condemned the feasting, dancing, meeting, playing, and running of men and maidens together, without all respect of honesty or modesty. And that which is worst, parents and masters will behold their pastime, and delight in the vanity of their wanton children, training them up in a dissolute life, and commending their indecent and unseemly behavior. Amend this negligence in the shell of infancy, and your children will grow up to your greater comfort, and prosper to their more happy welfare, and the occasion of many sins will be cut off, if we follow the counsel of the Spirit of God.

And so she abode. This is the conclusion of this chapter, and second part of this history showing unto us that *Ruth* followed the counsel of her mother, abiding with the maidens of *Boaz* to the end of barley and wheat harvest, and afterward dwelleth with her mother again. Where we observe another example of obedience in *Ruth*, that hearkened to the voice of her mother, and went forth with the maidens of *Boaz*. And surely it is commonly seen, that such as the mother is, such is the

Gen. 18.30
Gen. 31.32
Exod. 15.20

Judg. 11.37

daughter: for more *Naomis* would make more *Ruths*, and more good mothers would make more good daughters: And in these days all the faults of children may justly be imputed to the folly of parents, as the old crab goeth, so goeth the young, and as the old cock croweth, so croweth the young: a Serpent hatcheth a Serpent not an Eel, so evil parents bring forth evil and ungodly children; but good fathers, by diligent instruction and tender admonition, by praying with, and for their children, as *Job* did, shall live to see their generations as blessed as his was. | Job 1.5 | Job 42.12

    Secondly, by this we learn an excellent example of godly liberality, in that *Boaz* suffered *Ruth* to gather wheat as well as barley, the best as well as the meaner. In like manner must we as willingly depart with, for Christ's sake, our wine as our water, our drink as our draff, and as we commonly speak, our white bread as our brown: and truly in this, many good men offend, not because they give it not, but because they think it too much to give: as if our best gifts were not best accepted in the presence of God. He which fed the Israelites with Angel's food, would also that we should feed him in the godly poor, with our worshipful and daintiest fare. This I speak not, that those which ask, should be discontented with the meanest and fittest for them, for the proverb is, beggars must not be choosers, as it is covetousness not to vouchsafe the best we have (if need require) to the poor, so it is scornfulness for the poor, like the Israelites which loathed Manna, and desired flesh, to be discontented with their necessary and present food, and to lust for that which is above their vocation. But the use of this point is, to persuade to be like minded unto *Boaz* in this, to the godly poor, that we every one, without partiality or grudging, when necessity requireth, give our gold as well as our silver, and distribute our dearest alms to our poorest brethren.

    Thirdly, harvest being done, *Ruth* abideth with

her mother in law, for none of the godly will make a daily and continual trade of asking alms, or forsake their own parents or poor habitations, for worldly respects, as appeareth by this example of *Ruth*. For it is no doubt, she fared well every day with the servants of *Boaz*, and much better than her poor mother could provide for her at home, but she is not drawn away therewith, but is as contented to eat the hungry morsels with her mother at home, as the plentiful abroad. And it is great pity that any should be succored, which are not contented to live hardly at home, and then to ask, when there is no other honest means left to live. And this condemneth the common walking-mates, which neither have houses nor honesty, and it is greatest pity that they either should be succored or suffered so to do, for they are drones, which never come in hives, but to the hurt of other; they waste all, but get nothing, neither have they any other care, but to charge the godly and charitable people. Unto such give not, as we have often said, for they which will not live of the sweat of their brows, let them not eat of the bread of our labors. Now let us give praise to God.

The end of the Seventh Lecture.

The Eighth Lecture

Ruth Chapter 3. verses 1-6

1 *Afterward,* Naomi *her mother in law said unto her, shall I not seek rest for thee my daughter, that thou mayest prosper.*

2 *And now, is not* Boaz *our kinsman, with whose maids thou was, behold he winnoweth barley in the floor this night.*

3 *Wash thee therefore and anoint thee, and put on thy clothes, and go down into the floor, and let not the man know thee, until he have made an end to eat and drink.*

4 *But when he lieth down, mark the place where he lieth: then come thou, and uncover the place of his feet, and lie down, and he shall tell thee what thou shalt do.*

5 *And she said unto her, whatsoever thou hast command-ed me, that will I do.*

6 *And so she went down into the floor, and did altogether as her mother in law had commanded her.*

This third Chapter is the second occasion of this marriage, wherein *Naomi* espe-cially dealeth with *Ruth,* how she should make known her suit to *Boaz.* The whole Chapter hath these two parts, first the counsel of *Naomi* to *Ruth*: secondly the effect of that coun-sel. The counsel is contained in these six verses now read, consisting also of two parts: first, her care for *Ruth,* verse 1. that her desire is to procure her prosperity: secondly, the means whereby *Ruth* might perform that which she advised: first because *Boaz* was then alone in the floor winnowing of barley: secondly, she must prepare herself to go to him: first, in her body, by washing and anointing it: secondly, in her ornament, that she put on her best clothes, and so go down to the floor: after she was come thither, she instructeth her, how to behave herself: first by keeping out of his sight and knowledge, till he had supped: secondly, by marking the place of his bed, and lying down at his feet, and declaring her suit unto him; and that he would tell her what she should do. After all this, *Ruth* promiseth obedience, verses 5,6. and accomplisheth her mother's desire. Of these parts let us briefly speak, as the Spirit of God shall assist us, and the time permit.

Afterward Naomi. In these words is declared unto us the great care that *Naomi* had of her daughter in law *Ruth*, for they are thus much in effect. Now both of us are in quiet, and peaceable rest at home, yet I see that our welfare cannot alway endure, for I am old, and the grave gapeth after me; thou art young, and a good marriage tarrieth for thee: it is my duty to look for thy welfare, and to provide for thy continual rest, if I be taken away: and being careful of it, I have now invented the means, etc. Out of the which we note these two profitable doctrines.

First, that it is the duty of parents to provide for their children, when themselves shall be taken away, yea though they have no certain assurance, whether they shall need it or not. This we may see here practiced by *Naomi*: for she was never in better case since her arrival at Bethlehem, then she was at this present: Harvest was ended, provision obtained, household furnished, and these two poor widows living lovingly together, yet then we see in her best estate, she is most careful for the marriage of *Ruth*. And truly this is required of all them that have any children, to provide for them, that they should not care only for their present maintenance, but also for their future commodity. And this maketh many godly persons to marvel, why men do trouble their houses with their children, when they are able honestly to provide for them abroad. Why do many permit and suffer their sons and daughters, to spend the best of their youth in single estate, when it is rather required that while they are young, they should be bestowed. Truly this maketh so many marriages against the parents' minds, when they are negligent to look to their children, and then the children provide for themselves. Men look for offers, as the mariner looketh for wind, and when the wind serveth, the tide falleth; so many would provide for their children when it is too late. This injury is all heaped on the children; they match without wealth or blessing: they are detained in the best time of their days; and finally, are discredited by their own parents. Would God, you that are natural parents would learn of *Naomi*, which was but a stepmother. She differed not the time; she knew it a sin against nature, that youth should be wasted, and not in marriage: she had a conscience of her duty; and a care to her daughter in law, that her welfare might increase, her solitary life be comforted, her name advanced, and her Religion rewarded, with a temporal blessing of a godly husband, and eternal salvation in the kingdom of heaven.

Secondly, by this we gather that for many causes marriage is better than the unmarried estate of women, if with the fear of God it be undertaken. For in this place *Naomi* calleth it rest, as she did in the first Chapter: and therefore by relation, the unmarried life is disquietness, and as rest is better than trouble, so the married life is better than the other. And truly, in the unmarried life, we find many inconveniences: First, the heart is never satisfied: if a man have riches, honor, pleasure, health, and favor; yet wanting a convenient marriage, he is not at rest, but desireth that. If he be in sickness, the dili- verse 9 gence and care of a wife is better than a physician. Nature biddeth him marry to increase his name. The world biddeth him marry, to multiply mankind. The Lord biddeth him marry, to prepare some heirs for the kingdom of heaven: So that if Nature; World, and Religion require it, who shall speak against it? Secondly, in the unmarried estate, is either too too much solitariness, or too too much pleasure: the mean between both is marriage, where he shall alway find company to expel sorrow, and joyful care to drive away over-merry pastimes: it calleth a man to gravity, it admonisheth of death, it showeth the world to be vanity, and hath no hope but in heaven. Therefore *Solomon* speaking of one kind, and alluding to both, saith: He that findeth a wife, findeth a good thing, and receiveth favor of the Lord: even so may a woman say, if she find a godly husband, she hath a great favor. Christ taketh greatest delight in his Church, and his Church in Christ. Such is marriage, when the heart of one resteth in another, that is, the rest which is to be required. As for temporal blessings which further it, they must be sought for by diligent labor, and prayed for by faithful supplication, because it is the Lord that giveth power to get riches, grace to use them, and his blessing to increase them. We know, all the fathers so soon as their children were grown up, they willed and wished them to marry, that their minds might first be stayed at home, as it were the foundation, and then their actions would be wiser abroad, which would make a perfect building. But some will say, *Paul* affirmeth, it is not good for a man to touch a woman, that is, to marry. I answer, that saying of *Paul* is because of troubles that are incident to marriage, by reason of the wickedness of the world. The merchant that ventureth on the sea, hath greatest gain, and suddenest loss, not as if the sea were in fault, but because the storms fall on the sea; even so, if any find their marriages bitter unto them, let them know, the fault is not in the thing, but in the time, place,

Prov. 18.22

Deut. 8.18

1 Cor. 7.1

or persons: and though troubles follow it, it is but sour
sauce to sweet meat: as the furnace doth purge the gold,
that their love might be manifested, their fidelity tried,
their patience approved, and their religion, if they have
any, declared.

Again, they will object, the same Apostle saith in
the same Chapter, He that giveth in marriage doth well,
but he that giveth not in marriage doth better: therefore the unmarried life is better than the married: to
which I answer, first, he speaketh to them that have the
gift of chastity, but we know the fewest part are endued
therewith: Secondly, his speech is for those troublesome
days of persecution, when the faithful were in continual
troubles and fear of their lives, then was it better to die
single, than leave many helpless widows behind, that
they might the better fly in danger, be constant in affliction, and have no lets, or pull-backs, to keep them from
Christ: so he wisheth and protesteth, that their troubles
were means to keep them from marriage, in which sense
the Apostle calleth it better not to marry, and yet yieldeth the other to be good and lawful. But in times of
peace, where there is plenty and liberty, the swelling nature will not be appeased, but only by marriage, where
the gift is not, and the Apostle saith, in those dangerous
times, that it was better to marry than to burn, that is, to
be vexed with a daily desire, through the feeling of our
own necessity.

Thirdly, they may object that the unmarried care
for the things of God, but the married to please their
husbands and wives: to the which I answer, that marriage hindereth not the service of God, but furthereth
it in many respects: first, because a household is a little
Church, where the married persons are the ministers of
their family, by private instruction to draw both children and servants to the kingdom of heaven. Secondly, it putteth them in mind of the love of God to them,
when they love one another, and admonisheth them of

their duties, which is to love God again. Thirdly, they have more private blessings, as the seals of God his favor toward them, which also stirreth them up to serve the Lord. Fourthly, two are better than one: for if one be negligent in the worship of God, the other may whet his fellow on, and their prayers are more acceptable, because the number of them that pray is greater. And if any omit these duties, the fault is in the persons, not in the marriage: for that is it which the Apostle Saint *Paul* condemneth, when either party are so much inclined to one another, that they weigh not the love of God, and care of heavenly things, for the fondness over themselves and travail for earthly commodities: but we must be married, as if we were unmarried in this respect, we must use the world, as if we used it not, and rejoice in the company of one another, as if we rejoiced not. Therefore, to conclude, marriage is honorable in all, instituted by God himself, observed by the Fathers before Christ, both princes, priests, and prophets, commanded by our Savior and his apostles, to be undertaken, that such persons as have not the gift of continency, might marry and keep themselves the undefiled members of Christ's mystical body. Let us then be exhorted to be patient in the troubles that accompany it, for although a bitter shell do compass the nut, yet how sweet is the kernel that lieth within: although it have as many miseries, as the winter hath cold days, yet unspeakable is the comfort of it, to them that are equally minded. And as our labor in innocency was nothing but pleasure, which now is nothing but sorrow. So marriage was then more sweet, though now for sin it is become more bitter: but the hardest labor hath some profit, and the poorest marriage hath much comfort. But most accursed are they, which for to avoid the troubles they have conceived of marriage, do give their bodies to most filthy whoredoms, and wretched adulteries: Of whom Saint *Paul* saith, That God shall judge them, that is, utterly condemn them: for they shall never be made the members of Christ, which have incorporated them to be the members of harlots, and heirs of eternal and everlasting damnation.

And is not Boaz. As in the former verse we have heard the diligent carefulness of *Naomi* for *Ruth*, to prepare her some rest, that is, a marriage. So now we are to entreat or speak of the means whereby this might be accomplished, which *Naomi* expresseth in this verse, to this effect. By my daily study I have found out a means, whereby thou mayest come to more continual rest, *Boaz*, with whose maidens thou hast gleaned, and did so courteously entreat thee, he is our kinsman and defender, by the law, and even now he is alone in the floor, winnowing his barley, to whom if thou wilt go, and follow my counsel, he will show thee the way that tendeth to thy wealth. Out of the which we gather an example of ancient nobility, how they followed not their daily pleasure, but continual labor: how they honored the wealth that God hath given them, with the diligent labor of their of their own persons: that even this poorest work, of winnowing and threshing, as we read of *Gideon*, was not only committed to their servants, but performed by themselves. Whereby we are taught that it is no such unseemly thing, as many would make it for men of wealth to follow their basest labors. This *Boaz* had a prince to his grandfather, and he was the heir unto all his possessions, yet here we find him alone winnowing his own corn. We read of *Judah* the son of *Jacob*, a progenitor of this *Boaz*, that he went in his own person to the shearing of his sheep: and so did the sons of king *David*, when *Amnon* was slain by the servants of *Absalom*, because he defiled his sister *Tamar*. Examples of this are more plentiful, than the time will suffer me to rehearse, which are all left to us for patterns of thankfulness in their diligent labors, and witnesses of our unworthiness in all our possessions. *Adam* could not dwell in paradise, except in his own person he tilled it, but many with us, I think would deride him

Judg. 6.11

Gen. 38.13

2 Sam. 13.24

Ruth Chapter 3. verses 1-6

and all their fathers, if they saw them in anything but the gentleman's trade: for being hindered neither by the magistracy, nor by the ministery, they had rather follow hawking or hunting; gaming, or playing, than at any time to foil their hands with their own labors, but wasting their wealth in unprofitable pleasure, while they might increase their substance by godly travail. Cast away therefore this worshipful idleness, for men think nothing maketh them gentlemen, but abstinence from bodily labor, whereas that one thing is the greatest blot to our latest nobility, that they have cast of the care of their labors to others, applying their time to greater liberty, opening by idleness the passage to all manner of iniquity. Remember, the fattest Ox cometh first to the slaughter, when the laboring beast is merry in the yoke: even so the idlest bodies are soonest seized by sickness, and consumed by death: whereas laboring persons have many days; insomuch as it seemeth a matter of murder, by idleness to hasten the death of our bodies. Therefore, some loathing labor take themselves to licentious riot, and sweat out their sickness in unlawful pastimes: but bodily exercise profiteth little, and will rather in the end procure the pains they most of all abhor, like the hair

2 Sam. 18.9 of *Absalom*, wherein he most delighted, with which was wrought his death. But the conclusion of all this is, that those which are the chiefest in spending, should be the chiefest in working: and the princes of the possessions, must be the principal in the labors.

Wash thee therefore. These words contain the preparation, which she counselleth *Ruth*, before she descend to *Boaz* in the floor, that she wash her, and anoint her: Two usual things in those countries: and the meaning of *Naomi* is, that *Ruth* prepare herself in most comely manner to go down unto him, whom she desired to be her husband. For these actions of washing and anointing, were, and are very common in those places: washing, to scour off the filth of the bodies; and anointing, to make them look cheerfully. So we read of *David*, after he had long fasted for his adulterous child, hearing it was dead, he washed and anointed himself: and as *Bathsheba* was washing herself, it happened that he saw her; whereby his heart was taken with her love, and drawn from God at one time. Insomuch as we see it an usual and accustomed thing in those days the washing of men and women, and for anointing our Savior speaketh, that when we fast we anoint ourselves, that we seem not unto men to fast. Here then we see *Naomi* commandeth *Ruth* no unseemly addressing of herself, but such as was usual, and common among her own people, and lawful also for her to put in practice. Whereby we first of all observe, that comely ornaments, and modest addressing of ourselves, either of men, or women, is a thing required of them that fear God; for the outward cleansing and washing away of the filth of our bodies, being the savor of sin reigning in us: insomuch as it is a brutish thing to go in their bodies (as many will) without all respect of person or humanity, hands spotted, face besmeared, countenance disfigured: and their natural complexion defaced in them, through their daily, uncivil, and unnatural behavior and negligence, who by their cruel laboring to get the world, lose the comfort of their own bodies, while in swinish attire they wallow in the company of God and men.

2 Sam. 12.20
2 Sam. 11.12

Matt. 6.17

Secondly, by this we gather, that the Lord hath given the fruits of the earth, as well for our ornament, as for our nourishment, because it is as necessary in some respects for the comeliness of the body, to be raised up to handsomeness, being nourished: as that it should be nourished being weak. Therefore saith *David*, With wine he refresheth the heart of man, and he hath given oil to make him have a cheerful countenance: and in the verse before he saith, He maketh the grass to grow for the beast, and the green herb for the use of man: not simply for the meat, but for the service and use of man. And notable is the history of a woman, that came to

Psal. 104.14, 15

Ruth Chapter 3. verses 1-6

Mark 14.3,4
anoint our Savior before his death, that poured on him a rich and costly box of ointment, and he excused her, and commended her for it. And it was an use in old time to anoint the bodies of them that were dead, as we may see how those three women, *Mary Magdalene*, and *Mary* the Mark 16.1 mother of *James*, and also *Salome*, came to anoint the body of Christ lying in the grave. If this was lawful to be done to the dead carcasses, much more is it to the living bodies of God his Saints.

And here by the way we may profitably describe, what is to be thought of starching, because the godly are much troubled therewith: for some think it utterly unlawful: some suppose it to be indifferent; but other imagine it to be necessary: and every one of those do mutually condemn one another: Therefore let us hear the reasons that are brought against it, if they be weighty receive them; if light and of little force, we will leave it to the discretion of the faithful.

First, they say against it, that it consumeth the grain of wheat, whereof it is made, so that the same which was ordained for food, is transferred to another use, which is unlawful. To which I answer, so was oil ordained for nourishment, as well as wheat; yet the godly might take that most comfortable creature, and apply it to the adorning and setting forth of their bodies: which was lawful for them, and therefore the other for us, if it be sparingly used. But they will say, oil was applied to the body, but this is only in the apparel, therefore the reason of them is not alike: To which I answer; that which is done to the apparel, is done to the body, because it Gen. 27.19 is done for the body's sake, as we read of *Isaac*, which smelled the savor of *Esau's* garments, that *Jacob* wore when he got the blessing, and upon that pronounced his blessing.

But they reply again, and say, it maintaineth pride, and therefore is unlawful, but I answer, it is hard to condemn, except we knew the heart, for that is the seat of pride, and not the apparel. Again, if any do so abuse it, they more offend in that by a thousand parts, than if the thing itself were utterly unlawful: therefore the fault lieth in the persons, not in the manner of addressing themselves.

But they object again: That it is a great loss of time, for it asketh much more labor than simple washing: but I answer, so did this anointing, and if the reason be good against the one, it availeth also against the other: so that of the three former judgments, I think it in the mean to be indifferent. And thus in a word, and briefly I have touched it as a thing not worth any farther handling, and have uttered my poor judgment in the same, in the behalf of them that indifferently use it, because some have slanderously given out, that none but proud and singular persons use it: others have scornfully answered, that none but precise fools mislike it. But let us in the spirit of meekness and gentleness neither condemn them that use it, nor contemn those that do forbid it. Neither do I speak this to persuade any to embrace it, whose consciences have always been against it: but I charitably desire them, to bear with their brethren, and in these unnecessary trifles; to suffer all the faithful to enjoy their Christian liberty. But especially let us learn to praise the Lord, which hath thus carefully and plentifully provided for us every way: outwardly in our bodies, making his creatures to comfort us: and inwardly in our souls, giving his own spirit to be the earnest of our salvation: that we might want nothing to draw us away from his majesty: but in all thanksgiving to walk before him in the profession of the Gospel, being compassed about with the helps of this life, as *Elisha* was with the mountains of Angels: that the comfortless sorrows of worldly miseries may never drive us to desperation.

And put thy garments. This is the second thing which *Naomi* willeth *Ruth* in her preparation to go down to *Boaz*, for first she commanded her to dress her body:

Ruth Chapter 3. verses 1-6

so now she willeth her to put on her best apparel, as the goodliest ornaments of her body: for we must not imagine, that *Ruth* went naked in the house, although she bid her put on her apparel, but her meaning is, that she should put on her best apparel, that every way she might be furnished to deal with so noble a personage, and so weighty a cause: Out of the which we note. First, another duty of humanity, that if God give any blessing unto us, we should also be careful in these bodies of sin, to provide for ourselves change of apparel. For we know after *Adam* had sinned, the first thing he thought on, was somewhat to cover his nakedness. By the which we may learn that the first entrance or occasion of clothing was given by sin, that we might cover the shame of our bodies, for if *Adam* had continued in his estate of innocency, there had been no shame of nakedness, no cause of garments, no fear of cold, or terror of heat, and therefore before all things he sowed some fig leaves together, for the hiding of his offence, but God made them garments of skins. So then we must be very careful for the conscience of sin, that we cover our bodies with outward apparel, which indeed is a type, to show, how our souls must be clothed with Jesus Christ. For this cause it was usual in ancient time, that they not only provided simply a garment for the present necessity, but many changes for their body's commodities. And as the world grew, so sin increased, and as sin increased, the miseries of our bodies multiplied: like a ruinous house, that every day falleth to decay more and more: Therefore more helps were invented in the days of *Abraham*, than in the life of *Adam*: and more in the time of *Moses* than in *Abraham's*, and more in *Solomon's*, than in all the residue or former: for as the sore spread itself, so the salve must be lengthened; now the air is intemperate, the earth unfruitful, the bodies of mankind molested by a thousand diseases, and every herb which was the first man's nourishment, is our surfeit; insomuch as the avoiding of all these must be

Gen. 3.7

carefully provided by lawful devises, which the Fathers' ordained and appointed by long experience, to be not a little holpe [*helped*] by the change of apparel. And here we see these poor people have this benefit for their bodies, as well as the rich.

Now, because in some the excess hereof is so great, that they pass all humanity: and in other the want is so indecent, that it shameth mankind, to see their brethren go so basely: Some being able, yet like asses laden with much wealth, they have no power to bestow it on themselves or other: again, many poor souls, which have nothing to provide, or to cover them, are neglected by them that are able: Therefore, in this place we must set down some rules out of the word of God, to take away all these extremities. And the first thing that must be known, is the cause for which it is not only needful, but also lawful to provide apparel, which already we have showed you, to be the sin of *Adam* which wrought in us the shame of our naked bodies, and brought upon us cold and heat, sickness and sores, surfeits and death: so then the bodies covered by clothing are made comely again, are armed against heat, warmed against cold, strengthened against sickness, and the days of health lengthened, life prolonged, and death avoided: For as the prisoner looking upon his irons, thinketh upon his theft, so everyone, when he seeth his garments, must think on his sins. And this one consideration striketh down all devises of fashions, or conceits of pride: for alas, what glory hath the thief in his bands, or what profit by their making; for now he is clogged with them, but anon he is tucked up with the halter: so proud persons are now pranked up while they look on their feathers, but anon are paid for their fashions with eternal damnation. For the Lord crieth out by the prophet, that he will take vengeance of the princes and the sons of the king, for using strange apparel. Zeph. 1.8

Secondly, there may be a difference of apparel,

Ruth Chapter 3. verses 1-6

one kind for the rich, another for the poor; one for the prince, another for the people. One for the noble man, and another for the gentleman: for our Savior speaking of the royalty of *Solomon* in all his apparel, doth not discommend it: and we have heard already of the apparel of *Esau* lying in his father *Isaac's* house. And this may be also in many Suiters [*wardrobes*]; as *Jacob* had sent him by his son *Joseph*, and *Joseph* gave his brethren to every one garments, but to *Benjamin* he gave five changes. But some will say, our Savior biddeth us not to have two coats, and therefore this change is unlawful. To which I answer, that it is unlawful to possess change, or variety of garments, when we see and behold our brother hath none: therefore our Savior Christ addeth, that he that hath two coats must give to him that hath none: So that our abundance must never be to the want and necessity of our brethren.

But alas, where is this difference in manner of garments? I speak for the matter wherefore they are made: we may make the old complaint of a Christian father, a thing worthy to be seen, yea rather to be lamented: The maid followeth the mistress in such bravery of apparel, that it is hard to know whether maid or mistress goeth foremost. Such confusion of degrees, consuming of wealth and goods, condemning the humble, and advancing of base persons by apparel into the place of worthy men, is the overthrow and destruction of a whole country, the ruin of a commonwealth, and the defacing of the Church of Christ. But all this while the naked may go naked still, for any clothing they can get of these that have such plenty and abundance: so that men clothe themselves in the finest silks, feed themselves with the fattest Calves, and ease themselves in the softest beds; while Christ in his members is harborless without houses, hungry without bread, and naked without any raiment to cast upon him. Oh, woe be to you dainty persons, that thus provide for your own maintenance,

Matt. 6.30

Gen. 27.29

Gen. 45.22

and neglect the substance of the poor: you are clothed in soft and gorgeous apparel, and fare deliciously every day: you eat up the needy like bread: you are deaf at their cries, blind at their nakedness, and like the *citizens of Sodom*, unmerciful to their miseries: consider, that their eating and drinking brought brimstone from heaven, with fire to burn up their cities and souls. *Consider the end* of that rich glutton in the Gospel, which was so tormented in the pains of hell, that he desired but a drop of water, and could not obtain it. Your bravery shall be turned into shame, your pride into pains, your ease into restless trouble, your abundance into everlasting want, your friends into devils, your honor into hell, your unmerciful hearts into insufferable plagues, and your pleasures repaid with eternal destruction both of body and soul. The like may be said of those covetous persons, which go as far under their calling as other above, and will hardly bestow any garments on themselves worth the wearing, and disgrace the proportion of mankind through their base apparel, and unreverent addressing themselves, without all respect of honesty, regard of Religion, conscience of their places, and knowledge of the true use of the benefits of God. But many spend all that they can get upon their bellies, never caring how simply they go in the face of the world; so they have anything to cover their nakedness: and we know what kind of beasts are the punishment of such slothfulness. Therefore, let us everyone help those that are not able to provide, yea, and to buy them apparel: and let us all learn hereby, what care we ought to have of the change of our bodies, that if we will be ruled by the example of the godly, we must rather study and travail for our covering, than for our nourishing; Therefore, we must pray for our clothing of him that clotheth the Lilies of the field, in such measure as we may be comforted, our nakedness covered, our shame abated our uncomeliness adorned, and the savor of sin expelled, that we might praise his power for ever-

Ezek. 16.58

Luke 17.18

Luke 16.19

Ruth Chapter 3. verses 1-6

more.

Secondly, by this we also may note, what reverence, we owe to magistrates, and to men in authority, that we must be careful in their presence to give no offence, even in our apparel: for here we see *Ruth* going to *Boaz*, an elder of Bethlehem, she is commanded by *Naomi* to put on her best apparel, as a duty of all the faithful, that they make not their presence odious in the sight of their rulers, and for this cause we read in stories, that when any were wont to come before the magistrates, having any suit unto them, they were appareled with white, which signified the innocency of the person, and purity of the cause, and also they had one suit, that in all decent manner they might deliver their minds in the presence of the magistrate; for the baseness of apparel, is loathsomeness to many. But this shall suffice for the touching of this matter.

Let not the man. After she had commanded her to prepare herself, she descendeth to instruct her, of her behavior: after she cometh down to the place; which was this, that she let not him know of her till he had supped, and were gone to lie down in his bed, which she advertiseth her diligently to mark, and to come and bestow herself at his feet. Where it may seem that *Naomi* counselleth her daughter an unlawful thing, yea, rather to play the whore, than to get her a husband by a lawful means; for she biddeth her to trim and smooth herself up, she warneth her not to come to the man till he were laid to his rest, and finally, she counselleth her to lie down at his feet. Truly, in outward show it seemeth unlawful, yet in substance very honest, if we consider every circumstance. First, I demand, what is it that seemeth dishonest in this whole discourse? some will say, first, the dressing of herself is scant the part of an honest woman, for it is very likely, *Naomi* had this intention, by this means, to draw the old man in love with her, for she took him as it were at advantage alone in the floor, and

such, saith *Solomon,* is the part of whores. I answer, that
the mother of *Solomon* saith, that it is also the point of
a wise and a godly woman to watch in the night, to be
finely appareled, to clothe her household, and such like.
Therefore, seeing an honest woman may do these things.
Ruth did no dishonesty in this. Again, this kind of dressing in *Ruth* was needful, because she had to deal with
an honorable man, and therefore the more carefully and
comely she must appear in his presence. But you will
say, that *Naomi* had some such meaning, because she bid
her that she should not let herself be known till the man
were gone to his rest: I answer, this she did, that they
might more freely talk together of the matter of her marriage, for if she had come before he went to supper, the
day would not have sufficed to commune of the cause of
her coming, neither would the old man have gone to his
lodging, if he had known a woman to be present. Then
you will say, why did she not come to his own house at
home, and that in the daytime? I answer, because it was
a reproach to *Ruth,* to be known to deal publicly in her
own marriage, which must needs be known if it had
been done in the city, or in the daytime: and therefore
seeing time and place were now convenient, the man
being alone, they took opportunity by the forelock, and
prepare themselves for the adventure of her marriage.

Why then will some say: what moved *Naomi* to
give such counsel unto *Ruth,* seeing she knew it might be
defamed? I answer, *Naomi* knew *Boaz* to be an old man,
not given to such lewd and filthy conditions, but especially she knew him to fear God, and *Ruth* her daughter in law to be a virtuous woman, and trusting to his
age, and both their godliness, she is emboldened to give
this advice. And this may suffice any sober minds, from
suspicion of *Naomi's* counsel, *Ruth's* dishonesty, or the
Religion of Boaz. But some will say, if the matter be so
clear as you will make it, then may we also follow the
example and do the like. To which I answer, if any do so,

Prov. 7.9,10,
11
Prov. 31.10,21

it is much amiss: for we must not imitate every example we read of in the Scripture, as that of *Rebecca's* counsel to her son *Jacob*, whereby he got away the blessing from *Esau*. There is no cause that can move us, as there was *Naomi*, for *Ruth* must be married in her kindred, we need not: she was bound to one or twain, but we are free to many thousands: she might challenge in her own behalf, for the Law of God, but we cannot do so, except there be a promise of marriage: therefore neither must we follow this example, nor yet suspect the actions of either.

And Ruth. Now the counsel propounded, and the means for the execution thereof declared, *Ruth* approveth her mother's advice, by promise of obedience, that first she would do it: and in the sixth verse, she doth perform it. Where we have a good example, in the matter of marriage for all children to depend upon their godly and religious parents. If any ask me, whether they be bound upon necessity so to obey their parents, that if they offer them husbands, or wives, they cannot refuse them, but their parents may compel them: to whom I answer, first, if it be possible, hearken to the voice of thy parents; but if thou canst not, thy parents cannot command thee against thy mind, for they must propound it conditionally, not absolutely. In thy body (concerning thy labor) thou must obey them in all things, because they are the parents of thy body, but thy mind or soul which cometh from God, is alway at liberty. So that disobedience to parents is the refusing of their temporal commandment, but marriage is everlasting to the death of a man.

Secondly, children may refuse, because the Lord many times revealeth that to the child which he showed not to the parents: as we may see in the example of *Sampson*, when he would marry with a Philistine woman: for his parents gainsaying it, the Scripture showeth the reason of it, because they knew it not to come from

Judg. 14.2-4

the Lord: but *Sampson* did, and therefore stood in it, and his parents harkened unto him in the end, and got him that woman for his wife. By the which we gather, that no children may lawfully celebrate their marriage without the parents' consent: secondly, that parents must be very circumspect to marry their children: thirdly, that they cannot in any good conscience deny their consents to their children to keep them from honest marriage, if there be any equality between the parties, or hope of honesty in the time of loving. But of this matter we have often spoke: and therefore this shall suffice for this time. Now let us give praise to God.

The end of the Eighth Lecture.

The Ninth Lecture

Ruth Chapter 3. verses 7-13

7 *And when* Boaz *had eaten and drunken, and made his heart merry, he went and lay down beside the heap of corn, and she came softly and uncovered the place of his feet, and lay down.*

8 *And at midnight the man was afraid, and turned himself hither and thither: and behold, a woman lay at his feet.*

9 *To whom he said, who art thou? and she said, I am* Ruth, *thy handmaid, spread the wing of thy garment over thy handmaid, for thou art the kinsman.*

10 *And he said, Blessed be thou of the Lord, my daughter, for thou hast performed more kindness at the last, than at the first, because thou followedst not young men, were they poor or rich.*

11 *Now therefore, my daughter, fear not, whatsoever thou sayest, I will do unto thee, for every one within the gates of my people knoweth thee to be a virtuous woman:*

12 *Now indeed it is true that I am thy kinsman, yet there is one nearer than I.*

13 *Sleep here this night, in the morning if he will do the part of a kinsman, let him: but if he will not do the kinsman's duty, I will do the kinsman's duty, as the Lord liveth, sleep until the morning.*

ow it followeth, in this Scripture to speak of the effect of this counsel, and of those things that happened after *Ruth* came down into the floor; and the happy success she had with *Boaz*: The words do easily divide themselves into two parts: the first respecteth *Boaz*, the other *Ruth*.

The first part concerning *Boaz*, is that which he did after his work, and before his sleep, verse 7. that he ate and drank and made his heart merry, and lay down beside his corn. For, that he did after his sleep, verse 8. First, he feared when he felt a woman at his feet: and secondly, he asketh who she was. After he knew her, he blessed her, verse 10. Secondly, he comforteth her, verse, 11. In these words fear not my daughter. His comfort hath two parts: first, his confession that he was her kinsman, verse, 12. Secondly, the counsel he giveth to her, verse 13. to tarry until the morning, and then he would try her other kinsman: if he refused, *Boaz* promiseth by oath to the confirm her right, and do her kinsman's duty: and therefore biddeth her to sleep until the morning.

The second part, which concerneth *Ruth*, is her behavior after she came to the place appointed, and hath these two branches: first, that which she did alone, verse 7. That she came and lay down at his feet: secondly, that which she did with *Boaz*: first, she telleth him her name, when she perceived the man was afraid: secondly, she showeth him her petition, desiring him to spread the wing of his garment over her, verse 9. Of these parts let us speak in order as they lie, by the assistance of the Spirit of God, and permission of the time.

And when *Boaz*: These words concern *Boaz* and that which he did after his work, the day being ended and his body being wearied, he went to his meat, eating

Lecture 9

and drinking, refreshing his stomach, and cheering his heart with those blessings of God which he had present: afterwards getting him to his lodging at the end of his corn; instead of a softer bed, he harboreth upon the straw. Out of the which we observe these things.

First, the blessing of God upon his creatures, that are moderately taken; for it is said that he cheered his heart after his eating and drinking; his body was not only nourished, his hunger abated, and his stomach filled, but also his heart was cheered thereby: as if the holy Ghost had said, Here is my blessing upon meat that is moderately received, that the powers of the soul are refreshed by it: therefore we read in the preacher, that a whole land is blessed by the moderate receiving of these benefits in eating and drinking. The experience whereof is plainly proved every day among us. For what is the fruit of this immoderate devouring the benefits of God, but as *Solomon* saith, the corruption of the body, the swelling and redness of the eyes, wounds without cause, quarrels and contentions to the woe of many, wherein they that rejoice are void of all reason, which ought to be the ground of all our mirth: but like beasts some from feeding to sleeping convey themselves: other from eating to gaming turn their bodies, delighting in naught but vanity, being as far from this cheerfulness of heart by their meat and nourishment, as *Nabal* was after his feast, when one word of *David's* anger stroke his heart dead. But this *Boaz* was here alone and none beside him: and yet you see, that in his solitary barn, void of companions, he made himself merry, with the fellowship of the blessing of God upon his meat. Even so assuredly, if the hands of many could guide their mouths, their mouths rule their appetites, and both were governed with the Spirit of God, that they received for strength to nourish their weakness, not for gluttony to stuff up their stomachs, they should with greater comfort sit down to their meals, and exceeding joyfully, rise up again. But since

Eccles. 10.17

Prov. 23.29

Ruth Chapter 3. verses 7-13

our minds have as many devises, as our stomachs receive morsels, we eat, and yet we are not satisfied, we drink, and yet we are not merry: but overcome with the good creatures of God, we seek after idle songs, vain jesting, and unprofitable fables of falsehood, and forged conceits in ungodly books, which drowneth our spiritual joy, and plungeth our minds in the gulf of worldly mirth and woeful misery. Then let us learn the wisdom of Christ, and look for joy which standeth not in laughter, but in the inward comfort of the assurance of the Spirit, being persuaded we feed in the presence of God, we may have Christ at our temporal and worldly meals, that we may eat and drink with him in his everlasting kingdom.

Here we see, that *Boaz* after his labor both eateth and drinketh; for so in ancient time, he did not drink much that did not eat much. The wicked were wont to be a generation of Vipers, a cruel and vile kind of Serpent; but now they are no less vile, yet they are become Dipsads, and not Vipers only, for they die of thirst, drinking more than they eat. And as the moral is of the Falconer, that while he gazed at the birds on the tree, to shoot and kill them, suddenly a Serpent bit him by the foot, and killed him by her poison. Even so is it with these wretches, while they give themselves to lift their pots, and swill in the destruction of the Lord's creatures, the Devil like a Serpent in that way, giveth their souls mortal wounds. I am ashamed to write, how in this age of the Gospel, drinking overcometh all: so that I may say as Isaiah 5.22. *They are strong to drink wine, and mighty to suck in strong drink.* Yet lest our drunkards should think this a virtue, the Prophet pronounceth a woe against them: and no marvel, for saith Hosea 4.11. *Fornication and wine take away the heart.* When a certain profane fellow boasted of his great drinking, a Heathen man could answer him, that it was praise to drink much, for Asses and Mules could drink more than he, and yet they were not commended for that. It was writ-

ten of *Darius* upon his tomb, *Hic jacet qui uinum mul-
tum potuit hibere & probe ferre*: Here lies the man, which
had no other praise, but that he could drink much wine,
and carry it away. In like manner, the beasts of our time,
when they die, leave no other remembrance of their actions behind them, for they spoil both the liquor and
themselves. For drunkenness taketh away the memory,
dissipateth the senses, and confoundeth the understanding, saith Saint *Augustine*, it maketh of a wise man a fool,
of a strong man, a weakling, and of a man a beast: yea,
saith Saint *Chrysostom*, whosoever leadeth a drunken
life, is under the devil, for drunkenness is a smiling devil,
a sweet poison, a pleasing sin, but yet the shame and reproach of mankind. If a woman in times past had killed
a King in his drunkenness, she was not only acquitted
from punishment, but also for her reward, married to
the next heir of the crown. *Ariadne* the wife of *Zeno*,
finding her husband so often drunk, at last buried him
in his drunken fit, where he miserably perished. Even so
let them perish, O Lord, that delight in drinking more
than temperance.

Secondly, by this we observe, that our meat after
our labor is much more joyful to our hearts, and profitable to our bodies, than if it be received in an idle life:
for *Boaz* had wrought hard all this day, and the reward of
his labor, is the work of his meat, which in the end of all,
maketh his heart merry. In consideration whereof, the
Lord inflicted this as a punishment upon mankind, that
their meat should be unprofitable, unless it were eaten in
the sweat of our brows: for as sleep to a man that hath
long watched, so is meat to a man that hath long labored,
and as the coursing of the Hart [*male deer*] maketh him
to breathe for the water springs; so labor causeth men
to hunger more vehemently, to eat more liberally, and
digest more effectually their desired morsels. We read
of *Jonathan* the son of king *Saul*, when he had wearied
himself in the slaughter of the Philistines, and being very

Gen. 3.19

Psal. 42.1

1 Sam. 24.27

Ruth Chapter 3. verses 7-13

hungry did but dip the top of his bat in a honeycomb, and putting it to his mouth, his eyes received sight: so acceptable are the crumbs and drops to them that labor, that they restore the life and power of the body, and for this cause the greatest persons in the first and purest age (when the life of man was many hundred years) were not exempted from bodily labor. On the other side, as *Solomon* saith, they which sit long at wine, and seek after strong drink; meaning those which with idleness follow their bellies, are most noisome to the world, unwholesome to themselves, and woeful forever: for their end will be as the biting of a Serpent and the stinging of a Cockatrice: teaching us that laboring men's morsels are most sweet: and if we should joyfully recreate ourselves in the benefits of God, we must diligently prepare our stomachs in some honest travails, that the basest fare may be acceptable meat unto us; for the health of the body is preserved by labor, as the planted corn by the diligence of the husbandman: for he which tilleth the earth is satisfied with bread; but idleness is nearest kinsman to madness. Against this we have often spoken heretofore, and let this suffice for this time.

Prov. 23.20

Prov. 12.14

Thirdly, we must note, what manner of mirth or cheerfulness was this of *Boaz*: it could not be in talking, for he was alone, nor yet in jesting, for the former reason: nor yet was it in outward in singing, for it is said his heart was cheerful, as if there were a mirth that were not outward. And truly, where the holy Ghost dwelleth, there abideth this inward joy. Which proceedeth from it, as a stream from a fountain, or heat from a fire. *Saul* could be merry when *David* played on his harp, the King of Babylon was merry in the midst of his delicates, *Ahasuerus* was merry among his princes, and *Nabal* was merry in the midst of his reapers: but what maketh the godly merry among the wild beasts, joyful in the dungeons of the earth, and sing heartily when they receive brown bread? nothing but this joy of *Boaz*, which is the

Rom. 14.17
Eph. 5.22

1 Sam. 16.16

Dan. 5.4
Esther 1.10
1 Sam. 25.36

joy of the holy Ghost. This maketh men joyful in death, merry in misery, and leaping under the yoke of Christian troubles: which all the princes in the world cannot do upon their thrones of majesty: this is mixed with no fear, because it proceedeth from so excellent a root. Why do men marvel, that so many godly persons live so solitarily? the bird had rather be in the wilderness alone, than with thousands of her fellows sitting in a cage, and the godly are most merry when they are farthest from worldly company. If the godly be a company together, this their joy must be expressed by singing of Psalms, as *James* saith, and our *Savior, with his disciples, practiced this at his last Supper*, for when they had done, they sung a Psalm, and went out into the mount of Olives; yea even then, when Christ had prophesied of his death, and they were sorrowful, yet this inward and spiritual joy was not extinguished: wherein we see an excellent commendation of singing after meat, that it might be an outward testimony of our inward joy. This striketh down all foolish talking for stirring up of mirth, and answereth to them that say, if they follow not vain pastimes, they cannot be merry: Truly that pleaseth the flesh, but displeaseth the spirit: and let them assure themselves, whosoever they be, that this temporal and wanton sporting, will bring upon them everlasting lamenting.

James 5.13
Mark 14.26

But some will say, is this singing and mirth at tables commendable, seeing the prophet speaketh so against it? They sing to the viol, and frame to themselves songs like the songs of *David*, etc. I answer, all curiosity and pleasure in outward singing at our feastings is forbidden by the prophet, which he doth notably describe in the same place, by these marks. First, when it is used to forget their sins, and to drive away the terrors of their consciences. Secondly, when it is added for pleasure and ease. Thirdly, that with greedier appetites, they might devour their meat and drink, to draw away their minds from the remembrance of the Lord. Fourthly, such

Amos 6.5,6

Verse 3

Verse 4

Ruth Chapter 3. verses 7-13

mirth as maketh them forget the afflictions of the church
of God. If any desire mirth for these causes, the woe of
the prophet taketh hold upon them. And surely, here is
condemned all playing on instruments, and singing at
table, when we eat our meat, as a thing against which
the prophet much aimeth, and is too much used among
us here in England, for nothing maketh us more readily
to forget the affliction of *Joseph,* than that doth: when
two occasions of mirth are joined together, meat and
music, it is like two diverse plasters laid to one wound,
which by their vehement operation, increase the sore. In
like manner, we are more apt to be made worse, than to
be amended by the benefits of God. For as too much
rain drowneth and overfloweth, and too much drought
chippeth and cleaveth the earth: so too much mirth and
pleasure overcometh the heart of man. This I speak, not
to discommend music, which I acknowledge freely with
all the godly, to be holy and lawful: but I exhort and admonish, that it may not be used at the present time of
eating, but sparingly before or after our feasting. And
let us all choose rather to sing one Psalm from a feeling
spirit, with a grace in our hearts and minds, than to hear
a thousand songs upon instruments of pleasant music,
without inward comfort.

    But I cannot so pass over the merriments and
pleasures of men, which are his disciples in the Gospel,
that bade his soul live at ease, eat, drink and be merry.
They have indeed, with *Boaz,* land and corn, revenues
and riches, but they apply it all to pleasure and merriments. They buy pleasant things for their sleep, for their
watching, for their garments, for their meats, for their
ointments, for perfumes. In their ears are the continual sound of music or flatterers, which they maintain,
in their eyes, nothing but variety of colors and pleasant
things, never looking after a poor or distressed Christian: those they permit not to come in their sight, for fear
their mirth be hindered. What are their garments but

purple, silk, or very rich every day. For this cause they change their dwellings, and have variety of houses: as the Kings of *Assur* had Babylon for the Winter, Persepolis for the Spring, Ecbatane for the Summer, and Susis for the Autumn: so these now in one corner of their Land, now in another, now in the City, anon in the country, floating up and down for pleasure, as if they were cursed upon the earth, and might long dwell nowhere.

We read of the Sybarites, a voluptuous people of Calabria, the selfsame things that are now in practice in England: first, they were so costly in their feasts, that they were long in providing, and bade their guests sometimes a year before. They suffered not a Smith, or any trade which might offend their ears with nose, to tarry among them; and for that cause they kept no cocks in their Cities, lest their early crowing should awake them. They nourished little dogs, which their women carried about; and when they were disposed to go into the country, they procured them easy Litters or Coaches, and went not so many miles in three days, as other do in one. They would not let a laboring man come into their presence, and they measured nothing which they used, except only their water, which they put into their wine. Thus lived the wretched Sybarites, and almost so live we: so they perished by pleasure, for mirth and pleasure is a Serpent, it will kill if it be nourished; but as the thorns harm not much, being lightly touched, no more do pleasures, but as thorns, the more they be grappled and embraced, prick the deeper, and draw more blood, even so do pleasures and merriments which are the joy of the idle.

He went to lie down. Now we are come to the second part of that which he did alone, which in these words is declared to be the choice of his lodging, at the end or one side of his corn. Where we note another usage or custom of ancient nobility: instead of a palace, they had a cottage: instead of attenders and waiters, they had the instruments of their labors: and as this *Boaz*, a heap of straw, instead of a bed of down: such as his toil and labor was, such is his lodging: a hard work, a hard bed; for he that is wearied with travail or labor, can sleep and quietly take his rest on the grass. And this putteth us in mind, of the estate of all our forefathers many years ago, before this softness and tenderness was invented, they were glad, we see, though they were great Lords, yet to be laborers: and although their possessions excelled ours, yet they had less bodily ease than we: for the richest and highest estate or dignity, is not the quietest life. By the which we are admonished, with all kindness, to harbor the poor and needy, though it be but in a pad of straw, considering they be the images of the ancient nobility, who were contented with the like entertainment: and the poor are exhorted with patience to abide their tedious travails and hard lodgings, seeing the Lords of the world, had no better estate; they which had most wealth had least ease, and we which have scant one man's inheritance among twenty, do peaceable enjoy more worldly security, and truly this maketh us to feel, that every commodity is tempered with some molestation: the Israelites being delivered from *Pharaoh,* thought they were well, but then they were driven to go through the bottom of the sea, and being come to the land of Canaan, they found many enemies, and did not overcome them all, till the reign of *David*: so that every pleasure is mingled with some worldly sorrow: they which use the sea, get much wealth, but yet with great danger, and they which are on the land, are in safety, though not in such wealth. And thus must we frame our minds, that when we enjoy the end of our desires, yet it bringeth with it alway some occasion of dislike: therefore it is better to be contented with hard fare, than discontented with dainty cheer, to like in hard harbor, than dislike in the softest beds: and better is a little thing with a quiet mind, than the possession of a kingdom, with the trouble thereof.

Which thing let no man accuse or misinterpret, for (as is already said) *Ruth* obeyed herein the counsel of *Naomi*, and *Naomi* (for my opinion) of God. Yet I will not strive so much to purge these women of all blame: for it needeth not, seeing the Saints of God were holy, and better instructed than these, have had their several infirmities, as are most notoriously known. Yet such they were as were worthy of excuse, not of defense, and such is this of *Ruth* and *Naomi*, which if it cannot find so much favor and charity, as to be cleared from all blame, yet let it be deemed a sin of woman's frailty, nature's necessity, and a fault not to be censured by man, which is so little spotted by the holy Ghost.

 And Ruth came. *Boaz* being weary with his labors, and sufficed with his meat, no doubt but being quietly laid, a sleep had soon taken him: and *Ruth*, when she had spied a convenient time, came, and conveyed herself softly to the place of his feet, which at midnight was perceived by *Boaz,* and not before. For she so laid herself, as he being awaked, might quickly espy her: whereby we see the occasion that moved *Naomi* to counsel *Ruth* to come so near him, which was this, that *Boaz* might first be grieved, and then should *Ruth* best utter her suit. But of all this we have spoken before, and therefore to the petition of *Ruth.*

 Spread the wing. *Ruth* omitting no opportunity, so soon as she had uttered her name, she putteth up her petition, and by a figurative speech, desireth him to be her husband and defender. For to spread the wing, we know, is taken from birds, who keep their young ones under their wings. And this speech of *Ruth* to *Boaz,* is indeed to entreat him to be her husband: for we read the sense of these words to be spoken to *Sara* by *Abimelech* Gen. 20.16 the king of Gerar, that her husband *Abraham* should be unto her a cover, against all those that would oppress her. And therefore in ancient time, women were wont to be covered in the presence of their husbands. And *Ruth* saith to *Boaz*, spread thy wing over me, that is, be thou my husband to cover me: for in times past it was a thing very odious to be without husbands, even as odious as to be stark naked, or a masterless dog, as the proverb is: Which appeareth by that complaint of the prophet *Isaiah*, That seven women should lay hold upon one man, and desire to be called by his name, promising to provide their own living. So that this figurative speech, doth most notably describe, the duty of husbands towards their wives. First, the wing signifieth protection; for it is the duty of husbands to defend their wives, to be able and willing to shield them from injuries, provide for them necessaries, cover them in dangers, minister to them comfort and strength in their weakness. But truly it is pity to see what married men we have in these days, and how little commodity many helpless wives receive by their retchless [*reckless*] husbands, that surely they are driven with *Abigail*, many times to shift for their own lives, and the lives of their families. These roistering companions, hasty and heady husbands, which for every light occasion forsake their families, or weary their wives with their presence; minister neither covering nor comfort, according to their bounden duty: but like perjured and forsworn caitiffs [*wretches*], that have falsified their faith to God, the church, and their wives, run headlong to their own destruction, and decay of their posterity. Oh how sorrowful is the estate of women, if they be not supported with the kindeness of their yokefellows. Bearing of children is nothing in comparison of this: for that is their deserved punishment of God; but the other, the intolerable hand of the Devil. We read, that the Pelican will tear out her own breast to feed her young ones: but we read of few so unkind, as to feed upon their young ones, save only these unnatural husbands. We read that the Storks are always fed so long by their young ones, when they are old, as they nourished them when they were young. But these godless fathers care neither for to

Isa. 4.1

Psal. 63.7

nourish their little ones being young, nor how they shall be maintained when they are old.

Finally, by this, wives are instructed their obedience to their husbands, that as the little bird is at the call of his dame, so wives must be ready at the beck of their husbands. And let us look upon the brute beasts for examples of lives, who in their brutish kind condemn our humanity. The Emmet [*ant*] laboreth and provideth for winter, that condemneth sluggards. The Ass knoweth his owner, and the Ox his master's crib: These condemn unthankfulness to God. The Doves teach us innocency, the Serpents wisdom: the dogs watchfulness, the Foxes wariness, the Lions courage, and the little birds our duties to wives and children. Therefore let us not be more graceless than these, lest their diligence, like the voice of *Balaam's* Ass, condemn our disobedience to perpetual misery.

Blessed be thou of the Lord. Now cometh the second part of the conference between *Boaz* and *Ruth* to be handled: wherein only *Boaz* speaketh. And first of all, he blesseth or prayeth for her, saying, *Blessed be thou of the Lord, for this latter favor is greater than the former*: Then thou forsookest thy country to come with thy mother in law, but now thou forsakest young and youthful husbands, to come to me a diseased old man: neither wealth nor poverty can alter or change thy mind, from following the commandment of God to thy own hindrance. So in this example we have an excellent pattern of true and unfeigned Religion, which is this: when *Ruth* is obedient to the ordinance of God, even in that which seemeth to her own discommodity and earthly consolation: for she was a young woman, and therefore by nature desired a young companion, and not to be troubled with a withered old man, from whom she could receive but little bodily comfort: yet because by the law she was tied to her nearest kinsman of her deceased husband, forsaking all other, she cleaveth to him, making the law her choice,

Ruth Chapter 3. verses 7-13

his age her honor, and the trial of his former courtesy, as bands of assurance for his future kindness. This was the faith of *Ruth*, that caused her like *Levi* to forsake his custom: like *Zacchaeus,* to depart from his wealth: like the courtiers of *Herod,* to forgo their honor, and also the saints of God to forsake their dearest friends, to follow the voice of the Gospel.

Luke 5.28
Luke 19.8,9
Acts 13.1

And this teacheth us, to cast of earthly commodities in worldly business, to forsake nature and natural affection, to forgo life and living, and account all things but dung in regard of obedience to the word of God. This is it that toucheth the quick, and will prove the heart of every Christian. If this condition were propounded, Christ saith, That for him we must forsake all that we have: Now, if this law were made, that whosoever went to hearing of the word, should presently confiscate his goods at the pleasure of the Law-maker: Who would in this case be obedient rather to the bare voice of Christ, than to the threatening words of the law? Examine beloved, and arraign every man his own heart, for this point and then you shall see, whether the love and desire of the world hath not drove out the love of the Father. Every dastard [*base coward*] will offer and make show to fight hardly, till he come to approach the field, but in the face of the enemy, if he abide, there is the trial: nay, if he see but one way to escape, he will surely take that, though it be to his own discredit. So I fear me, I fear me, many, if danger were, would not only turn from us, but fight hotly against us, for all their fair faces to us. They which now will hardly of one hundred pounds give one to the Gospel, will not then leave the principal to follow the truth: but as the glare-worm doth not glister but in the night, so true Christians will not be known, till the days of darkness and error come, when these dissembling hypocrites shall be found to be nothing but rotten wood, good for nothing. But to come to *Ruth*; she performeth her promise to God, as *David* saith, though it be

Psal. 15.4

to her own hindrance, she knoweth it with the apostles, better to obey God than men, to follow Christ and not Acts 4.19 the flesh, for the world itself shall be shortly consumed and then the lovers thereof shall be utterly condemned. Oh, then let us practice the denial of ourselves before the time of trial come, let us as the martyrs did, try the burning of our fingers, before we venture our whole bodies: let us give some of our wealth to the poor now, rather than keep all to be spoiled by the wicked apostates then: but how will men do this at the fiery trial, when now in peace they will forsake and forswear the Lord, some for their merchandise, other for rents and revenues, some to bring the poor *Naboths* into destruction, many for worldly profit and temporal gain: but this queen of worldly desire, shall one day be meat for the dogs; as was *Jezebel*, when it shall be said, that happy are all you, that in wealth and poverty have followed the Son of righteousness in sincerity.

Fear not my daughter. His prayer and the reason thereof being ended, now followeth the consolation he giveth to *Ruth*, in these words, bidding her to cast away fear, for whatsoever lieth in his power he would do: for the whole city would testify the estate of her person, and uprightness in her living: and therefore he should be much to blame, if he denied so lawful a request. Out of the which we note.

First, here is set down the duty of all magistrates, which is with meekness and gentleness to hear the petitions of their suitors: for *Boaz* was a public person, or else *Naomi* had complained to the magistrate; but himself being a godly elder, the suit is first privately handled with him. Therefore, they must follow the example of *Boaz* here declared, which is with the kindest words to entreat them, and just judgments to proceed for them, alway yielding to equity, where the cause is required. Luke 18.3-5 For our Savior accounteth a magistrate that is contrary minded, neither to fear God, nor to respect man: that

Ruth Chapter 3. verses 7-13

is, such a one is hated of God and man: For if magistrates love God, or regard their subjects, they must be easily entreated by the voices of their suitors. Therefore is that everlasting commendation of *Moses*, that he sat in the door of his tent in judgment, from evening until morning, where all the people might freely have access to his presence, and godly conference with his person, the which all the Judges in Christendom might imitate, without impeachment to their honors. Old *Samuel*, when he had anointed and appointed *Saul* to reign in his stead over all Israel, appealed to the people what injury he had done to any, and the people justified him in all things: now he was easily come unto at all times, when *Saul* and his father's servant seeking for Asses would go to the man of God, meaning *Samuel*. Oh that all that are in authority would hearken to these examples, that with all gentleness they might entreat the people of God, committed to their government, that they might freely come to them, and friendly speak with them, that at the day of their deaths, they might have the poor saints of God praying for their deliverance, their consciences unburdened, their duties discharged, their subjects satisfied, justice offered, and their souls everlastingly saved.

1 Sam. 12.2-5

Secondly, by this we gather, that Judges and justices must especially look to the godly: for *Boaz* saith, that all the city knew *Ruth* to be a godly woman: So that he bindeth himself by her Religion, to be as careful for her, being a stranger, as if she were his natural daughter. For as all the city knew her religious, so they would all rejoice to see her advanced. And this is the cause wherefore the Lord hath so much commended unto us the estate of widows and fatherless children, because for the most part they are oppressed, and not oppressors: vexed, and not vexers: receivers, and not doers of injury. And surely, such are simple godly men, they will bear many burdens before they complain; and for every trifle they will not trouble a magistrate. Therefore every magis-

Deut. 10.18
Prov. 3.3

trate must say with *David*, My eyes shall be on them that
speak truth on the earth, and they that walk uprightly
shall be my servants: so have you respect of persons,
though not in judgment, yet in common opinion: for
the professors of religion are your dearest friends, who
without ceasing pour forth their prayers for you, that in
equity you might draw your sword for them. Oh how
lamentable is it to hear, how poor godly men are daily
blasphemed and reproached for their religion: when
wicked Atheists, carnal persons, common swearers, and
godless wretches, have their heart's desire at the hands
of the magistrate. Surely such persons, who desire your
aid against others, deserve your swords of justice against
themselves: for they never come into your presence, but
to the dishonor of God. Execute judgment therefore, for
them, and upon them.

Psal. 101.6

Thirdly, by this we gather, what it is that most
commendeth women: for *Boaz* saith virtue; and if all the
world cry the contrary, yet *Bathsheba* the mother of King
Solomon will confirm it: for thus she saith, Favor is deceitful, beauty is but vain; but a woman that feareth God,
she will get praise to herself: for virtue and the fear of the
Lord are both one thing. So that this is the thing they
are most commended for, if religion will take any root
in their hearts: for beauty is worn by age, proportion of
body lost by sickness, love of men at the wagging of a
hand, and brave apparel when wealth decayeth, only the
fear of the Lord endureth forever. We read that *Vashti*
the queen of *Ahasuerus* was exceeding beautiful, but she
disobeyed her husband, and was put from her princely
room, when godly *Esther* was taken in her stead. If the
fear of God had been in the former, to obey her husband,
Esther had not so soon come into her place. But the
Lord, that he might punish the pride of the one, and reward the religion of the other, lifted up virtuous *Esther*,
and cast down that stately *Vashti*: to show unto us, that
much better is the fear of the Lord, than all the beauty

Prov. 31.30

Esther 1.16

Ruth Chapter 3. verses 7-13

and glory of the world.

We find many commended in the word of God, for their faith, but few for their fairness, that all should 1 Pet. 3.4 learn more earnestly to labor, that the hid man of the heart may be found in incorruption of a gentle and a quiet spirit, which is very precious in the sight of the Lord.

Lastly, let us all learn by this, as well rich as poor, governors as subjects, men as women, that above all things we follow the example of *Ruth*, to please God more than ourselves, to labor for virtue and Religion as for a treasure hid in the ground, to search for it, as for gold and silver, that we may boldly come before the Judges of the Lord, and plead as subjects, seeing the knowledge of the Law resteth in our hearts. And let us diligently labor for good reports, that the magistrates may speak for us, as *Boaz* doth for *Ruth*, to her singular comfort, that we may with boldness stand to be judged, Eccles. 7.1 and not to suffer as evil doers. For a *good name* is better than a precious ointment, and the godly and guiltless are most honorable, when they are causeless accused: even as *Joseph*; the nearest way for him to come to the king's favor, was first of all to be wrongfully imprisoned. So if we study to lead holy conversations, let them draw us to the judgment seat as offenders; yet our Religion shall speak for us, not guilty: and though all the world should unjustly condemn us, yet the Son of God shall sue out our pardon.

And true it is, I am thy. We showed you in the beginning, that his consolation had two parts. The first his confession in this verse: and the other his counsel in the next. Now then cometh his confession to be handled, wherein he granteth himself a kinsman, and therefore bound unto that duty she required of him: but yet withal he soberly telleth her, there is one nearer than I: meaning to show her, that the whole care of the matter doeth not chiefly depend upon him. Whereby we gather, the sin-

gular conscience and humility of *Boaz*: for if the fear of
God had not hindered him, he might like scornful persons, have denied that he had any kindred so base: and
therefore he might have told her, that she was come to
a wrong man, that she had mistaken her mark, that she
must not look so high, as the choice man in Bethlehem,
and some baser husband will beseem a Moabitess. But
he doth not so, for he confesseth against himself, that
her suit was equal, and he bound to deal in it. Where
again we have another worthy example for all magistrates to imitate; even to pronounce judgment against
their own causes, and give evidence against their own
commodity. For what a simple thing was it for *Boaz* to
marry with so poor a woman as *Ruth*, by whom he could
hope for no great portion, but only Religion? Oh that
this uprightness would enter into the hearts of men in
our days, when they handle their mutual affairs, to speak
the truth indifferently, as well against, as for themselves,
yea, and forsake their dearest friends in unlawful suits.
But rather it rejoiceth them at the heart, to see bad matters bolstered up, and wrong judgments through ignorance unjustly pronounced: whereas the plaintiffs, and
defendants themselves, do either of them in their own
conscience know their cause to be naught: yet against
both conscience, justice, and equity, will spend their
money and hearts also to be thoroughly revenged on
their Christian neighbors, to overthrow their cause, be
it never so equal: yet this is their drift, to make the righteous law, the only defender of all their unrighteous and
ungodly dealings. How, if there were no law nor magistrate, would these malicious persons behave themselves,
that dare to wrest the helm of justice by corruption in
these peaceable days? they are more fit to be the inhabitants of Sodom and Gomorrah, than the fellow dwellers with the godly and faithful? Would God, that every
offender were bound to restore for every default, four
times so much, then would our quietness be greater, our

Ruth Chapter 3. verses 7-13

suits uprighter, the truth uttered before danger, causes ended without chargeable costs, wise men should be the lawyers, the truth should be the evidence, conscience and equity should give judgment against ourselves.

Tarry this night. This is the counsel that *Boaz* giveth unto *Ruth*, that seeing it was night, she should tarry till the morning, and then he will deal with her kinsman in the behalf of his right, which if he will do unto her, *Boaz* cannot withstand him, but if he refuse, then will *Boaz* perform the duty. Which promise he confirmeth by an oath, *As the Lord liveth*: bidding her to sleep until the morning. Where we see first of all the kindness of the man, that would not presently thrust a poor woman from the place of her lodging, but quietly suffered her to harbor beside him, yea, and biddeth her to tarry at her rest, and to sleep until the morning. Where I cannot but excuse this good old man from all suspicion of dishonesty or uncleanness: seeing he talketh of virtue, he neither lost it in himself, nor destroyed it in her, he knew not the other kinsman's mind, therefore he would not defile her, lest he had committed adultery. Neither let this seem strange unto us, for why should not old *Boaz* be as chaste as young *Joseph*, Genesis 39.10? or why should we not as well believe this, as that of *Joseph* and *Mary*, who after our Savior's birth never touched or tempted each other? A time there was that adultery was not known in Lacedaemon: The young Men and Maids of Chij were wont to dance and sacrifice together; yea, all night to converse with either Sex, and yet it was never known that one of them was with child before marriage. The like was said of the old Germans, where they never found adultery, they loved not marriage so much as husbands and wives, that is, they preferred not the work of marriage before honest love: and good manners, were more worth among them than in other places good Laws. I will say no more but that of *Thomas 2.* An Archbishop of York, who being sick and persuaded by his Physician to lie with a woman to save his life, he would not: *Pudicitiam amittere propter salutem carnis tandem moriture*, Lose his honesty to save his life for a little while: and no doubt *Boaz* had the same mind.

Secondly, he would do nothing which might prejudice the cause of her other kinsman, before he had gotten his consent to the delivery of his right: teaching us thereby, that it is not lawful to enter into the least part of our neighbor's titles, though we may seem to have as great right in it, as *Boaz* had in *Ruth*, without the free and willing agreement of him that hath any property or interest therein.

Lastly, *Boaz* confirmeth his promise with an oath, which is the last speech unto the woman, for her assurance to depend on his credit, and the last thing that must be used in all our communications: But of these matters we have already spoken, and therefore thus much for this time. Now let us give praise to God.

The end of the Ninth Lecture.

Ruth Chapter 3. verses 7-13

The Tenth Lecture

14 *And so she lay at his feet until the morning, and then she arose when one knew not another. For* Boaz *said, Let no man know that a woman came into the floor.*

15 *And then he said, Give me the sheet wherewithal thou art covered, and hold it up: then he measured six measures of barley, and laid it upon her: afterward he went into the City.*

16 *But she came to her mother in law, which said, who art thou, my daughter? and she declared whatsoever the man had done unto her.*

17 *And she said also, he gave me these six measures of barley, for he said, thou shalt not return empty to thy mother in law.*

18 *Then said she, Be of good comfort until thou know how the matter will fall out, for the man will not rest unless he end it this day.*

These words are the last part of this Chapter: wherein is showed unto us how *Boaz* dismisseth *Ruth*, after they had slept till the morning: and *Ruth* returneth joyfully to her mother again.

The words contain two parts, generally in them: The first part is between *Boaz* and *Ruth*, verses 14,15. The second is between *Ruth* and *Naomi*, in the three next verses following. The first part between *Boaz* and *Ruth*, is of those things which they did together in the barn. First, that *Ruth* lay at his feet until the morning. Secondly, that she arose early before day, because *Boaz* would have none to know that a woman came into the floor. After they were both risen: *Boaz* giveth to her six measures of barley, layeth them upon her, and sendeth her away. Secondly, he himself goeth into the city, verse 15. to perform that which he had promised unto her.

The other part between *Ruth* and *Naomi*, in the three next verses, containeth a declaration of those things which passed between them twain after she came from *Boaz*. Wherein *Naomi* first asketh who she was, because coming home early before the day, she could not know her by her countenance: To whom *Ruth* declareth all things which passed between *Boaz* and her, showing unto her the six measures of barley which the man gave unto her for *Naomi's* sake, verses 16,17. Secondly, after *Naomi* understood the proceedings of *Ruth*, she comforteth her, verse 18. assuring her of the diligence of *Boaz*, that he would not sleep till he had ended the matter the very same day. Of these parts let us briefly speak in order, as the Spirit of God shall give utterance, and the time permit.

And so she lay at his feet until the morning. As we have heard in the former verses, the conference had between *Boaz* and *Ruth*, the end and conclusion whereof was this, that *Ruth* should content herself to tarry with him, and sleep until the morning. So in this place, the performance thereof is noted unto us. For the holy Ghost undoubtedly expressing these words, doth it to signify unto us these two things: First, that *Ruth* remained satisfied with the answer of *Boaz*, and troubled him no more with further talk. Secondly, that he might deliver these two innocent persons, from all suspicion of incontinency: for neither talked they any more, or turned one to another, but either of them both contented with their hard lodging, gave themselves to quiet sleep until the morning.

Where we first of all note that the gift of continency or chastity, is not in nature or the power of man, but is a holy fruit of true and unfeigned religion, yea, a special work of the spirit of God, as appeareth in both these godly persons: for if either of both had been given over, no doubt but nature hath put them forward to the satisfying of their carnal lusts: But seeing, as Christ saith, none can have it but them to whom it is given, and every gift cometh down from the Father of lights. This among other, is a special and extraordinary blessing of God, upon many persons truly religious: not for any other cause, but that thereby they might more freely give themselves to please the Lord, as *Joseph* answered his wanton mistress, how shall I do this, seeing I fear God? The use of this point is this, seeing we acknowledge this benefit, to come from the Lord, let us among our prayers desire the same, that we might crucify the works of the old man within us, sanctify the powers of our souls and bodies, be strengthened to resist the temptations of Satan, and bring every wanton desire, and wavering affection into subjection of the spirit of God, which ruleth and reigneth in the hearts of the faithful. And above all things let us earnestly labor for the fear of the Lord, that we may have the tree as well as the fruit, the fountain as well as the stream, the root from whence it springeth, as well as the blade, and increase of the same, for except the stream be supplied by the spring, it will quickly die, except the blade be nourished by the root, it will soon be withered, except the fire of the holy Ghost be increased with the coals of the knowledge of God, it will soon be quenched with the cold water of human infirmitiy; or else willingly go out of itself. And if ever this exhortation were needful, it is most necessary in these our unclean and filthy days: wherein fornications, adulteries, whoredoms, and all actions of incontinency did never

Matt. 19.11

Jam. 1.17

Gen. 39.9

Gal. 5.25

more abound and the reason hereof is this, because men and women, have refused the knowledge of God: and therefore as the Apostle saith, he hath given them over to work filthiness one with another. As the flesh lusteth against the spirit, so the spirit lusteth against the flesh: the one is carnal and bringeth damnation: the pure knowledge of God is spiritual and worketh salvation: but if the bodies of men were made the temples of the holy Ghost, how could they convert them to the members of harlots? But be not deceived, for God who is true, is not mocked: you which now delight your bodies in the pleasures of uncleanness, shall lament your woes in the sorrows of bitterness: when your souls and bodies for their wonted follies, shall eternally curse themselves, and cry vengeance, vengeance, to all their deserts: yea though the Almighty should grant you repentance, yet the consideration of your whoredoms will trouble your consciences, that it will be much longer before your hearts be eased, or sins released, for such as is the festered wound, such must be the searching and purging corrosive: he that stole little, hath but little to restore; but he that stole much, must recompense much again.

Secondly, by this we note, the diversity of the distribution of the gifts of God, for many godly persons are clear from one sin which reigneth in other, and have some proper gifts which are denied to other, some are subject to one sin and some to another. In this place *Boaz* and *Ruth* are declared, and commended for continent persons, but in another place *David* and *Bathsheba* godly also, are overtaken with this folly: *Judah* the son of *Jacob* was a good man, yet he lay with his daughter in law *Tamar*, sitting in the likeness of a whore; *Joseph* his brother also feared God, yet he refused his Lady and Mistress: And as it is in this, so it falleth out in all other, for some that have great gifts of God his spirit, yet are too much given to the love of money; others again like *Zacchaeus* distribute the greatest part of their posses-

Rom. 1.24

2 Sam. 11.4

Gen. 38.18

Gen. 39.9

Luke 19.8

sions, to satisfy their injuries and relieve the poor: other of the faithful like the Apostles *James* and *John*, desire the superiority, and chiefest places in the Church: but many, like the other Apostles, envy and disdain them for it.

And thus the Lord which delivereth his Spirit by measure, giveth to some a less, and to some a greater measure thereof, even as a rich man distributeth his alms, giving to one a good reward, and to another a small, so the Lord leaveth some to be overcome by their lusts, other by their money, many by their honor, some by their office, other by their pride, and every man hath some special sin that reigneth in him above other: for diverse men being called to one hope, and obtaining the like precious faith in regard of Christ, yet are diversely affected and infected with sin.

And this teacheth us these doctrines: first, that we never condemn the persons of the sinners, but the sinful acts they do commit: who should condemn *Noah* for drunkenness, *David* for murder, *Judah* for incest, or the Apostles for desiring superiority? surely, they were godly persons, and had their several falls, that the mercy of God might be magnified in their raising up again: for none of the godly are able to go upon the waters, as *Peter* would, but they must sink as *Peter* did, and yet they perish not, but are lifted up, and saved by Christ, as *Peter* was: though our old *Adam* cause us to commit many sins, yet our new *Adam* will remove all: we must judge charitably of all our brethren that are overtaken in their several sins: *Sara* lied unto the Lord himself. *Onesimus* was a thief and a run away from *Philemon*, *Rebecca* caused *Jacob* her son to beguile his own father, and all the holy Patriarchs had many wives, yet none must be so bold as to condemn any of them, notwithstanding their several and manifold faults: Even so in these our days, though we see and behold our brethren, some overcome with the world, other by promotion, many by their lusts

Ruth Chapter 3. verses 14-18

and concupiscences, other in their brave apparel: nay if they steal and rob, yet we must not judge but charitably of them. I speak not this to encourage any hereunto: for if grace abound above sin, yet cursed are they that sin, that grace and blessing might abound unto them: for if we may not do evil, where we certainly know good may ensue thereof, much less may we do evil, to make the mercy of God the bawd of our sins, but this we must remember, that there is no condemnation to the righteous, although they fall seven times a day, but if any sin upon presumption of God his mercies, their damnation is just, and are like a thief that stealeth, because he seeth one among twenty pardoned by the Prince.

Secondly, there are many that condemn the whole profession, because they live not all in the same perfection, and bring not forth the same fruits which by this doctrine we see here condemned: For as the grapes of the vine have some less and some more sweetness, yet all are grapes, and grow of the vine: so the Saints of God, have some more purity and some less, and yet all are nourished by Christ the vine: what if some (saith the Apostle) have not believed, shall the grace of God be made of none effect? and what if some have often fallen into sin, shall the whole Gospel for their sakes be discredited? nay, the Lord hath alway some that live so purely, such as *Isaac, Joseph, Boaz, Daniel, Zacharias* and *Elizabeth*, whom all the world can never blemish: howsoever others have their public faults, first that the work of repentance, which is a grace of God, might be practiced: Secondly, that God his mercy in saving great sinners, might be magnified. Thirdly, that the faithful (seeing their daily falls) might more earnestly desire their final deliverance. Lastly, that the wicked by this means might have occasion, by their blasphemies to work their own damnation.

Afterward she arose, for Boaz *said*: Now the night well passed in quiet sleep, and the dawning of the day

John 15.1

Rom. 11.12

2 Pet. 2.1
1 Cor. 11.6

approaching, *Ruth* at the commandment of *Boaz* ariseth
before the daylight, lest any should know she had tarried
with him all that night, whereby the good old man signifieth unto us, that it is no new thing in the world, that
slanders should be raised, for this was the thing that *Boaz*
feared, that if any should have seen the woman with him,
they would presently conceive it were for no goodness.
For the world museth as it useth, and they will soonest
espy a mote in the eye of a godly man: it ever was, is, and
will be, that causeless surmises and reproaches, shall be
brought up upon the godly, for princes nor people can
be freed there from: the which *David* felt well enough,
when he said in a certain place, that one blessedness in
God his Kingdom, shall be this, *to be kept from the strife* Psal. 31.20
of tongues, thereby insinuating, that they must needs endure them in this life present. We know what our Savior Matt. 11.18,
reporteth of the Pharisees, how they accused him to be a 19
friend of publicans, harlots, and sinners; and *John Baptist* to have a Devil. Therefore this must work patience in
the faithful, that are like affected and afflicted with ven-
omous tongues, for we are not better than those fathers
are, who many years ago sustained the same reproaches,
and left the burden behind them, to be borne by us, for
the world is no changeling: that which then they spoke
against them, now they spit against us, and though the
authors of these slanders be many years since departed,
yet their manners and heirs shall abide while the world
standeth. But to come to the words, wherein the mind
of *Boaz* is, that none should know that women were with
him, at such a suspected time: Why? will some say, is it
such a matter to talk with a woman privately and alone, 1 Thess. 5.22
we may do it publicly, and who can say nay unto it? I
grant, we may, and with less offence, yet *Boaz* would give
no occasion of offence, because we must abstain from all
appearance of evil: we must not only be careful we sin
not, but Christians must be careful to avoid all suspicion
of sin: it is not lawful for Christians commonly to com-

Ruth Chapter 3. verses 14-18

pany and keep with enemies, because it may be thought that they are secretly in league with them: it is not lawful for a Christian to go into the house of a harlot, because it will discredit his name, it is not lawful for a Christian to go into a Temple of idols, unless it be to deface them, because it may be thought he goeth to worship: the like may be said of all other in the like kind, where men are as guilty that look on, as they that are the principles.

And behold, I would to God that this carefulness, to avoid and shun the outward appearance of iniquity were well considered: the extraordinary charges in diet or apparel would be eschewed, lest we be accounted dainty and prodigal, or proud: slackness in going to sermons would be amended, lest we be deemed idle and secure Atheists: buying, selling, playing, and gaming on the Sabbath day, would be punished, lest it be thought we have no fear or care to worship the Lord: the daily and most lamentable swearing of rich and poor, old and young, parents and children, masters and servants, husbands and wives, men and women, would with terror of the Lord's judgments be restrained, idleness would be reformed, drunkenness in every degree would be corrected, dalliance and wantonness ashamed, cozening and deceiving simple persons be banished, and finally, if this fearing the shadow of sin would rest in the hearts of mankind, neither should the substance thereof overcome them, the pleasures allure them, the hope deceive them, the profit compel them, the glory provoke them, or the end thereof condemn them. Let us therefore beloved, neither frequent or approach to persons that are suspected, or places that are corrupted: we can touch no pitch but we must be polluted, nor any unclean thing, but we are defiled: sin is a contagious disease, it will infect the walls and the garments where it is committed, and what agreement is between the children of God and *Belial*? touch not their meats, handle not their pleasures, and taste not their companies, for the world seeth thee and will slander, the Lord seeth thee, and will recompense. We avoid the sight of Serpents, as *Moses* fled from his rod, why should not we then fly from the sight of that old Serpent the Father of lies, which by all means possible seeketh to deface the name of Christ, and the nature of the faithful? we come not to the picture of the Devil, which is devised by a painter, but we loathe the presence, and abhor the proportion of it, why should we not then, as much the works of himself, whereby he is more slyly communicated unto us, than in all the pictures and images of the world? We avoid the air where the Cockatrice layeth her eggs, because she poisoneth the same: but alas, we daily delight in the paths of unrighteousness, where is greater danger to our souls, than all the poisons of the world can bring to the body, thus we escape out of the snare, but we fall into the ditch; we strain at Gnats but we swallow up Camels: we play with the Lion, and are afraid of the Lamb: death is at the end of our journey, and yet we will not see it. Therefore, again, and again, beware of offences, that is, take heed you bring not the glorious names of Christians to discredit, your faith to ignominy, your hope to shame, your liberty to slavery, and fill not the mouths of the wicked, with your unwise and intemperate walking.

Secondly, by this we note, that we must not only abstain from the appearance of evil things, but we must also beware, we make not good things evil, for *Boaz* knew it was lawful for him to talk privately or publicly, day or night, alone or in company with any woman living: but he was afraid lest any should take his example, as a rule or defense for their private wantonness, or judge his company with *Ruth* to be utterly unlawful, whereby the name of a magistrate, the title of an Elder, and the credit of two faithful servants of God might be impaired. Therefore to stop these occasions, with timely arising, he was careful that the knowledge thereof should come unto none, that a lawful thing misunderstood or conceived should not be made unlawful. And truly, this teacheth us also, in Christian wisdom, to weigh all our doings by the rule of the Apostle, when he 1 Cor. 6.12   saith, all things are lawful, but all things are not expedient, all things are lawful, but I will not be brought into bondage of any: where he willeth us not only to see what we may do without danger to ourselves, but also without danger to any other: Secondly, that in nothing we prejudice our Christian liberty: whereby we gather that everything must be considered with the circumstance of time, place, and persons, a lawful thing in time may be out of place, and being lawful for time and place, yet it may be unlawful for the persons, this we will make plain by the examples of alms fasting, which our savior Christ himself used. It is lawful and a holy thing, to give alms at all times, yet if it be done in a market place, or with a Matt. 6.1-5   public sign, as to blow a trumpet, or toll a bell, or such like, it is hypocrisy by the sentence of our Savior, and therefore unlawful: even so, to pray continually is a good thing, but if it be done in the corners of the streets, or in the Churches while all the congregation be hearing the preacher, it is utterly unlawful: the same may be said of preaching and reading, eating and drinking, laughing and weeping, working and playing, buying and selling, watching and sleeping, with such like, all which are good necessary and lawful, yet as they exceed in time, place and persons, they may be unlawful, and therefore not to be done. By this let all the godly learn, to use the mean in all their indifferent actions; and specially according to this present scripture of *Boaz* and *Ruth*, I would to God, that this too common accompanying of men and women together, were altogether buried and banished from us, I mean such as is in this wanton manner, not only in the married, who with their open and public dalliance give great offence to sober minds, but also in the unmarried, in their unseemly meetings, dangerous conventicles, wanton feasts, and immodest running and dancing together, which in many unstaid persons, stirreth up the fire of concupiscence, that ought rather to be quenched. Even as *Phinehas* stroke the Israelite and the Midianitish woman, together upon one spear, so would God our *Zimris* and *Cozbis* had some punishment, to stay other from committing the like in every age, for it is much to be feared, that the heavy hand of God is gone out against us, by reason of our open and public whoredoms, for even now the children are infected with the example of their elders, and what hope can there be of the ages to come, when those that must be the parents of them, are thus poisoned with sin, in the days of their youth: surely as the rotten seed bringeth but a sorrowful harvest, so corrupted and wicked children will bring forth a woeful and lamentable posterity. Put away therefore this evil, of laying stumbling blocks before the blind, giving offences to the weak brethren, breeding the slander of the holy Gospel, grieving the hearts of the sober minded, drawing the curse from heaven upon us, and utterly drowning ourselves, and all our progeny in everlasting destruction.

Num. 25.8

  And when he had said give me thy sheet. This is the first thing which the holy Ghost reporteth of *Boaz,* since he awaked from sleep, and arose from his lodging, wherein he calleth for the sheet wherewithal *Ruth* was covered, (which no doubt but she brought from home with her) the which he filleth with six measures of barley, the which measures, as I take it, were hins, and contained an ephah, which we have showed you was seven gallons and a half of our English measure, for so much gathered *Ruth* the first day of her gleaning. Out of the which we note the duty of every godly man, which is this, never to be weary of distributing to the Church: for *Boaz* had often bestowed much upon *Ruth* and *Naomi,* yet we see so often as he could conveniently, he still continueth his liberality. For this cause *Paul* willeth us never to be weary of well doing, for he which needeth our

2 Thess. 3.13

Ruth Chapter 3. verses 14-18

liberality today, will also want our relief tomorrow, and so often as a faithful brother cometh and complaineth, so often are we bound (if we have) to succor his necessity. I know many are willing to do good once or twice to one person, but to give so often as *Boaz* did to *Naomi*, they cannot abide, yet this is our weakness and hardness of heart, for as we pray every day for our daily bread, so every day (having enough) we must distribute our bread: therefore we must follow the counsel of *Paul*, not to slack in doing of good, for in due time we shall reap if we faint not, and therefore while we have time, let us do good unto all, but especially to the household of faith, for as a father doeth every day sustain and provide for his own household, so should we which are the stewards of the Lord's possessions, give of his own to his poor servants, for we shame his majesty, if we suffer his family to want. We read that our Savior came often to one house, yet was not accounted a chargeable guest. We read that all the poor in the primitive Church, were daily maintained at the cost of the wealthy: Our Savior hath told us that we shall alway have the poor among us, to whom we may do good, not that we should once or twice bestow liberally, and ever after close up our benevolence, but that the same poor persons that dwell among us should daily receive their daily relief. For how shall we desire of God to finish his work of redemption, begun in our souls, when we cease to perfect our liberality bestowed on the poor. And now beloved in the Lord, if ever you did put on compassionate hearts towards your poor brethren, in this time of dearth, then think not sufficient to distribute once, but stretch out your hands again and again, to help the necessities of the poor saints, which daily cry unto you, give, give, that your love may increase, your compassion augment, and your fellow-feeling of the same hunger, may work a fellow feeding on the same relief.

And she came home. Now we are come to the second part of this Scripture, which concerneth *Naomi*

Gal. 6.9,10

and *Ruth*. And first here is set down her coming home to her mother in law before day, to whom she declareth how the man had used her, what promise he made her, and what gift he sent her, where we see the diligence of *Ruth*, who hasted to her mother in law, to show her the news, and to avoid the slander which we spoke of before. And this teacheth us a mutual concord in the duties of our profession, that the weaker should be warned by the elder, as *Ruth* was by *Boaz*, for we must not let any be lost through default of our negligence, but the wisest must govern, and the other must obey, if any be weary, let them lay their heads upon our advice, for the credit of the Gospel pertaineth to all, and therefore all must be careful to maintain the same.

Then said she. *Naomi* hearing the report of this prosperous success, and seeing the corn that *Boaz* had given her, comforteth her daughter to tarry the issue, looking for a joyful end of so happy a beginning; for she knew *Boaz* would not faint in the cause that so much concerned his credit, as this did, nor sleep till he had ended his intended devise. Whereby we first of all note, that here is a godly example for parents to imitate, to stay their children by exhortation, to depend in all things upon the leisure of the Lord: for if they be sick, the comfort of parents is much worth, if in trouble, the counsel of parents may ease them, if in labor, the parents' advice will much encourage them, if in danger, the care of their parents may deliver them, and if they be obstinate, who but parents can reclaim them, for as *Abraham* answered *Isaac* his son, when he asked him for a sacrifice, the Lord said, he will provide a sacrifice, even so parents must show their children, the providence of God to maintain them, his love to embrace them, his care to defend them, his word to instruct them, and the merits of Christ to save them. Secondly, by this we gather a worthy example of a godly Magistrate, who by his wonted and accustomed diligence, had won and deserved this com-

Ruth Chapter 3. verses 14-18

mendation that here *Naomi* giveth of him, that he would not rest till he had finished the matter, and followed the suit of the widow to the end, which is a worthy example for men in authority to imitate, that for conscience they should labor as faithfully in the cause of the poor, as if they were hired by fee in the suit of the wealthy, and would God this could enter into their minds, which like dull Horses will travel no further, than the spur of money pricketh them forward; how far are they from the uprightness of *Job*, which was an eye to the blind, feet to the lame, father to the poor, and diligently sought out the strife which he knew not: they are no Rulers, that in meekness entreat them not, in mercy forbear them not, and in justice reward them not. But of this we have spoken before: now let us give praise to God for that which hath been spoken.

The end of the Tenth Lecture.

The Eleventh Lecture

Ruth Chapter 4. verses 1-6

1 *And* Boaz *went up to the gate and sat down there, when behold, the kinsman came by, of whom* Boaz *had spoken, to whom he said, ho, such a one, come hither and sit down here; who came and sat down.*

2 *Then* Boaz *took ten men of the elders of the City, and said to them, sit down here, and they sat down.*

3 *Afterward he said to the kinsman,* Naomi *that is come again out of the country of Moab, will sell a parcel of land, which was our kinsman* Elimelech's.

4 *And I thought to advertise thee, saying, buy it before the assistants and the elders of my people, if thou wilt redeem it, redeem it, but if thou wilt not redeem it, tell me, for I know there is none beside thee to redeem it, and I am after thee. Then he answered, I will redeem it.*

5 *Then said* Boaz, *what day thou buyest the field of the hand of* Naomi, *thou must also buy it of* Ruth *the* Moabitess, *the wife of the dead, to stir up the name of the dead upon his inheritance.*

6 *And the kinsman answered, I cannot redeem it, lest I destroy mine own inheritance; redeem my right to thee, for I cannot redeem it.*

ow, by the permission of the Almighty, we are come to the last Chapter, and last part of this history, wherein the Holy Ghost showeth unto us, how *Boaz* performeth his promise made unto *Ruth* in the former chapter, and taketh her to be his wife: the whole

Chapter containeth two parts, the first is the marriage of *Boaz*, and the second is the description of his kindred, as well his ancestors, as his offspring. The first part of his marriage is described in the first fifteen verses of this Chapter, with all the circumstances thereof necessary to be known, and we will divide it into two parts: first, must be considered that which passed between the other kinsman and *Boaz* in the first ten verses: secondly, the manner and circumstances of the marriage, unto the end of the fifteenth verse. The things that passed between *Boaz* and his other kinsman, are first their conference about the matter in these first six verses: secondly, the alienation of the right from the other kinsman to *Boaz*, in the four next verses: the conference is described by the place, that it was at the gate of the City, verse 1. secondly, by the witnesses, that it was before the elders of the City, verse 2. The matter being thus prepared, *Boaz* propoundeth the cause of their meeting in two parts, first, for the redeeming of the land at the hand of *Naomi*, which was the inheritance of their kinsman *Elimelech*: whereunto he answereth, that he will redeem it, verse 4. secondly, he propoundeth unto him the marriage of *Ruth*, that the case so standeth, if he redeem the inheritance, he must also marry with the widow, for otherwise she would not agree, and this is in the fifth verse. Unto which latter condition the kinsman answereth, that he cannot do it, first, showing the reason of it, lest he destroy his own inheritance: secondly, yielding him power to redeem his right in his behalf, verse 6. Of these parts let us briefly speak as the Spirit of God shall give utterance, and the time permit.

Chap. 3.15

And Boaz *went up to the gate.* We have heard in the former Chapter, how *Boaz*, after he had dispatched *Ruth* back again to her mother in law, himself went into the City, to finish up the matter, now in this verse we see the place mentioned where *Boaz* bestowed himself after he was come thither, which is the gate of the City,

where he waited till he could see his kinsman come in or
out, and seeing him, called, who came unto him, and sat
down beside him. Now the gates of the Cities in those
ancient days, were the public places of judgment, as appeareth in many places of Scripture, among other, when   Gen. 34.20
Hamor and *Shechem* would persuade their people to be
circumcised, it is said, they sat in the gate of the City;
the like is that of *Moses,* that the obstinate son should
be brought by his own parents to the elders of his City,
and to the gate of the place; likewise if any man should
accuse his wife not to be a virgin at the day of her mar- Deut. 21.19;
riage, then her parents should bring the signs of her vir- 22.15
ginity to the elders of the City, and the gate thereof. But
we must also know, that the public judgments and trials were done so openly for diverse causes. First, that
no truth might be concealed, and so wrong judgment
pronounced, for thither everyone might freely come and
speak their minds. Secondly, that strangers might have
law and justice, as well as their natural and native inhabitants, and therefore it was at the very entrance of
their Cities: so we see *Abraham* a stranger, in the judg-   Gen. 23.10
ment place was heard before *Hebron* and *Heth*, when he   Gen. 22.17
bought his burying place. Lastly, because the munition,   Gen. 14.60
strength, furniture, power and defense of the City lay in   Rebecca
the gates: as God blesseth *Abraham*, so also *Laban* and   Matt. 16.16,
his mother bless their sister *Rebekah*, that their seed   18
should possess the gates of their enemies, that is, their
strongest defenses. And our Savior Christ, showing his
Apostles that he would build his Church upon the faith
which they had confessed, saith, that the gates of hell
should not prevail against it, meaning the whole power
of the Devil should never overcome it.

And this teacheth us by many things, first, that
in matters of trial, equity and justice, it is an injury, if
public faults be privately adjudged: for *Abraham* dealing but for a piece of land with *Hebron*, which was but
a private matter, could not obtain it, till it came to the

Ruth Chapter 4. verses 1-6

gate of the City, the public place of judgment, and if a matter so honest and lawful could not be ended, without such an open and public assembly, much more open offences, which are in themselves wicked and dishonest: 1 Tim. 5.20 for the Apostle saith, that those which sin openly must Deut. 24.17 be openly rebuked. Surely there is none of us that are ignorant of the great evil, which cometh by the private handling of offences, for thereby guilty persons escape unpunished, unjust matters are by consent confirmed, public peace is much abused, as if colors were discerned by blind men, or gold without the touchstone in the light: Yet herein are we much bound to magnify the Lord, who hath vouchsafed us open Courts for deciding of controversies, punishing of felons, and maintenance of peace, some for weightier, and some for lighter contentions; for as the wax melteth before the sun, so the subtlety of offenders at the examination of the magistrate.

Secondly, by this we note, that we must in judgment have regard both to the stranger, and to the freeborn, to the poor, and to the rich, to the widow, and to the married; and finally both alike to women and men, for thus the Lord commandeth, Pervert not the right of the stranger or infant, neither take the garment of a widow to pledge. For we must remember that *Abraham*, *Isaac*, and *Jacob*, the fathers of the faithful, were all their lives strangers in other lands, and therefore we which either would or should be their children, by doing injury to harborless strangers, do revile and oppress our spiritual fathers, when we love not their persons, maintain not their right, receive not their suits, and hear not their supplications, though they were against our own selves, if we justly deserve them; but of this matter we have spoken in the first and second Chapters. Thirdly, by this we learn, that public Judges, Justices and Judgments, should be defended by public authority; for as these Judges sat in the gate where the munitions were, that if any should refuse them, they had power and strength to compel them: even so, if men of wisdom have not authority, who seeth not that every disordered person doth contemn them. But if they have authority, and do not show it in punishing offenders, without fear or favor of men, they are like to *Saul,* when God had commanded him 1 Sam. 15.33 to kill the Amalekites, and spare neither man, woman, child, or beast alive, yet contrary to this commandment, he saved King *Agag,* but the Lord refused him, and cast him out of favor, and *Agag* was hewn in pieces by the prophet *Samuel:* even so it is to be feared, that there are a great many *Sauls* in every place, whose affections stand for law, sparing their friends for favor, and great men for fear, who are likewise reprobated of the Lord, and rebuked by his ministers. And here we have good occasion to be thankful to the Lord, which hath given our Magistrates this power, that all things are done in the name of the Prince, and assisted by the country, for the punishment of offenders: and I pray God increase more obedience to their authority in others, and more courage in themselves, to strike asunder with the sword of justice, the indissoluble knots of injurious and contentious persons, and to give the offenders their deserved reward. Then here we have *Boaz* sitting in the judgment place, as one that was not ashamed of his lawful cause, and the Lord which guideth all things, and would now reward the Religion of *Ruth,* bringeth the other kinsman to the sight of *Boaz,* who calleth him, and he cometh at the request of *Boaz,* and there tarrieth and sitteth down, where we will leave him, and go to the second part, which is the witness of this conference.

Then Boaz took ten men. The witnesses of the actions, which are to pass in this place, we hear in these words to be ten men of the elders of the City: there are only ten, in my judgment, because every City of the Israelites had twelve governors, according to the number of the tribes of Israel, to whom appertained the ordering of all civil causes among them, for they meddled not with

Ruth Chapter 4. verses 1-6

religion: now it is very likely that *Boaz* and this other kinsman, being men of so great kindred and wealth, were two of the number of the elders, who being the parties in suit, had the residue of their fellows, to be witnesses of the actions that passed between them. And this interpretation is confirmed, by the diligent examination of the place, for it is said that *Boaz* took them, as if he were equal or greater in authority than they, and the other being a man of great wealth, as appeareth by this, that he was willing to redeem the inheritance of *Naomi*, which could be no small charge, considering the late troublesome days, and after we shall hear in the sixth verse, that he would not take *Ruth* for fear his own name should be put out in Israel, whereby appeareth his calling not to be mean, beside his linage which was to the greatest house in Judah, by the which it must needs follow that he was an elder or ruler among them, which being plain both by this and other places of Scripture, that the civil government of the people was exercised by elders, and that the elders themselves could do nothing without the consent of their fellows. We see here noted unto us this excellent doctrine, namely, that men in authority and government must exercise nothing without the due execution of their own law and decrees: we see here this *Boaz*, a man of great authority, and lead by the Spirit of God, having a cause for himself, would not desire, or go about to accomplish it, but in the judgment-seat and presence of the elders, so that no favor of persons may break the course of justice, whereby a commonwealth is ruled. Some think it a base thing that great men shall stand to be judged in the place of common persons: and I think it as great a fault that common persons should have any access to Magistrates to be judged by them, for as it debaseth their estate to be joined with these in judgment, so it troubleth their quietness to be Judges over them. But some, and they of the greater sort, which have the law in their own hands, deal with it as *Judah* did, when it was told him, that his daughter *Tamar* was with child, then there was nothing but fire and fagot to punish her for her whoredom, till she showed him that he was the man by whom it came, as *Nathan* did with *David*, but then the heat of the fire was well cooled, when himself was found to be the greatest offender: even so many deal against the weaker and poorer sort, the laws are executed to the uttermost, but the rich and wealthy which offer all the injury, gather all the friendship, which is not only a fault to others, but in their own consciences, for how can they judge another when the same offence condemneth themselves? and therefore, as there was one general place of judgment, so there was but one common manner of trial: like as God judgeth the rich and poor, so a good Magistrate should equally receive both, and be as willing to be judged themselves, as to give sentence upon other.

Secondly, by this example of *Boaz* and the elders of Bethlehem we observe that in our public business, we must resort especially to the Magistrates, even in those things that require nothing but record and witness-bearing. This *Boaz* might have gotten some of his private friends, before whom he might have effected the matter, but we see him here the solicitor of his own cause, and craveth no friendship, but the witness of the elders, by the which this doctrine is confirmed: and therefore our Savior having cleansed a leper, biddeth him go show Matt. 8.3,4 himself to the Priests, for a witness unto them: and for this cause it was commanded in the law, that the weighty matters should be brought before the Priests, for Magistrates must hear as well the conclusions of peace, as the contentions of disquietness between man and man. Wherein we are bound to render most humble and earnest thanks to almighty God, who hath vouchsafed us this blessing, that the contracts of matrimony, the conveyance of possessions, the redeeming of mortgaged lands, the records of inheritances, and the purchase

Ruth Chapter 4. verses 1-6

of every lawful thing remaineth written in the several courts and offices of credit, that they might be everlasting testimonies for the posterities succeeding.

Afterward Boaz said. *Boaz* like a wise man concealeth his mind from the elders and kinsman, till they were all quietly set together, and then he beginneth with one part of his suit, telling the kinsman of the land of *Elimelech*, which was to be redeemed by his nearest kinsman, the which *Boaz* propoundeth, but very obscurely, that thereby he might thoroughly try his mind and good will toward *Naomi*, and making it known in the presence of the elders, he might by no means recall his words. And this teacheth us not only innocent uprightness, but also godly policy, that we be careful for the speaking in judgment, so much as may further our just and lawful cause, and not hinder it. For thus dealeth *Boaz*, he did not at the first show the drift, and secret of his mind, which was the marriage of *Ruth*, whereof as yet he knoweth nothing, but beginning the matter with the redemption of the lands, coloreth the marriage by the restoring of the inheritance, for by this means he openeth the secrets of his kinsman's heart, that he bore some goodwill to the cause of *Naomi*, but of this matter enough.

Wherefore he determined. In the former verse, and in this, *Boaz* propoundeth the matter to his kinsman, testifying thereby, that of duty and conscience he did it in the behalf of the widow, and requireth him for his duty and conscience, to perform the part of a kinsman, which is either to redeem the right, or to render it up, showing that beside them two, there is not one that was bound unto it: and also promising, that if he refused, then he himself would discharge that duty. Where we see first of all a holy example, teaching us to deal with our neighbors, for ourselves, or for other, even as *Boaz* did in this place: for he might have charged his kinsman, that he had no love or care to *Naomi*, that he had omitted his duty, in not redeeming the inheritance before this day, that his covetousness was so great, that he had forgot the very Law of God: and finally, he might have called upon the Magistrates for some punishment to be inflicted on him for his disobedience to the law of God, and neglect of his duty toward *Naomi*. But he doth none of these, but soberly in the presence of the elders, he turneth his gentle speech to the party, and having propounded the matter, requireth a present answer. Whereby we are admonished, that with the like charity we handle our neighbors, if we have them at any advantage, for this is that meekness that causeth to inherit the earth, for thereby we follow Christ, with whom we shall find rest for our souls, for love dealeth not churlishly, it seeketh not his own, it is not bitter, it thinketh no evil. Therefore as *Paul* entreated the Ephesians, so must I entreat you, that we so walk, as is worthy our vocation, unto the which we are called, in all modesty, meekness, and gentleness of mind, bearing with one another through charity. Oh how ungodly are these clamorous accusations among us, for which many lie in wait, that they might have any cause to draw their brethren, as it were, stark naked into the presence of the magistrates, that is, with most impudent and shameless untruths, to charge and examine them upon their own suspicions, never thinking on the injuries they offer unto them, or looking for the same measure again at the hands of other. Some there are also, which for every trifling farthing, will call their neighbors before the Magistrate, delighting in their own injuries, the troubles of their friends, the disquietness of the Magistrates, and the abuse of the Law; whose impatient constitution calleth for vengeance at the hands of the Lord, and the curse of the land is gone out against them, nothing is wanting, but that the branches of their unquiet spirits, should be pruned by the sword of justice, by them to whom they make their complaints.

Matt. 5.5,29

1 Cor. 13.5

Eph. 4.1,2

Secondly, by this example of *Boaz* we gather,

Ruth Chapter 4. verses 1-6

that the only cause of bringing suits before the elders, and magistrates, was the peace and quietness of the people, not for the kindling, but the quenching of contention before it arose, that the daily brawling, railing, chiding, and quarrelling, might be prevented by the wisdom of the Magistrates; for as the Philistines took away all the armor of the Israelites, to keep them from rebellion: so Magistrates hearing of causes with severity and justice, should take away the instruments of oppressions, and the weapons of contentious persons from the commonwealth. Thirdly, by this also we gather the diversity of proceeding in judicial causes in these days, and in times past. Then men in their own persons did plead in judgment their own causes, but now others make gain of it, then suits were not so tedious, as now they are, then men sought not out such sliding shifts to cover their falsehood, but they did as *Boaz* and his kinsman doth, the one simply propounded his grief, and the other gently answered his question, for so should everyone utter the truth indifferently, both to their benefit and damage: then the world was not troubled with writs, fees, or counselors, but every man brought his cause and his witness, so the injury was quickly confessed, easily tried, and speedily remedied: finally, we retain almost nothing of the ancient manners in this point, but only the bare and outward names. By the which we are admonished of human misery, for as the world groweth, the troubles thereof are increased: in the first age they had no wars, in the second age they had no certain dwellings, in the third age they had no chargeable suits, in the fourth age they had no quietness, and ever since wars have multiplied blood, one country carried to another, men's lawful inheritances are taken by violence, the church is spoiled of her liberty, the world of her peace, our bodies of their health, our goods of their continuance, our names of their credit, our corn of increase, our lands of their fruits, and all our lives of their natural benefits.

Lecture 11

Our Savior showed us, that before the end, the love of many should wax cold, but surely it is not only cold, but frozen in our lamentable age: the Apostle hath showed us, that men should be lovers of themselves, and lovers of pleasures more than God, when shall these days be, if they be not now? may we not see that every man taketh for his profit, as the Eagle raveneth for her pray, if they may get house or land, leases or farms, goods or cattle, money or meat, apparel or ease, they care not though all other lie harborless in the fields, naked in the streets, and pining in their weary and daily labors. Doth not now the Gentleman make more account of his worship, than the worship of God, the Merchant of his profit, than of Jesus Christ: the husbandman of his fruits, than of the fear of the Lord, the laborer of his wages, than the wealth of his soul, the beggar of his alms, than of unfeigned devotion: and every craftsman of his trade, more than of true Religion: when shall the day of vengeance come? for the Church of God travaileth with child of these miseries, and every day is a thousand till she be delivered, surely the day cannot be long before the final remedy appear.

But Boaz said. After he had entered with the land, and the other had granted to redeem it, he proceedeth also to the second part of his speech, telling him, if he redeem it, he must redeem it at the hand of *Ruth* the Moabitess, the wife of the dead, with whom he must marry, to raise up the name of the dead upon his inheritance. This law for a man to marry with the widow of his deceased brother, as it is commanded by the Lord, so Deut. 25.5,6 it had a special regard to many things, first, for the continuance of the first born in every family, who were the Lord's by the law; signifying thereby, that Christ the first born of the Almighty, should remain with all his Church, like the first born of this world, to be the heirs of grace forever and ever. And as he would not suffer any family to want a first born, because it was the Lord's, so not one of the faithful can be lost, because they are the Lord's.

Ruth Chapter 4. verses 1-6

Secondly, because it was an image of the resurrection, for as a man being dead without issue, his brother taketh his wife, begetteth a son, which shall be called the son of the deceased, and he which is dead shall live in him, in as much as his name is revived: even so the body laid dead in the grave, shall be revived at the last day by the powerful working of the Almighty, for as the first is wonderful, so the second is admirable. Thirdly, by this law of subrogation, is signified the great care which the Lord had for the temporal augmenting of every family among the Israelites, and in that, the love of God in Christ to his Church, that though we die without fruit in barrenness, yet the Lord will give us a name, whereby after a few days we shall live with him forever.

But in these words we first of all note, when he saith that he must buy it at the hand of *Ruth* the Moabitess, the wife of the deceased; that one cause, both of the redemption of lands, and marriage of the brother or next heir to the widow, was for the woman's or widow's sake, namely, that she should not be left destitute: for we read in the Gospel of *Luke*, that barrenness was a great reproach among women in those days: now we know that this law was only for barren widows, and not for them that were fruitful, and who would marry with such a woman, whom in his own heart he feared would be fruitless: therefore the Lord to succor these poor desolate widows, gave this for a law, that the brother or nearest kinsman to their husbands deceased, should take them to be their wives: where he again commendeth unto us the careful estate of destitute widows: if they be oppressed, we must ease them, if rejected, we must receive them: if forsaken, we must comfort them: if reproached, we must acquit them: and finally, if they will marry, they may, yea their own friends, or the Church must provide them husbands. And seeing the Lord would thus decree by a law, the safeguard of those that were despised, much more would he defend by judgment the cause of poor

Luke 1.2,5

fruitful widows, the mothers of many children. Now although we are not bound to this law of marriage, yet we are tied to do good to the widows, for the nature of the Law being long since abrogated, yet the use thereof remaineth forever and ever. For maintenance by the word of God must be allowed them wherewithal they may live, their husbands being dead. Therefore *Boaz* telleth his kinsman, that he must redeem the inheritance, at the hands of *Ruth* the Moabitess, because by her marriage, it is made the widow's, the husband dying without issue, like as in this place we observe that all the inheritance descendeth to the widow, and therefore she bestowed herself upon the next of the kindred, who indeed with us is the heir to all. Therefore by this we must all learn, but especially the married, or those that intend it hereafter, that it is one especial duty of a careful husband, to provide beforehand for the maintenance of their wives, that if death never so sudden take them away, yet they may not leave them as many have done, harborless without house, comfortless without friends, and wealthless without convenient maintenance.

By this we see, the commendable assurance of jointures and dowries in lands or money, which many parents do wisely take for their daughters, to be a thing allowable by the word of God: yet many offend in the excess that they will never match where they can have none, though there be never so great hope in time to come, so that wealth and nothing else is the end of most marriages. Then by this we see condemned, first all those which having sufficient, will hardly leave to their wives anything beside that which they cannot keep from them, and hence it is, that many leave to their children hundreds and thousands, but scant twenties or forties to their helpless widows. Other having many children, leave the greatest part of their wealth to their widows, through whose youthful marriages, many times, their whole posterity is brought to poverty. But a third sort

Ruth Chapter 4. verses 1-6

there are, which mind nothing save only marriage, and borrow a little for their festival day, but afterward let the world sink or swim, children without bread, wives without comfort, themselves as bare as the Grasshopper in winter, and their whole families most pitifully tormented: they repent, though all too late, the children wish they had never been born, the parents curse the day of their first acquaintance, the family complain of poverty, the country of charges, the people of necessity; but they poor silly souls, the innocent infants are left to the merciless world, to live in beggary. Oh that this godly forecast would enter into the minds of many headlong parents, that their lives might be more blessed, their children more happy, their families more contented, the country better furnished, and the poor better succored, that there might be no complaining in our streets, no leading into captivity, and not one feeble person among us, that our sons may be as the fruitful garners, and our daughters like the polished corners of the Temple: Oh blessed are the people that be in such a case, yea blessed are the people whose God is the Lord. Then should the name of God be honored by our lives, and praised in our deaths, when our widows are provided for, our children maintained, our families nourished, and our souls shall be blessed.

Then the kinsman said. This second question of marriage being propounded, the kinsman in these words answereth, that he cannot redeem the inheritance upon the condition, and giveth a reason thereof, because then to save another's, he should destroy his own, meaning if he had but one child by *Ruth*, that should be for *Mahlon* her deceased husband, and so his own name should be forgotten in his inheritance. Whereby we see that he opposeth the fear of the loss of his own name, against the severe commandment of God, and doubteth that if he follow the Law of God and custom of the faithful, his land may lack an heir, his house a master, and himself a son. The like unto this was that of *Onan* the second son of *Judah*, when he should have taken the wife of his deceased brother, would not perform his duty towards her, but abusing in filthiness his own body, because he would not benefit his brother, was therefore justly slain by the Lord. And I fear that a great many are sick of the same disease, that love the world above the Word, their land above the Law of God, their children more than charity requireth, who think they are born for nobody but only for themselves: but especially in marriage, they had rather have the land than the man, the portion than the woman, like this man which was willing to take the inheritance, but unwilling to marry the widow: for this cause they oppress both children and widows, they prefer their private gain, before public godliness, who for their posterity, some are occupied in bribery, some in usury, some in extortion, and many in unlawful bargaining, whose only and chief care is for nothing, but that they may die rich: but better is poor *Lazarus* at his death, than all the rich gluttons in the world; for wealth maketh not to die well, but rather choketh the soul with insatiable care, only Religion is the surest badge of a godly man, whose riches is poverty, whose pleasure pain, and whose reward is salvation. But this man is well contented to give over his right to *Boaz*, wherein surely he doth him a pleasure, but if there had been any profit in it, he would first have served himself: wherein we have a worthy example of a worldly mind, which granteth all things, till it touch his discommodity: for thus the world will hear us preach, till we rebuke their covetousness, or crave their benevolence, for everyone will go as far dry-foot as they can, but none will be wet for the Law of the Lord: that is, so long as we tell them of their faith, exhort them to repentance, persuade them from pleasure, and drunkenness, but once touch their purses, as *John Baptist* did *Herod's* whoredom, then farewell preaching, faith and repentance: but thus much shall suffice for this time.

Gen. 38.9

Ruth Chapter 4. verses 1-6

Now let us give praise to God.

The end of the Eleventh Lecture.

The Twelfth Lecture

7 *Now this was the manner before time in Israel, concerning the redeeming and changing for to establish all things, a man did pluck off his shoe, and gave it his neighbor, and this was a sure witness in Israel.*

8 *Therefore the kinsman said to* Boaz, *buy it for thee, and he drew off his shoe.*

9 *And* Boaz *said unto the elders, and unto all the people, ye are witnesses this day, that I have bought all that was* Elimelech's, *and all that was* Chilion's *and* Mahlon's, *of the hand of* Naomi.

10 *And moreover,* Ruth *the Moabitess the wife of* Mahlon, *have I bought to be my wife, to stir up the name of the dead, upon his inheritance, and that the name of the dead be not put out from among his brethren, and from the gate of his place, ye are witnesses this day.*

These words contain the finishing up of the matter between *Boaz* and his kinsman, how the one resigneth his right to the other, and the knitting up of the marriage. They consist of two parts: first, a description of the ancient manner of alienation, or changing of titles, rights, and properties, in the seventh verse, in these words: *Now this was the manner afore time, etc.* to the end of the verse. The second is the manner how this man doth give over, and resign his right to

Boaz, in the eighth, ninth, and tenth verses: and containeth two parts; the first respecteth the kinsman in the ninth verse: where first, he biddeth *Boaz* to buy or redeem it: Secondly, he draweth off his shoe.

The second part respecteth *Boaz*, and showeth how he receiveth it in the two next verses: wherein first he calleth witness of the elders and people, verse 10. Secondly, he accepteth the proffer, or purchase, which is double: first the land or inheritance, verse 10. Secondly, the widow or wife of *Mahlon*, verse 11. Of these let us briefly speak in order as they lie, with the assistance of God his spirit, and the permission of the time.

Now this was. First of all here is described the manner of God his people, how in ancient time, they were wont to alienate, or put off their right from one to another, which the holy Ghost setteth down for the better understanding of that which followeth. And this manner of changing or selling was commanded by the Lord himself, as we read in these words. *Then the Elders of his city shall call him and commune with him, if he stand and say, I will not take her: Then shall his kinswoman come unto him, in the presence of the Elders, and loose his shoe from his foot, and spit in his face, and answer and say, so shall it be done to him, that will not build up his brother's house. And his name shall be called in Israel, the house of him whose shoe is put off.* In the which words we note these things: First, that it was the duty of a woman to complain of such a man before the magistrates, as we may see in the seventh verse. Secondly, that the magistrates were bound to call and examine such persons, of the causes of their denial. Thirdly, that the woman should pull off the shoe, and also spit in his face, which the Lord did doubtless command for the poor comfortless woman's sake, that no excuse should be admitted of delay, but that they might either be presently received, or presently refused: for she which was not fit today, would not be tomorrow, where we gather the great care of the

Deut. 25.8-10

Lord for widows, which hath warned their friends to provide for them marriages, and armed the magistrates to defend their weakness, truly as they which are least accounted in the world, are most esteemed of the Lord, even so they which are most regarded of the world, are least respected of the Lord: for in this law the Almighty had an especial eye to the poor, for he knew the wealthy could want no husbands: Whereby we are taught first, to magnify the goodness of the Lord: which as *Mary* saith, looketh upon the poor degree of his servants, and beholdeth the rich afar off, his delight is in advancing of them that are cast down, and all his laws defend the causes of the oppressed. Secondly, that we make no light account or reckoning of those whom the Lord in his word doth so highly commend unto us: for it is an especial token of them that shall be saved, that they make much of them that fear the Lord: what though they be as poor as *Lazarus*, and never so contemptible in the eyes of the world: yet it is a thousand times more commendable to be friendly to such, than to all the rich gluttons of the world, but of this point we have spoken before, and it is sufficient to touch it now.

Luke 1.48

Psal. 15.4
Luke 16.25

      Secondly, by this we also note, that if there be any injury done to the children by their parents, or to widows, by their friends, in their marriages, it is lawful for them to appeal to the magistrates: As for example, if the parents would force their children, either not to marry at all, or else to marry against their minds, rather than they yield to either of both, they may and ought to sue to the magistrate. The which as it was lawful for the Jews by this law here mentioned, even so it is left to us to imitate, although the ceremonial use of it be ceased, which consisted only in the brother's marriage, and as long as magistrates are, so long the true use of it remaineth, as it doth in many others. Yet although the Gospel speak not of it, because it is a thing so far against nature, yet it commandeth that they which do evil should fear the sword

Ruth Chapter 4. verses 7-10

Rom. 13.1-4
Matt. 7.12

of the magistrate, because he beareth it not in vain: and moreover, it is flatly against the Gospel, that any should do unto other, which they would not have done to themselves: much more this forcible dealing with friends or children: And if it be lawful for the wife or husband to fly to the magistrate in private injuries, much more for the children, which are weaker, and therefore need more help. This I speak, not to stir up the minds of any against their parents; but with the Apostle I exhort and command that everyone obey their parents in all things lawful: for he is accursed that doth otherwise, but to this end I utter it, that we may know what is lawful, and what is unlawful: for the same God which hath commanded that parents should bring their unruly sons and daughters for to be punished, willeth also that they which do any hurt to their children, either in soul, to draw them from the Lord, or in body, as in unlawful or ungodly marriages, in unlawful and ungodly actions, their only refuge should be to the minister of God, the lawful magistrate, to whom they owe more obedience than to their own parents. Therefore, *Paul* willeth parents, that they provoke not their children to wrath, which is by their tyrannous commandments to bind their consciences, and their cruel authority to murder their minds: For if a private subject may sue against the Prince, and crave the law, much more a son or a daughter, being grieved by their parents: The use of this doctrine is to teach and instruct us, first what duty we owe to the magistrates, who have greater care and charge over us for the peace of our country, and public welfare, than parents for our maintenance, and private obedience: therefore *Paul* willeth to pray and give thanks for the magistrates, that under them we may live godly and quiet lives, for that is good and acceptable in the sight of God our Savior, whereby we may justly complain of the slackness of our unhappy age, wherein men murmur and grudge at any charge which ariseth for our prince, but especially that

1 Tim. 2.2,3

there are so few, which in all their lives have prayed for
Prince or Magistrates, and if they have, it was but a wish
and no more, that they might live in peace to gather
wealth, not in godliness, for the profit of their souls:
Again, by this all parents must be instructed, how to deal
with their children, that they reign not like Gods over
the fruits of their bodies, but entreat them in meekness,
being of years of discretion, like their fellow heirs of God
his Kingdom: even as they will answer to the Almighty,
who gave them such issue, and to the laws of our Prince,
that requireth account of them, for the chiefest stroke
lieth not in them, but in those that govern both church
and commonwealth, and we have already showed that
in some causes, it is a glory for their children, to decline
from their counsels: Lastly, all children must herein also
be schooled, that with all reverence they submit themselves to the advice of their parents: but especially like
free men in Christ, they listen alway what the word of
God saith: for that must be their judge, and parents also,
when it shall not go for payment, that they did it for fear
of their friends: but they which fear them more than
God, shall with them be excluded forever from God: and
let us evermore give thanks to the Almighty, which thus
provideth for our misery, to defend our innocency that
if we be in one place oppressed, we may be redressed in
another, appointing courts of appeal from our own parents, to his own magistrates:

  Thirdly, by this also we observe and note, when
he saith, that this was a sure witness in Israel, that it is
a thing required in our religion, that of our public affairs there may be public testimonies, as for example, our
purchasing, buying, or selling, ought by Religion and the
fear of God, to be done with open and public witness,
for the better assurance to buyers and sellers, to avoid
deceit in the one, and covetousness in the other; and
therefore it was said in the Law, that under the witness
of two or three shall every word stand. And further also,

Ruth Chapter 4. verses 7-10

there must be some outward sign to seal up the matter, in this place here is the putting of the shoe, which signifieth possession, and dispossession again, the rendering of a man's right to him that hath it. Therefore, in some places there is used striking of hands, as the shutting and making up of bargains and covenants, and who knoweth not that in the purchase of Land, there is seisin and delivery by a piece of earth and a twig; of houses, all go forth and the buyer entereth in alone, and there abideth, and this I may say, is a sure testimony in England. But you would know why the Lord beside the record of the magistrates, required such outward and open signs: To which I answer, he did it for this cause, that the simplest among them might not be deceived, but might have that as the evidence of his possession for evermore: witness faileth, magistrates die, people are unconstant; yea, and some will falsely swear and witness to any untruth, yet the shoe remained an everlasting testimony. Therefore among us there is writing and seal, by the which things are confirmed, which passed many ages ago, and this was taken from the ancient usage, wherein men's names were entered in brass and stone, and the quantity of their possessions described. Therefore doth the holy Ghost so precisely set down the purchase which *Abraham* made with *Ephron*: where the field is named, the borders or bounds of it is described, the cave is mentioned, and the very trees that grew in the same, are made sure unto him, the like may be said of the stones in Mount Gilead, that *Jacob* reared as a witness between him and *Laban*, and many other which serve to this end, that as *Paul* saith, We should not defraud one another: for if he were accursed that removed the landmark of his neighbor, what shall they be which get marks and lands both, some by deceiving, some by forged evidence, other by false witness, and some force their neighbors, will they, nill they [*willy-nilly*], to depart from their dwellings and possessions, and to leave them for little or nothing in the claws

Gen. 23.17

Gen. 31.52
1 Thess. 4.6

of these cormorants, their great possessions require great accounts, and I fear me, when that day shall come, they will be as ready to restore, as ever *Judas* was, but it shall be too late and without fruit, for the sentence is already pronounced, that fire shall consume their dwellings, and their children or posterity shall be vagabonds, but the righteous shall have the land in possession.

Therefore the kinsman. This verse showeth how the right was resigned, first the kinsman giveth *Boaz* authority, when he biddeth him buy it for himself: and secondly, he renounceth his own, when he pulleth off his shoe. Where first of all it may be demanded, why doth he pluck off his own shoe? seeing by the Law, the woman should do it, and also spit in his face; as we have heard already. Unto which I briefly answer: First the Law before said, wherein the woman was bound to pluck off the shoe, and to spit in her kinsman's face, was for such, as utterly denied both to redeem the inheritance, and to marry the widow, as also that would not provide any substitute to do it in their behalf: but this kinsman of *Naomi's*, got *Boaz* to redeem his right, as we may see in the sixth verse of this Chapter, in these words redeem my right to thee: Therefore that ceremony was needless: Secondly, I answer, that the woman by that Law was bound to complain to the magistrates: but neither *Naomi* nor *Ruth* did make any complaint, save only a private petition unto *Boaz,* for to marry her in his own behalf; and therefore the matter being confessed before the complaint, as he was willing to release his title unto *Boaz,* who was ready to receive it, so with less rigor the law was executed upon him: for a penitent offender is worthy of most favor. Thirdly, neither *Naomi* nor *Ruth* were present when this matter was in hearing, because they were uncertain of their kinsman's mind, who if he had granted, it had been immodesty for them, seeing they never asked him before, and if he denied as he did, by their presence they should seem to distrust the promise which *Boaz* made to *Ruth*: But seeing the consent of *Naomi* and *Ruth* was yielded to *Boaz*, and that being but the first motion, they needed not to be present, and the matter at the first confessed, was at the beginning dispatched: Out of the which we first observe, that it is a point of godliness, and worthy of friendship, that in our suits we should at the first confess our oppressions: if we have done any; I know many will commit their unjust dealing to the trial of the Law, looking for a doubtful issue of the same: and will say, if I be condemned, the charge is but the more to myself: but I reply and say, why doest thou not confess thy folly, and the injury which thou hast done, and save the charges which thou spendest in the trial, thou dost but add murder to thy malice, drunkenness to thy thirst, and prodigality to thy covetousness: Thou hast already robbed thy neighbor, by thy oppression, now thou wilt spoil the Lord, of those his goods, whereof he hath made the steward, by consuming them in Law to defend thy injuries. Follow the counsel of the Lord, agree with thy adversary quickly, whilest thou art in the way with him, lest he complain of thee to the Judge, and the Judge deliver thee to the Jailor, and so forth: Let wise men end your matters at home, abide not the verdict of the Law, it is too costly, for as you are accountable to your neighbor for the uttermost farthing, so you shall be answerable to the Lord for every mite, you have misspent, when the very money you have laid out shall rise in judgment against you, to condemn your contentions.

Matt. 5.25

Secondly, we note here in *Naomi* and *Ruth*: an excellent example of a godly mind: for if *Naomi* would, she might have dealt with her kinsman, and he denying, she might have done him all the disgrace set down in the Law, to have pulled of his shoe, to have spit in his face, to have defamed him and his house forever: but she dealeth not so, she would not revenge one injury by another, she maketh the matter sure beforehand, that if he refused,

Ruth might be married, and the other not disgraced: So dear is the name and credit of one's neighbor to a godly person, that they will adventure their own loss and hindrance, to save the honesty of the other. Therefore, saith *Peter*, it is the glory of a man to pass by the in- Gen. 39.17,18 firmities of his brother, *Joseph* might have disclosed the lusts of his mistress, and saved his own imprisonment: but he concealed it which wrought first his misery, and then his felicity. But, oh how few are there like *Joseph* in our days, which having their brethren at advantages, will not to their uttermost accuse them! We have many *Zibas* which accuse poor *Mephibosheth* to *David*, with 2 Sam. 16.3 gifts and with bribes, pretending simplicity, with words sweeter than honey: when war is in their hearts, their lips have learned their flattering style, they are of their father, that old accuser of God his children, but as he is cast down, so they shall be condemned, yea, even then Rev. 12.10 when it is no benefit to them, how doth it rejoice them Job 1.10 to see their neighbors imprisoned, their enemies slandered, their possessions removed, their wealth diminished, their credit abated, and they deprived of friends and favor at one time.

       Is this the thing that you would have them do to you? might not the Lord have suffered him to stand, and cast down you, that he might have laughed at your destruction. Consider yourselves, beloved in the Lord, and let us be the scholars of this godly *Naomi*, if we may get our own with fair speeches, let us not use these threatening words: If we must hide the truth for the benefit of our neighbors, much less must we conceal falsehood, that not one word of disgrace be uttered to the discredit of our neighbors. Oh that those which contend with their neighbors would be instructed in this doctrine; how much would it moderate their malice, for the benefit of their adversaries, and bring peace unto both, never to be repented of? Wherefore lay aside all maliciousness 1 Pet. 2.1,2 and guile, dissimulation, envy, and all evil speaking, as

Ruth Chapter 4. verses 7-10

innocent and newborn babes: and let us desire the sincere milk of the word of God, that we may grow to be perfect men in Jesus Christ, that as he suffered and gave no answer, being led as a sheep before the shearer, which openeth not his mouth: having many causes to allege against his adversaries, yet in silence endured both their judgment and reproaches, that we with the same lenity and meekness, should forgive other, even as he hath forgiven us.

Thirdly, by this also we observe that the laws both of God and men, be they never so sharp, yet in some causes they may be moderated, according to the discretion of the magistrate, especially when they respect private persons. In this place the spitting on the face, and the disgracing of the name of the man is omitted: which the magistrates might have constrained, if they pleased: neither are they to be blamed, for the party which was most grieved, by this denial was best pleased, neither did she call for extremity. And as Christ would not in his judgment, condemn or accuse the woman taken in adultery, but bid her sin no more, even so the rigor of the Law is not to be executed upon every offender, but where hope of amendment is, there may be a testimony of favor. This is worthy doctrine for our days, wherein men lie in wait as the Dragons do for the Elephants, to get their brethren within the compass of the law, and though God his word and their own consciences condemn them, yet if the law say it, deprive men of their livings, Christians of their liberty, servants of their freedom, in the service of God, parents of their children, wives of their husbands, Churches of their preachers, and no man dare open his mouth for them, that if Christ himself were on the earth again in his human shape, they need no other argument but this: we have a Law, and by our Law he ought to die: But woe be unto you saith the prophet, that urge the laws of *Omri*, that is, which dare maintain the decrees of princes against any of the Lord's

John 8.1-11

Micah 6.16

servants: Surely, it is an argument that men fear the creature above the Creator, which will not be drawn from
their laws, be they never so childish: but in our days it is
most lamentable, that any good laws should be wrested
against the course of the Gospel, which were made for
the enlarging thereof, such as is the forcing of men to
abide with dumb ministers, when the Gospel preached,
calleth for them at the next Church: But I speak not one
word against lawful authority, or against the law, but
only the partiality of the executioners thereof, is worthy
of blame, many times punishing severely, where is no,
or little offence, and pardoning by sufferance notorious
blasphemers.   But let no magistrates think when they
may mitigate offences, that they may altogether bury the
force of the law, when they shut their ears against the
cry of them that complain, or execute it not for favor or
friendship: But on the contrary, they must not in matters
of judgment repel any information or evidence: but if
the party grieved require extremity, by wisdom they may
persuade him, but by authority they cannot deny him:
finally, in all things consider with the Apostle, not only
what is lawful, but also what is expedient, that charity
being joined with authority, love may rather amend our
faults than law, and severity put unto justice, the greatest faults may have the sharpest punishments, that not
the words, but the mind of the Law-maker may ever be
considered.

    And Boaz *said unto the elders.* Now the cere-
mony being ended, the resignation delivered, the holy
Ghost proceedeth to express how *Boaz* received it,
where he first of all calleth witness of the elders, and of
the people, that now he hath bought the inheritance of
Elimelech's, and whatsoever was *Mahlon's*, and whatsoever was *Chilion's*, he hath bought at the hand of *Naomi*:
So that here he testifieth with the witness before said,
that it shall be as his own in possession forever.

    Where first of all here cometh in question

Ruth Chapter 4. verses 7-10

1 Kings 21.3

Lev. 25.23

whether then it were, or now is lawful to sell inheritances, which by this place appeareth to be very lawful, seeing *Boaz* buyeth that which was *Elimelech's*: and if it be so lawful, then was *Naboth* in great fault, that he did not depart from his in *Jezreel*: and so might have saved his life. But *Naboth* had the express law of God on his side, which commanded that the land should not be sold to be cut off from any family: and giveth this reason of it, because they were but strangers in the land, and sojourners, but the fee-simple (as we call it) was only the Lord's: Therefore *Naboth* was not wrong, but had the Law of God for his defense: nor yet *Boaz* did not amiss, which bought *Elimelech's* possession or inheritance of *Naomi*. Therefore we must briefly set down the conditions of sale, as they may be gathered out of the law of God.

Lev. 25.25-28

First, therefore these are the words: *If thy brother be impoverished, and sell his possession, then his redeemer shall come, even his near kinsman, and buy out that which his brother hath sold: And if he have no redeemer, but his hand hath gotten to buy it out. Then shall he count the years of his sale, and restore the overplus to whom he sold it: so shall he return to his possession. But if he cannot get sufficient to restore to him, then that which is sold, shall remain in his hand that bought it, until the year of Jubilee: and in the Jubilee it shall come out, and he shall return to his possession.*

Out of these words we gather these propositions for certain truth. First, that for poverty it was lawful for men to sell away their inheritance: Secondly, that the next kinsman might redeem it, and no man else beside him that sold it: and they might at any time redeem it, neither could the possessor deny them. Thirdly, that no sale of any land was good or effectual for any time after the year of Jubilee: By these three conclusions we may try the title: Naomi was now impoverished, and therefore she might sell her inheritance to whom she pleased;

Boaz was by substitution, the next kinsman: therefore he might lawfully buy it: For *Naboth*, he was neither poor nor wanted, neither was *Ahab* any of his kindred, and if it had once got into the king's inheritance, who could ever have required it again.

Therefore *Naboth* was without blame in denying to sell his vineyard, and *Boaz* without fault and blame for buying of *Naomi's*: And *Boaz* knew that he had the consent of the seller, and therefore he was the bolder. Then by this we may gather, in what cause it is lawful to buy or to sell one's inheritance.

First, it is lawful to buy with the consent and good will of him that selleth: so we read how *Abraham* Gen. 23.17 bought a field of *Ephron*, after he had first communed with his sons, and had their liking of his suit, and after at the gate of the city, he had his assurance, and without this it is not lawful at all to deal, for except the will be free and not compelled, it is no bargain before the Lord, but plain robbery, and unjust dispossessing, because in the last commandment the Lord saith, Thou shalt not covet thy neighbor's field, or his house, or his Ox, or his Ass, or anything that is his, whereby is forbidden every thought of covetousness, much more forcible and unjust dealing to compel men to depart from their inheritance. Therefore *Ahab* was blamed by *Elijah* (though only *Jezebel* wrought the murder) because he knew it was forcible dealing, and he ought not to have entered, seeing the means of his death. But how many constrained purchases are there made, the Lord only knoweth, and the country everywhere ringeth of them, where many by one means or other, are driven to depart from their patrimonies, are left destitute of dwelling places, wives without maintenance, children without inheritance, families brought to poverty, by such daily and usual purchasing.

Secondly, it is lawful to buy if it be publicly done, not only for the conveyance or assurance, but also

Ruth Chapter 4. verses 7-10

for the price: Therefore *Ephron* made *Abraham* the price of four hundred shekels, in the gate of the City, and here *Boaz* doth it before the elders. This is a most worthy consideration, because by the neglect of this point it cometh to pass, that great livings are done away for a song, as the proverb is, young men privately sell their patrimonies, their fathers being alive, for little or nothing: others which have not so much worldly wit, as were to be wished, make private bargains of their lands, when they are in want or poverty, wherein they sell them half for nothing. And thus young men are deceived with the sight of a little gold, unwise and unthrifty persons are cozened, with nothing in regard of the value of their inheritance, widows left comfortless, children left harborless, and the country troubled and pestered with such covetous encroachers, and why? because they make subtle and deceitful bargains in secret, whereof they would be ashamed, if either before Judges, Elders, or Magistrates, this sale were propounded. Therefore, by the rule of God his word, we hold him a thief and a robber, which hath thus bought to the hindrance of the seller.

Thirdly, it is lawful to buy for necessity, house, or lands, or any other thing lawful to be sold, the former conditions always observed, but it must not be for vainglory, or for the advancing of their children or posterity, or that they might be land-lords to many: Not everyone that is wealthy, and hath much money, must alway purchase land: the former example of *Abraham* proveth this: who being a very wealthy man; yet he never offered to buy any land, till Sara his wife was dead, and that was for necessity to bury her in. So did *Jacob* his son buy a parcel of land of *Hamor* the father of *Shechem* for an hundred pieces of silver, whereon he pitched his tent, and built an Altar: He might have bought and purchased much more, as he was able, but he would not; only a dwelling place and an Altar room he provided: surely, we have an infinite and great number that buy

Gen. 33.19

dwelling places, but few that give any of their lands or livings to build altars or Churches on. Nay, who seeth not how men sue daily to pull down the altars, and to make arable land where they stand; that is, they pull personages and spiritual livings to their nests, they get away tithes and oblations, they enter upon the lands and profits of the ministry, and, I think verily, in many places they are grieved that the Churches and Churchyards are so big, because they would have the more profit, these persons, I warrant you, are none of *Jacob's* children, nor *Abraham's* neither, which have taken to themselves the houses of God in possession. Against these the Prophet crieth, woe be unto them that join house to house, and field to field, that there might be no more place, that ye may be placed by yourselves in the midst of the earth: therefore hear their punishment. This, saith the Lord, is in my ears; surely many houses shall be desolate, even great and fair houses without inhabitants. This shall be the end of these covetous cormorants, who desire to be the Lords of the earth: And if good King *David's* posterity within a thousand years after him, had not one house to lodge in, but even in the same, which was their father's: *Joseph* and *Mary* were fain to harbor in the stables; fear not you, but your posterities will be beggared within a hundred years after you, which neither are so wealthy, or so godly as *David* was; but I may sooner pour out my very heart, than make any forsake their purchasing, so loving a sin is the desire of wealth, that men choose it with abundance here for a season, and damnation there forever, but let the godly use the world, as if they used it not, for the desire of money is the root of all evil.

Isa. 5.8,9

But now we have labored for the buyers, whom I know will be more careful of their profit, than my instruction, let us in a word direct the sellers also before we go from this point. If any demand wherefore, or for what causes they ought, or it may be lawful for them to sell their possessions, I answer briefly, for these causes

Ruth Chapter 4. verses 7-10

a man may, and for none else. First, to relieve his poverty, as being in sickness, for to recover his health, being imprisoned for some good cause or lawful debt, being taken a captive, to pay his ransom, or such like, all this is understood by the name of poverty, or any other means whereby a man may come into poverty: for the Lord which gave inheritances, gave them for the benefit of the possessors, that they might be helps unto them in this miserable life; for they must ever esteem more of their life than of their lands, of their liberty than their inheritance, of their welfare and health than riches or wealth, and therefore the Lord permitted the Jews to do away their inheritance: and mention is made of a godly woman in the Gospel, that had spent all the substance she had upon Physicians, which is reported to magnify the goodness of our Savior unto her, which cured her for nothing, and deferred to help her, till she had spent all, that she might account more of her health, than her wealth, of the kindness of Christ, than the cunning of the Physicians, but I need not many reasons to prove this, and therefore I will leave it.

Gen. 47.18-20

Mark 5.25,26

Secondly, a man may lawfully depart with some of his inheritance, to help him that hath none at all, either to sell it or give it. So did *Ephron* sell *Machpelah* to *Abraham* that had none; so did *Hamor* sell a parcel of land to *Jacob* that had none, and unto this I may refer the threshing floor of *Araunah*, which *David* bought to build an altar on, when the Lord stayed the plague, after he had numbered the people: this was to special use, and therefore for some special causes I think it lawful for men to give or sell their inheritance. By this we learn what to judge of them, which are so far from giving or selling, that it is a heart-sore unto them, to see such goodly hospitals and alms houses erected for the poor, although not of their cost, yet to their grief, for they had rather be fatted with the rent of the houses, than poor and miserable maimed people should be fed with the revenues:

2 Sam. 24.24, 25

Lecture 12

these persons think nothing well spent, but that which
is bestowed in surfeiting and pleasures, in costly apparel
and dainty fare, thinking the time long till these poor
alms-men's gowns be turned into velvet coats, but I pray
God their possessions may be hospitals, not hospitals
their possessions. Other think much if a poor body get
a little Cottage to be built upon the Commons or waste
grounds, they had rather have stys for their swine, than
dwellings for such destitute souls: surely let them take
heed, that their own stys, I mean their houses, wherein
such fat hogs as themselves are, living in pleasure and in
follies, be not made worse than the silly hovel of the other, and God curse them and their posterity, because they
have hated him in his poverty: for if he which giveth to
the poor, do lend to the Lord, then he which revileth the
poor, revileth or (as Solomon saith) scorneth his maker,
then he which taketh from the poor shall rob the Lord,
and sure his judgment shall be very severe, and his damnation very swift.

Thirdly, it is lawful to sell inheritances, and to
bestow or employ the money upon the Church, so we
read of the primitive Church, how they which had land,
sold it, and brought the money, and laid it down at the
Apostles' feet, and therefore is that excellent and fearful
history of *Ananias* and *Sapphira* his wife, who keeping
back but a part of the money that was their own, and
confirming it with a lie, were suddenly stroke dead. I
would to God the niggards of our age would consider
this, which will deprive the poor of that which they owe
them, and pluck from Church and ministry, that which
is given them. But of this latter disease, few are sick
in our days, that they will sell their land to give to the
Church, rather spend it in gluttony for their belly, than
liberality for their soul; in good fellowship among ruffians, than Christian charity among the faithful, clothing themselves above their calling, that for a season they
may live like Gentlemen, and ever after in woeful slav-

Acts 2.45

ery: these singing fools of all other are most miserable, for their friends will not comfort them, their fellows will forsake them, their wealth will decay, but their woe shall be everlasting.

Lastly, by this verse we note, that women or widows had the rule of their husbands' inheritances, if they died without heirs, for here it is said, that *Boaz* buyeth it at the hand of *Naomi*, because she was her husband's heir, and being past childbearing, had given over her right to *Ruth*: this we have already showed you, was the singular care which the Lord hath over poor desolate widows, that they should not be despised, although they were barren, and therefore, for their better preferment, willed the inheritance to descend unto them: whereby we may see it is no new thing that women should be inheritors, for the daughters of *Job* had inheritances among their brethren, the daughters of *Zelophehad* had their father's lot, and *Caleb* gave his daughter *Achsah* with an inheritance unto his kinsman *Othniel*, which may suffice for proof of this matter, for the perpetuities of inheritances are condemned by God and man; but I would to God that the wealth of many women were not their undoing, and their riches the cause of their casting away; especially where friends have aspiring minds, there the misery of maidens and widows falleth in nothing sooner, for setting them aloft with wealthy portions, and forgetting what they are in nature, their riches fall to unthrifts, and themselves to lamentable want.

And moreover. After the lands, he descendeth to his marriage, which is described in this verse: wherein he protesteth that he taketh the lands, that he might also marry with the woman, and he marrieth the woman for no other cause, but to stir up the name of the dead, according to the commandment of God: for what else should move an old man, to do that in his withered age, which he refused in his lusty youth? By the which we first of all note, how wisely *Naomi* dealt with her hus-

Job 12.15
Num. 26.6,7
Judg. 1.13,14

band's inheritance: she might have kept it to get herself a good marriage, yet she giveth it to Ruth: she might have sold it to fill her purse, but she bestoweth it to prefer her daughter. Wherein she teacheth us, with what love we must do for our children, namely, that for them we must depart with our own maintenance, and unto their good, not only to the uttermost, but also beyond our power. And this is worthy to be noted of widows, which are wealthily left by their husbands, who are wont but little to care for their children, but to bestow their goods upon youthful companions: see here this *Naomi* having but a daughter in law, she giveth her the whole inheritance, as if she had been born for it: and truly, the only cause (in regard of ourselves) of all our wealth, is, that we might bestow it upon our children: how grievous is it in many places to see both lands and livings consumed by them, which never sweat for them, and many poor children, to whom of right they do pertain, to be destitute both of friends and maintenance, and all through the wanton marriages of their youthful mothers: but of this matter we have spoken already, and shall be sufficient to remember at this time.

Secondly, by this we may gather, that a marriage was a mere civil action, because in the finishing thereof, there is not used either Priest or Levite, as we may see in this place, but is only pronounced by the man in the presence of the elders, even in the place of judgment. Hence it cometh, that in ancient time we read of marriages, but never celebrated in Churches, but in private assemblies, except Princes, which were wont to make great and general feasts. For this institution that marriages should be kept in Churches, came up of late, many hundred years since the days of the Apostles: but yet must not be disannulled, but observed as a holy and commendable order: first, for the avoiding of confusion, that those which are fit, might be joined together before the faithful: secondly, for the more honor of the estate of matrimony, that

Marriage was first brought into the church in the year of Christ, 1000.

Ruth Chapter 4. verses 7-10

they might know it was with all reverence to be undertaken, seeing they came, as it were, before the face of the Almighty, there to be united. Thirdly, that they might be begun with most earnest and fervent prayers, and thereupon came the Ministers to have a hand in it. Fourthly, that it might be publicly known among all the congregation. Fifthly, that those marriages which were privately kept and concluded, might be accounted suspicious and unlawful. Wherefore we must not in any wise break this godly order of the Church of God, for as it was lawful for the godly in old time to keep them in houses, much more may the company of the faithful now celebrate them in Churches, always remembering, that we make it no article of our faith, but hold it necessary only for order and unity.

Thirdly, by this we also observe the end of all marriages, which is first for the commandment of God, and secondly for the increase of the Church. Both these are here set down by *Boaz* in these words, *To stir up the name of the dead upon his inheritance, and that the name of the dead be not put out from among his brethren.* This was the special commandment of God, that he should marry his kinsman's wife, and raise up seed to his kinsman, which was, as we lately showed you, for the multiplying of the Church. By the which we may examine all the intentions of marriage, whatsoever. First, if we do not take it in hand for the commandment of God, what hope can they ever have of the blessing of the Lord upon them; like as a laborer which setteth himself to another man's work without his consent, hath nothing for his pains: even so all they, whatsoever they be, which have married of their own brain, without respect to the Law of God, can never have or crave any blessing of the Lord, upon themselves or their posterity: Oh fearful consideration, worthy to be considered of all them, which unadvisedly go about to marry; for a wild tree bringeth forth sour fruit, and wicked parents which have no regard of

holiness in their marriages, do seldom bring any wholesome fruit to the Lord. But some will say, how shall we
know how, or in what sort to behave ourselves, that before we marry we might aim at nothing beside the commandment of God? Hearken a little, and I will briefly
instruct you out of the word of God.

First of all, the care of those that will be married, must be for the only blessing of God, which is the
very final cause of this institution. Therefore after the
flood, the Lord in the restoring all things, amongst other
confirming marriage: *Moses* saith: *And he blessed* Noah
and his sons, and said, Increase and multiply, so that they
which look for any increase or fruit of their marriage,
must first of all be assured that the Lord hath blessed
them. But how shall we obtain this blessing of God? I
answer, by diligent reading of his Word, and by prayer.
David asking this question, wherewithal a young man
shall cleanse his way? and then he answereth himself,
and saith, even by taking heed unto thy word. And *Paul*
saith, that the unmarried care for the things that please
the Lord, as if he had said, they must remain unmarried for no other cause but that they might the more
freely give themselves to the service of God. If a man
want faith, he may obtain it by prayer, and if he want the
blessing of God upon his marriage, which is a less thing
than faith, may he not obtain it by prayer? *Isaac* having been married twenty years, yet was without children,
and then he prayed for issue, and the Lord gave him two
at one time: and may not prayer obtain this for the unmarried as well as for the married? Yes verily, if either
would take the pains to use it. But oh who are they that
ever in their lives once offered up their prayers to God,
to bless them with wives or husbands? that is, that they
might be so married as the name of God might be glorified by them. Nay, what young man or woman among
a thousand in these days, that is delighted with either
prayer or preaching, but rather affect liberty, pleasure,

Gen. 9.17

Psal. 119.9

1 Cor. 7.34

Gen. 25.21,22

Ruth Chapter 4. verses 7-10

and pastime, they never think of any need they stand of these things, but rather imagine that their youthful days and years must be consumed in riotous sports, and wanton wanderings, so that most men and maidens come by their wives and husbands at feasting and dancing, by dallying and playing, chosen by outward apparel, not inward and secret virtues, which are won with vanity, kept with pride, and forsaken to the destruction of wives and husbands, therefore first seek the kingdom of God, and the righteousness thereof, and all other things shall be cast upon you.

Secondly, the intention of them that marry for the commandment of God, is that thereby they might live more soberly in their several vocations; for as the wanton ox is bridled in the yoke, so unruled youth is governed by marriage, for if we regard the mind of them that marry, it is stayed upon one, if the company of the body, it is bound to one, if life, it cannot be solitary, if wealth, it must not be possessed alone. Therefore *Peter* said, husbands dwell with your wives like men of knowledge; as if he had said, in your unmarried time you were wanderers, but now you are married, you are dwellers; in your unmarried age you were inconstant, but now you are married you are as unmoveable as a house; when you were single, you were ignorant, but now you be married, be men of knowledge: and finally, when you were young, you were troubled with the desire of many, but now you are married, you are comforted with the love of one; and as a man without a dwelling place, so is the unmarried without a companion. Such is the commodity of marriage, if it be duly considered, and each party rightly instructed, that it is as sleep to a weary man, as wine to the thirsty, as a house to the harborless, and as a garment against winter; and therefore is it compared to the fellowship of Christ with his Church. How then cometh it to pass, that men live more riotously being married, than when they are unmarried, for they amend nothing,

1 Pet. 3.7

Eph. 5.5-9

but think all things as lawful for them then, as it was before, their houses without their presence, their wives without their company, their families without their government, so that you shall see married persons wandering abroad, as if they were unmarried, disporting themselves as shamefully and as loosely as any in the world: not living in sobriety and modesty, like the Turtle Dove, but in gaming and dancing like the wanton Goat; these parties never married for the commandment of God, but some rash desire possessed their minds, and a little youthful lust tickled their fancies, much like the savor of juniper, which continueth but a little while. Other are so far from this point to marry, that they might live more soberly, that they make their marriages the cover of their dishonesty, making the world believe they live in perfect chastity, because they are married, but privily they give themselves to most filthy adulteries: but the Apostle saith, marriage is honorable, but adulterers God will judge, that is, will utterly condemn; and if their behaviors were well examined, you should find this the cause, that their houses cannot hold them. The filthiness of these parties is condemned by the very brute beasts, and shall be punished by the severe judgment of God: for they which make the members of Christ the members of harlots, shall be with harlots the members of the Devil: therefore marry for modesty, not for filthiness, that your ungoverned age may be bridled with the consideration of your present estate, your wearied days may be quieted in the bed of godly, holy, and honorable marriage. *Heb. 13.4*

Thirdly, they which marry for obedience unto God, must only mind godly and not wealthy matches, they must look on the heart, not on the face, they must weigh the disposition, and not the riches, they must not say, as the Devil said to Christ, all this will I give, but they must say, as *Jacob's* sons said to *Shechem* and *Hamor*, if you will be circumcised, you shall have our sister: that is, if you fear God, and receive his true knowl- *Matt. 4* *Gen. 34.15*

Ruth Chapter 4. verses 7-10

edge, if you love his Word, and honor his sacraments, if you can benefit the souls as well as the bodies: But a man may weary himself many days, before he find any of this inclination, for parents will deny their consents, if they see not the riches for their daughters' husbands, or sons' wives, keeping them in continual burning, for lack of this wealthy liquor; And I know many parents which have cast off their children for poor marriages, but never any for the wealthy, were they never so wicked: therefore whosoever for this cause, denieth right to his child, shall be more faulty for their ungodly disposition, than the children for their unadvised marriage. Now in these days it is a wonder to see how the minds of men and women can love for wealth, that even as a harlot humbleth herself for money to him, whom otherwise she would not look upon, so men and women will marry themselves for wealth, where, if there were poverty, they would think them unworthy to be their servants. I marvel, if the heathen law were now in force, that no man should give anything to their daughter's marriage, in what time of their days would these men marry? truly I think they would never marry, except it were to make drudges of their wives. But these are not of *Boaz* his mind, for he marrieth a stranger, who had but little wealth, because the Lord so commanded to take his kinsman's wife; although he might have refused, yet he was contented for this cause, to buy her, as he saith in this verse: to teach us, that if God bid us to marry, that is, if we find in our own consciences that we cannot live otherwise, then rather adventure thy wealth, than the displeasure of God. But some will say, is it not lawful to desire and to sue for wealthy marriages? Yea verily with this affection, that thou like thy choice, as well if there were little, as now there is much. And therefore thou must evermore remember these cautions, both in the choosing and using of a wealthy marriage. First, that thou desire it, to the intent thou mayest be more able to

Acts 20.35

do good to thy brethren that want, for it is a more blessed thing to give than to receive. Secondly, that thou mayest the more freely give thyself privately, and publicly, to the service of God; for we know that poverty taketh our greatest time to labor for wife and family, but the wealthy need less labor, and may apply the more time to the service of God: therefore was it that *Paul* said, the married care for the things of this life to please their wives: showing, that it is one misery upon the poor, when they are married, that they are troubled about worldly and necessary provision, but if these things be supplied by a good marriage, thou mayest praise God with the greater diligence.

1 Cor. 7.34

But who are they which have desired or obtained a wealthy marriage for either of these causes? if the poor should go in collection for relief of them, which for this occasion have richly joined themselves, what should they gather, or how far should they go? to how many persons might they come, before they get a shilling? Truly for this cause they desire them, some, that they might lavish out the more in riotous expenses, with the rich man in the Gospel, to feed in pleasure, to be clothed in silk, to maintain dogs, hounds, hawks, horses, and retinues of idle men, but never the Church of God fareth the better for them. Again, by their wealth, they have idleness and time to wander abroad, here to feast and to make merry, there to play and disport themselves in bodily exercises, and worldly vanities, but never one hour the more is spent in the service of God, but much the less, for the Devil's sweet and pleasant baits draw away their minds from the consideration of their own miseries. Again, they are many times a thousand fold more clogged with the cares of their wealth, than the poorest soul to provide bread for his family by his bodily labor. Lastly, their desire is to leave great possessions to their posterity, that the honor of their houses may be increased, and the name of their memory might be ev-

Ruth Chapter 4. verses 7-10

erlastingly recorded, so that neither the glory of God,
the promoting of the Gospel, the relieving of the faithful, or the succoring of Jesus Christ himself, is any part
of the thought of these covetous wretches, but as they
desire the inheritances of the Lord, to be their portion
in this present life, so they have them for the canker of
their souls, the rust to consume them, the care to torment them, the fear to forsake them, the love to enjoy
them, the travail to increase them, and the reckoning
for abusing them, to their endless confusion. Therefore,
except the Lord do build the house, their labor is but in
vain that build it, except the Lord make the marriage, the
Psal. 37.16 riches of *Solomon* cannot continue them, for better is a
little that the righteous hath, than the great possessions
of the ungodly.

Lastly, he that marrieth for obedience unto God,
must have this care to provide beforehand things honest
and lawful for the present maintenance of wife and fam-
Gen. 24.35 ily. Therefore when *Abraham's* servants came to the City
of Nahor, among others, which he told unto *Laban*, and
Rebekah the mother of *Rebekah*, he showed them what cattle, and
flocks, servants and maidens, his master had, which all
should be *Isaac's*, thereby signifying, that all necessary
provision for their maintenance was already procured,
Gen. 30.32,33 and there wanted nothing, but a wife for *Isaac*. So *Jacob*
after his fourteen years' service with *Laban*, covenanteth
to have the profit of the flocks which should be spotted, and this was when he knew he was to depart from
his father in law, and therefore was bound to provide for
himself. Now this provision is not so meant, as though
everyone were bound to get all things beforehand, which
are needful to marriage, but it is required that everyone
should procure somewhat according to their degree, and
the maintenance of their calling. This point is clearer
than the sun, and it serveth to the reproving of them,
which run headlong to marry one day, but fall into woeful beggary the next, neither houses to dwell in, labor to

work on, meat to sustain them, money to procure them, friends to relieve them, or credit to help them, only wives and husbands they must needs have, not caring what shall become of them afterward. And truly, if the hurt did only redound to their own hindrance, the pity was the less: but woeful it is to tell, how their miserable posterity are thereby (even through their parents rashness) brought to everlasting poverty, and such as is most lamentable, for their minds are not instructed, they have no knowledge of the true God, neither can they pray to their comfort, or hope for any salvation. If it were but the labor and poverty of the body, it were much to be desired, and nothing to be feared; but being the endangering of both body and soul, how much is it to be disliked, that any for their own lusts should leave their wretched posterity to the power of the Devil. Therefore beloved, counsel your acquaintance to be careful for their children as well as themselves, first to try, and then trust, first to prepare somewhat, that if sickness come or charges come, or age overtake thee, yet then thou mayest comfort thyself with thy own gotten goods, and rather be helpful, than chargeable to any.

Fourthly, by this that *Boaz* saith, he taketh *Ruth* to wife, for to stir up the name of the dead, and that the name of the dead be no more forgotten among his brethren in the gate of his place: We note, that our marriages must be taken in hand also to this end, for the multiplying of the Church of God; we have already showed how one cause of this brother's marriage was for that use and purpose, and in this place not unnecessary to confirm. For the law of this marriage was special only for God his people, and therefore for the augmenting of the number of the Lord's flock. And as this was among the Jews, that every family might have some temporal inheritors, even so is it among the Gentiles, that if it be possible, everyone should bring one infant or other, to be an inheritor of the Lord's kingdom. By the which parents are taught to be more careful for the education and instruction of their children, than for their procreation and birth, for they are made the fathers and mothers of Christ in his members; therefore they must not leave him to *Herod*, that is, they must not give their children to the power of Satan, by their negligence and want of teaching: they are accursed that lay stumbling-blocks before the blind, and shall not they also that lead them into the sea, where is nothing but drowning? even so if godless parents do lead their children, and innocent babes, into damnable ignorance, who shall answer for their souls? shall not the authors of this destruction? Had not parents need then to look to themselves, for if they have as much gold as *Solomon* had, and as great inheritances as *Caleb* had, and as much possession of Cattle as *Job* had, yet if they be not able to bring up their children in the fear of God, it were better for parents and children they had never been born, than miserably to live in wealth, and be every hour in danger of damnation. But how then will you say, must we be careful for the instruction of our children? I answer, you must be careful for these two things: first, that you teach them that which is good: secondly, that you give no evil example unto them.

Concerning the first, for the teaching of them the truth, you must first teach them the matter of their faith, and secondly, how to pray. The matter of their faith is contained in the twelve Articles, commonly called our Creed or Belief, which every father and mother is bound to teach their children, with the pure understanding thereof, and as they be able to show them the proofs thereof, out of the Word of God, I mean, as the children be able to receive it. Herein, they must instruct them of the miserable estate of mankind after their fall, by the use and understanding of the Moral Law, contained in the two Tables of the ten Commandments, with the proofs thereof out of the Scripture, and the deliverance by the death and blood-sheading of Jesus Christ, the eternal and only begotten son of God.

Again, you must teach them to pray according as the Lord hath taught us in that form which we call the Lord's prayer, with the understanding thereof, out of the Word of God, for except you teach them what they pray Matt. 6.9 for by the understanding of it, you were as good to teach them in Greek or Latin, as in English. For there are many thousands in England that call God Father in their prayers, but I know not that there be any which know the meaning of the Word. I myself have reasoned with many both young and old, and of men of good calling in the world, about that one word, which is the easiest and plainest in all the word of God, but some few excepted, which have labored for knowledge in the hearing of Sermons: I never met with man, woman, nor child, that could give me any reasonable answer unto this question beside this, that God made them, and therefore is their Father, which every Jew, and almost every Pagan knoweth as well as they: Therefore as our righteousness must exceed the righteousness of the Scribes and Pharisees, Jews and Gentiles, so must our knowledge also, for by our knowledge of Christ we are justified to be his members. And although we repeat the Lord's Prayer a thousand times every day, and understand it not, we do but babble before the Lord, taking his name in vain, using it in our lips, when our hearts have no understanding, and therefore our prayers are without fruit.

Lastly, if you yourselves do not walk before them without reproof, in pure and sanctified conversations, whatsoever you teach them, you presently tread out again, for simple people and young children live by examples, and not by precept: if you teach them to worship God, you must also before their faces worship the same, that they may practice by your example. If you bid them that they swear not, you yourself must be careful not to swear, or else they will not believe you; for as the people look upon the life of their pastor, so the young

Ruth Chapter 4. verses 7-10

children behold the steps of their parents. And we see in brute beasts that examples are much more effectual than precepts; they cannot speak, yet how do they train up their young ones? It is reported of the Harts [*deer*] of Scythia, that they teach their young ones to leap from bank to bank, from rock to rock, from one turf to another by their own example, leaping before them, which otherwise they would never practice, by which means, when they are hunted, no beast can ever take them. Even so, if you go before your children in example while they are young, Satan the hunter and roaring Lion shall never have them for his pray. When they learn to speak, they take the words from our own mouths: even so when they shall learn to worship, fear, love, honor, and pray unto the Lord, let them take you for their examples, as *Jacob* did *Abraham* and *Isaac*. Now let us give praise to God.

Gen. 31.53

The Thirteenth Lecture

Ruth Chapter 4. verses 11,12

11 *And all the people that were in the gate, and the elders said, we are witnesses: the Lord make the wife that cometh into thy house, like* Rachel *and* Leah, *which twain did build the house of Israel, and that thou mayest do worthily in Ephratah, and be famous in Bethlehem.*

12 *And that thy house be like the house of* Pharez, *whom* Tamar *bore unto* Judah, *of the seed which the Lord shall give thee of this young woman.*

s we have hitherto heard of *Boaz* and his kinsman, the one in resigning, and the other in receiving his right, in the place of judgment, and the presence of the elders and people. So now the holy Ghost proceedeth to declare unto us, the behavior of this latter sort at this marriage of *Boaz*: which is their answer unto that speech of *Boaz*, when he calleth them to witness the bargain.

The words do easily divide themselves into two parts, the first is their confessions, to be witnesses of the contract, in these words: *Then spake all the people and elders, we are witnesses.* The second part is the prayer they make for *Boaz* and *Ruth* in the next words, consisting of two members; the first is the fruitfulness of *Ruth*, when they pray she may be like *Rachel* and *Leah*: that he may be wealthy in *Ephratah, and famous in Bethlehem*: The second member of this second part is for the blessing of God upon the posterity of these two new married persons: In the twelfth verse, that their house might be like the house of *Pharez* the son of *Judah*, which till that time, had the chiefest dignity in the tribe of *Judah*, and so continued till the Scepter was taken from *Judah*, and the Lawgiver from between his feet, which was almost fifteen hundred years, until the reign of the Idumean *Herod*. Of these parts let us briefly speak in order, by the assistance of God his heavenly Spirit, and the permission of the time.

And all the people. These words as we showed you, are the first part, wherein the rulers and people acknowledge their testimony with one consent, freely yielding unto the request of *Boaz*, and willingly rejoicing at that so strange a matter, when one of the chief of their elders, for love of the law of God, would to his own discommodity, marry with a stranger, and so base a woman, looking neither on birth nor wealth, but on the hidden man of the heart, making virtue his choice, and religion his portion. Out of the which we note.

First, that it is the duty of the godly, willingly in any good matter to give their testimony for their brethren: for men in this latter age are grown so fearful, that they will hardly testify the truth, for dread of some evil that might ensue thereby: these persons are not of the mind of these godly Jews, both Elders and others in this place, which of their own accord, give witness unto *Boaz* for the purchase of his land, and the marriage of his wife: so we read the people witnessed with *Samuel* when *Saul* was a chosen king: yea against their own selves, because they had refused him to be their king, and chose a king to reign over them, after the manner of the heathen. This is the more worthy to be considered in this place, because this people did not after any scoffing manner, but soberly and in the fear of God (as appeareth by their

1 Sam. 12.4,5

prayer) witness this contract unto *Boaz*: the world in these days, if the like thing should fall out, that an old man in the presence of so great a congregation, should take to his wife so young a woman, would rather mock, scorn and disdain it, than with such reverent modesty pray for it: For herein the world showeth itself, which is wont to condemn that in others, which in themselves they highly commend, and to look but upon the outward appearance, discerning and judging but with bodily eyes and carnal minds, yet here these Jews Bethlemites, shall speak for the godly, not deriding strange actions, not denying their voices to a lawful condition, not judging but with a spiritual eye, piercing through the bark of human body, into the soul of a godly old man: and this is the more commendable, because the magistrates and elders themselves join them to the people in so godly proceeding, by whose example, it is no doubt, the wavering multitude was much encouraged.

And this teacheth us how excellent is the profession and forwardness of men in authority, upon whom the eyes of the commonwealth dependeth: they are never alone, but as all beasts and creatures followed *Noah* into his ark, because he went before, so all sorts will follow their disposition, be it good or evil: We read of the wicked Judges of Jezreel which condemned innocent *Naboth*, had also wicked witnesses against him, for such as *Ahab* and *Jezebel* were, such were their Judges, and such as the Judges were, the same were the people: if they be godly, the lights of their lives will shine unto others; if they be profane, their darkness is like the darkness of Egypt, which spread itself over all the land. Oh how comfortable is your presence at our godly assemblies to the despised members of Christ: if you come, many come: if you abide at home, many follow your steps, the soldiers will follow their captains, into the hottest skirmishes, but without them, it is a grief to go into the easiest battles: so right Worshipful, if you continue your diligence in

1 Kings 21.12, 13

Ruth Chapter 4. verses 11,12

hearing the Gospel, we your underlings and servants will follow you to the farthest; but if you fall away, we are discouraged also: one word of your mouths in the commendation of goodness, is like golden apples in dishes of silver; but one step of your travail to the mountain of Sion in the company of the faithful, is like the company of *Jonathan* and his armor-bearer, to drive a whole army of ungodly Philistines from the tents of God's saints: If *Gideon* be once named, what are the company of the Midianites: if the magistrate or gentleman frequent the exercises of Religion, all the mouths of the swinish Atheists, which tread the pearls of the Gospel under their feet, are stopped. Look upon the Eunuch to Queen *Candace*, which came every year many hundred miles to worship at Jerusalem: he was a noble man, yet it was discredit to his honor to be diligent in God his service. Look upon that noble *Theophilus*, to whom *Luke* dedicateth his books, when all the world persecuted Christ, yet he suffered his name to be foremost in the Gospel, that none should be discouraged at the profession of Christ, when such a noble man would suffer his name to go publicly in the book. Look upon the noble woman of Thessalonica, which in greatest danger joined themselves to the profession of the Gospel. Look upon that excellent Lady, to whom *John* writeth his second Epistle, and her sister also, whose children favored and confessed the Gospel, as well as their parents, the day would not suffice to follow all that I might; these went before in the world, and before in the Lord, that is, they were noted in wealth, but notable in Religion, they were singular in authority, but excellent in Christianity, the memory of their wealth is lost, but the record of their faith remaineth registered in God his book forever. These men and women were worthy of their places, such as could rule their riches by the Word, feed their servants with the Gospel, and clothe their souls with Jesus Christ.

Secondly, by this we note, that seeing they all

1 Sam. 14.16

Judg. 7.20

Acts 8.27
Luke 14

Acts 1.1

Acts 17.4

witnessed, and they all prayed for *Boaz*: the duty of them that are gathered together in any godly assembly, which is to join themselves in the same holy exercises: if they hear, the other must hear; if they pray, the other must pray: if they sing, the other must also sing: for this is the fellowship of the saints, or else nothing is: When we read the church of God continued together in breaking bread: it is also said they continued in prayer, as if the holy Ghost had said, even as everyone did eat bread, so everyone did pray to the Lord: as it availeth not a hungry man to see another eat, and he have none, but rather increaseth his desire: so if you be every day and hour where prayers are made, and your selves taste not of them, it doth but increase your damnation: So we read when the Apostles were forbidden to preach in the name of Christ, they came to their fellows and lift up their voices with one accord to the Lord, and when they had prayed, the place was shaken where they were assembled, and they all were filled with the holy Ghost, and spake the word of God boldly, such is the effect of God his faithful, when they pray unto him with one accord, like the assault of the four winds upon Job's children's house, which not only shook but also overturned the same: many hands make a great labor to be lightly dispatched, and many men's prayers do pull down the mercies of God upon us. This I think is very needful for our days, wherein this dullness is grown so gross, that among a church full of hearers, you shall have very few which are not faulty in this doctrine: for it is a world to see how many have their bodies at the sermons, but their souls and affections are wandering in a thousand matters: these pray not when we pray, hear not when we preach, neither sing when we sing. What profit have these persons by our prayers, or preaching: surely, they are idols, they have tongue but speak not; ears but hear not; eyes but they see not. And this is most lamentable, to see many upon whom the Lord hath bestowed this gift of reading or learning, to

Acts 2.46

Acts 4.23,31

Ruth Chapter 4. verses 11,12

come hand over head to Churches, without either book or mind to profit themselves or other: Thus they bury the graces of God in them, they quench the fire of the holy Spirit; they lose the costs of their parents, which they bestowed to bring them to learning; they disdain to sing with the faithful, they abhor the labors of their youth, and mock the Lord with their presence: Look upon it my brethren, for if the Lord have given any of you learning, that you are able to read his word, then he hath planted you to bear fruit in his own orchard, but if you use not this gift, then you are fruitless trees, and the Lord will cut you down and cast you into unquenchable fire, if you say you have no books: I answer, the fault lieth in yourselves, for if you be poor, ask the godly and your want shall be supplied: if you be wealthy, save some of your idle expenses to spend upon such a holy business. If you say you forget your books behind you, I answer, it is a sign you care but little for your journey's end, for if you had that reverence, to come prepared to the exercises of the faithful, which you ought to have, you could not forget your Bibles, nay, you should rather forget your apparel, than your books, if you considered as it becometh you. But some say, they understand well enough, though they say not *Amen* to our prayers, and though they sing not to the Lord with us: but *Paul* saith to such, that they do no good to their brethren, because they edify them not, and that it is better in the Church to speak five words to instruct others, than ten thousand for his own benefit: for in the Church we are assembled for our brethren, not for ourselves only, and whosoever prayeth not with his brethren in the Church or congregation, doth break the fellowship of the faithful, and standeth for a cipher among the saints: Therefore if you have any care of your duty to the Lord, of the love of the faithful, of obedience to your parents, of increasing your talent of learning, or the salvation of your own souls, both magistrate and subject, elders and people, rich and poor, old

1 Cor. 14.16, 17

and young, men and women, fulfill the expectation of
the godly, pray when we pray, sing with us when we sing,
hear us when we preach: for with such sacrifice is the
Lord pleased.

The Lord make. Now we have made an end of
the first part, let us go to the second, which is the prayer
of these people and elders, the first member whereof
is contained in these words, wherein they pray for the
fruitfulness of *Ruth,* alleging an example to testify the
love they bear to *Boaz,* that they desire his wife to be as
fruitful as either *Leah,* or *Rachel,* who built the house of
Israel, so that they would have him the father of much
people, insomuch as his name both of wealth and children, might advance the dignity of *Bethlehem Ephratah.*

First, therefore hence we note the duty of all the
godly, which is to pray for the welfare one of another,
but especially in marriage, for the prayers of the faithful are as needful for the married as skillful mariners, in
the boat of passengers. Therefore we read of few godly
marriages in the Scripture, but they were celebrated with
prayer, when *Rebecca* was married to *Isaac,* her mother, Gen. 24.60
brother, and friends prayed that she might grow up into
thousand thousands, and her seed to possess their enemies' gate: and in this place these friends of *Boaz* pray
the like for *Ruth,* for what make the peoples' presence,
the multitude of lookers, the number of acquaintance, at
the time of celebrating marriages, except it be to pray for
the parties, we have showed you the last Sabbath, that for
the ignorance of the people, which could not pray, came
the ministers to have a hand in it, for supplying their
want: and how lamentable is it to see in many places,
and most persons that are married, where their company are none but godless ruffians, ignorant Atheists, profane swearers, and notable blasphemers, to be present at
their unhappy weddings, what prayers can these pour
forth, for their new married friends? can the Cockatrice
breathe forth anything but poison, or the Spider spin any

sounder cloth than her web? no more can these persons, but curse them with their prayers, not bless them with their cursings: is it not a world to see how many against their marriages compass the country, some to provide delicate diversities of meats, to feed both the belly and the eye, others to invite their friends, which come ruffling into the Churches, in silks, velvets, satins, and soft apparel, and some to deck up themselves in brave clothing, against their marriage day, but never one thought for the faithful prayer of the godly, that their prosperous life may be blessed in wedlock, this they ought to be most careful for, and yet not to leave the other undone, but godly prayers are better than great portions, and it is better to have poor Christ at our weddings, than a thousand thousand of these glistering gallants. Truly, in these days how do men and women provide for mirth, not for modesty, that their day of marriage may be joyful with worldly disports, not godly with Christian exercises: they buy and hire musicians, to pass the time in pleasant dancing, but never entreat or speak one word to the godly, to bestow their hearty prayers upon them. Let therefore beloved, this be our direction, that as we marry for the Lord, not for the world, so we study for prayer, and not for pleasure.

Secondly, by this we gather that the greatest blessing in marriage is the bearing of children, the blessing upon the vine, is to bring many grapes, the blessing upon the earth is to be fruitful in bringing and springing much corn and pastures: the blessing on the sea, is the multiplying of the fish, and the blessing of marriage is many children: Therefore in this place they pray that *Ruth* might be like *Rachel* and *Leah*, which built all Israel, that is, they were the mothers of a great nation, they multiplied in their posterity to a number like the stars of heaven. For this cause the first blessing upon mankind after the flood, was that they should increase and fill the earth, for this cause the fathers desired children so

Gen. 9.1

much, and the overlove of many children, increased the multitude of their wives: and for this cause the Apostle saith, that women through bearing of children shall be saved, if they continue in faith, and love, and holiness   1 Tim. 2.15 with modesty. For all other blessings may be had without marriage, wealth and riches, comfort and friends, honor and pleasure, quietness and rest, may be found in the lives of unmarried persons, only children must come of a grafted stock, which is a holy and sanctified marriage, or wedlock. When *Abraham* wanted a son, he prayed for one: when *Rebecca* was barren, *Isaac* prayed for her, and she conceived: When *Manoah* wanted children, he prayed, and the Lord gave him *Sampson*: when *Hannah* was barren, she prayed and obtained *Samuel*: and when *Zacharias* and *Elizabeth* had no issue, by prayer they obtained *John Baptist*. So they accounted of their marriage without children, as a fair and pleasant garden without fruits, and as the one doth fructify by seasonable showers, so the other doth multiply by faithful supplications: Therefore here this people of God pray for *Boaz* and *Ruth*, that many pleasant twigs may spring out of their fruitful bodies. By the which we see the ready remedy for barrenness, which are godly and zealous prayers, poured forth into the ears of the Almighty, that he would remove his hand from punishing, and withdraw the curse of barrenness from penitent sinners. But in our prayers we must alway take heed that we appoint not the Lord what he shall give us, either sons or daughters, but rest upon the will of God to receive either of both.

And indeed be it that children are the greatest blessing of marriage, yet all things considered, it is much happier to be barren, for our miserable days, and sinful lives call for a scourge, and once more the saying of Christ shall be fulfilled, that there shall be woe to them   Matt. 24 that are with child, and that give suck in those days, yea undoubtedly our posterity count them happy that are unborn, and themselves shall wish with *Job* and *Jeremiah* they had never seen the sun. Oh who are they that have any desire of many children? Look upon the world, it falleth to Atheism: look upon the Church, it declineth to error: look upon the Gospel, it is persecuted by the Devil, and view every degree, if corruption groweth not upon them: truly, truly as *Esau* said, the days of mourning for my father will shortly come, so may all the faithful say, the day of mourning for the Gospel and knowledge will one day come, and the Lord knoweth how soon. Therefore if you would leave your children to be Atheists, your issue to be heretics, your posterity to be afflicted, and all your offspring to be corrupted, and miserably punished in this life, or eternally plagued in the life to come, then desire little children. Be it, you can provide lands to maintain them, teachers to instruct them, learning to defend them, honor to advance them, friends to assist them, and castles of security to keep them from the hurt of the world: yet alas, alas, into how many thousand adversities may their souls descend, I speak not this to discourage any from desiring children, but I admonish from the Lord that you be wise in your petitions, and think as well of your infant's misery, as your own suffering: now you desire ease without pains, but they in all manner of afflictions may send up cries to the heavens and not be heard. Oh that all degrees both married and unmarried, would have pity on their posterity, before they be born, then should fewer be vagabonds than now are, and more be provided for than now can be, then should men and women for their children's sake amend their loose and desperate behavior not fit for Pagans, much less for Christians, lest the children should be plagued for the father's fault: Assuredly beloved, the Lord hath spoken it, that if your children prove wicked, they shall suffer and bear the sins of all their ancestors, yea though they be dead many hundred years ago.

Thirdly, by this prayer of these elders and peo-

Gen. 27.41

ple, we note that for the helping of our weakness in prayer, and relieving of our wants, we may set before us the goodness of God unto others. In this place they pray that *Ruth* may be as fruitful as *Rachel* and *Leah*, which were the wives of *Jacob*, who bare him eight sons and one daughter, expressing their hearty prayer for *Boaz* and *Ruth*, by the example of these twain. The like we may read of the Apostles, when they prayed after their Acts 4.25 deliverance from the rulers and elders, they allege *David* for their help, as he speaketh in the second Psalm. For we many times know not what to ask as we ought, but the spirit which wrought these gifts in the fathers, helpeth our infirmities by the examples of the ancient godly, that we should ask the same graces which they enjoyed, to lead the same lives which they lived, and obtain the same crown, wherewith they are all rewarded. Yet we must always remember the rule of the Apostle, that this is our assurance, if we crave anything according to 1 John 5.14 his will, we receive it: that is, we must not desire the least thing in worldly affairs, but under this condition, If it be thy will, O God, because the Lord is not bound to give us anything, no more than we are to give every beggar that asketh an alms of us, but if we absolutely crave without this exception, we break the law of prayer, and bring the majesty of God into bondage by our petitions.

    This teacheth us this profitable lesson, that before we pray, we should learn and consider our wants by the word of God, that we ask not at the hands of the Almighty, anything beside that which is godly, honest, and lawful: for many I am persuaded, do suddenly and unadvisedly start up into the presence of the Lord, with rash and ungodly desires, because they want the knowledge of the word of God, and the due consideration of those things which they want. Of this sort are all the prayers of the Papists, for they neither understand their prayers in a strange tongue, nor yet will examine them by the word of God: Unto these I add the prayers and wishes of

Ruth Chapter 4. verses 11,12

the ignorant multitude, which are as far from the prayers of the faithful, as the Moon is from the earth. For as it is impossible for a man to go without his legs, or to see without his eyes, so is it impossible for these to pray without the knowledge of the Gospel: For in our prayers we must speak to the Lord in his own tongue, as he speaketh in his word, but what can these persons bring out of the treasures of the holy Scriptures? scant one sentence in the whole Gospel rightly understood, how then can they bring the matter of their whole prayers, if they want but one thing that will suffice? but who is living which standeth not in need of many thousand mercies? But I know their old excuse, for they say they pray according to the Scripture, when they repeat the Lord's prayer, which is set down in the Scripture: to whom I answer, they do well if they understand it, but where do they find those wishes to grow rich, those curses upon them with whom they are angry, whether it be man or beast, and tell me the understanding of one petition in the Lord's prayer. Therefore beloved, pray in spirit, but pray in understanding also, use the Scripture for the rule of your supplication, for as no man can say that Jesus is the Lord, but only by the Spirit of God; so none can pray rightly, but by the knowledge of the Gospel: If you once entertain this knowledge of God his word, then you will do with it as a cunning workman in his trade: he will ever take delight in his work and occupation, even so if you had this this feeling, you would delight in prayer, which now is a hell unto many, then your hearts both privately would be as studious in meditating goodness, as ever they were desirous of worldly pleasure, and would publicly breathe after it as the Hart [deer] in his chase doth after the well-springs. But oh, dearly beloved, this condemneth men of hatred of God, of the pride of themselves, of ignorance in the truth, of coldness in Religion, of trusting in the world, misspending of time, loving of pleasure, and lack of devotion, that they are as hardly drawn to prayer, according to the common Proverb, as a Hare taken with a tabret. Think you that these persons, which absent themselves from public petitions and private prayers, have any love of God in them: nay, are not those condemned which are drawn to them against their will, and where shall these cursed companions appear, which forsake sermons, go out of Churches, lie idly at home, and are disporting themselves in bravery abroad, when the time of prayer calleth for their presence at home or in the Church? do they not separate themselves from the faithful in this life? and therefore they shall be miserably damned with the Devil and his angels, and everlastingly excluded from Christ and his Saints.

Fourthly, by this prayer of these elders we observe, that we must especially pray for the multiplying and augmenting of the faithful, for they pray that *Ruth* may be like, not to the daughters of *Lot*, of whom came the cursed *Moabites* and *Ammonites*: nor yet to *Rebecca*, of whom came the ungodly *Edomites*: nor yet to *Keturah*, from whom came the godless *Midianites* and *Arabians*, but to *Rachel* and *Leah,* which built the house of *Israel,* that is, which increased the Lord's people, which multiplied the heirs of the promised land, and augmented the number of the faithful. This our Savior commanded to be done, next to the glorifying of God: for first we say, Hallowed be thy name; and then, Thy kingdom come, which is, first that the Spirit might reign in our hearts, and then that more saints may be added to the Church. For we must pray for the multiplying of the friends, and not for the enemies of Christ. For this cause *Paul* compareth marriage to the conjunction between Christ and his Church: for as the one engendereth many saints, so the other must beget many faithful members: and truly as one pearl is worth ten thousand pebbles, so one good child is better to the parents, than many thousands of evil. The use of this doctrine is, that we should not be like the Jews, desirous of many children, because our fami-

Eph. 5.24,25

Ruth Chapter 4. verses 11,12

lies should grow great, but like the Doves which bring forth few, which might be the children of innocency: the Elephant being the greatest, and yet the meekest beast, conceaveth but once in all her time, whereas the lesser and more hurtful creatures increase many, yet it is better for the first to have but one, which are good and hurtless, than for the latter to have many, which are evil and harmful: even so beloved, it is good to increase Doves and not Serpents, Elephants and not Tigers, and better is one *Isaac* the son of promise, than a thousand *Ishmaels,* the children of bondage: We know the most precious herbs bring the least fruits, and that is not the best which doth most of all multiply, so the godly like good trees, must rather desire one or two children like themselves, and to bring forth and grow in issue sparingly, by little and little, than suddenly to swell up like the waves of the

Gen. 25.16,21   sea. We read that *Ishmael* had twelve sons, all princes, but *Isaac* his brother had only twain, *Jacob* and *Esau*, and them he obtained by prayer, so hardly the godly are born and conceived, when with the wicked they come as thick as the hailstones in Egypt, for the confusion of the fruit of the land. Therefore as the seed is cast in vain upon the land, which the Fowls do presently devour, so those children had been better they had never been born, whom darkness blindeth, ignorance possesseth, malice ruleth, ungodliness leadeth, and Satan tormenteth: for the fewest number are the godliest posterity, in whom light shineth, knowledge dwelleth, meekness reigneth, godliness guideth, and Christ eternally blesseth.

Fifthly, by the prayer of these people we note, the second blessing of a godly marriage, which is to gather by lawful means much wealth: for that which in the English is, *do worthily in Ephratah;* in the Hebrew is, *gather wealth in Ephratah*: For it is more general in the English, than in the original, for to gather wealth by honest means, is to do worthily, because it is the blessing of God: Therefore we will take the surest and the safest interpretation, by the which this collection is confirmed, and their meaning is, that *Boaz* which in his marriage respected not riches, should by his godly choice enjoy a virtuous wife, to bring up faithful children, and increase his substance by the blessing of God, that he might advance the honor of their Country and City. Neither is this unknown that after children, the growing in wealth is the next blessing of the Lord, as *Abraham's* servant telleth *Laban*, the Lord hath blessed my master exceedingly, and made him very great, for he hath given him flocks and herds, silver and gold, servants and maidens, Camels and Asses, all this did the Lord bless *Abraham* with after his marriage with *Sara*: Again, the holy Ghost describing *Job*, after his children, which were seven sons and three daughters, he reckoneth his wealth, and saith: His possession was seven thousand Cattle, three thousand Camels, five hundred yoke of Oxen and five hundred she Asses, with a great household. For wealth in marriage, is the best servant that can be entertained, I might speak of many more, but few persuasions will suffice in this point, because wealth was wont to be the maid, and godliness the mistress: but now riches is become the mistress, and Religion the maid: For wealth, men rise early and go late to bed, labor diligently, and fare hardly, travail earnestly, and sweat painfully, and I can find no fault but with too much following this wealthy trade: For first of all, I must complain with *Solomon*, that there is but one and not a second, who hath neither brother nor son, yet there is no end of his labor, neither is his eye satisfied with riches, for this old canker infecteth every age, whereby it is a pleasure to certain covetous wretches, to toil their bodies with untimely labors, to clog their minds with golden cares, and to weary their senses in numbering their wealth: and what is the end hereof? surely this, the gatherer is like an Ass which carrieth the treasure but cannot use it, being laid on his back it must be taken off again: the heirs like the drones spend all, but gather none, for

Gen. 24.35

Job 1.3

Eccles. 4.8

Eccles. 6.2

Ruth Chapter 4. verses 11,12

as they sweat not for it, as it was in getting, so they spare not as long as it lasteth, lavishing out that in riotous company, which was gathered in covetous encroaching. Others, that they may thrive, count all things lawful: for they say God hath given the earth to the children of men, therefore they spend the sabbaths in buying and selling, in bargaining and laboring: they get by right and wrong, forgery and deceit, play and work, neither lands nor cattle come amiss to them, so they may have them: But we must alway remember, that we neither go to the right hand nor to the left, that is if thou have many children, thou must use no unlawful means to keep them: if thou have none, thou must not hoard up thy wealth, as if thou haddest some, but remember the day of adversity, and deal somewhat for thy present need, and not altogether for thy own commodity.

But you will say, show us some brief rules, by which we may practice the truth: by your favorable audience I will give you these three rules: the first is in getting, the second in keeping, and the third in departing from it.

Concerning the first, which is getting of wealth; first our only care must be for the blessing of God to increase us: we have an excellent example in *Jacob*, having nothing in the world beside his wives and children, yet would receive no wages of *Laban*, but promised his service for the spotted Lambs, choosing rather to depend upon the blessing of God, than the policy of his own wit, to testify his uprightness in the presence of *Laban*, and to teach us all, that thriving cometh more by the favor of the Lord, than the wisdom of the world. For *Laban* thought he had made a good bargain for himself, which indeed proved to his great hindrance, even so when men think they have compassed the world to increase their profit, suddenly the Lord sendeth a cross to disappoint their purpose, that they might know that to be true which *Moses* saith, that it is the Lord which giveth power to get

Gen. 30.33

Deut. 8.18

wealth: against this those offend which increase their wealth, and live upon usury, for they depend not upon the blessing of God, but bind their debtors in bands, win or lose, they will have both principal and increase. Again, others are so greedily bent upon their profits, that their only desire is to wax rich, of whom *Paul* speaketh. They which will wax rich fall into many temptations, and snares; and many foolish and damnable lusts, which drown men in everlasting destruction: for the love of money is the root of all evil, which while some desired, they erred from the faith, and pierced themselves with many sorrows. This striketh to the earth false measures, naughty wares, breaking of promises, detaining of heirs, raising of rents, oppressing the poor, deceitful bargains, and unlawful trades; for none of these depend upon the Lord, but give their souls to the Devil, for increasing their wealth.

1 Tim. 6.9,10

Secondly, you must know how to use your wealth according to the word of God: which is thus, according to the counsel of the Apostle, if thou have little, be contented, for godliness is great gain, if a man be contented with that he hath, for we brought nothing into the world, neither shall we carry anything out of the world: this is the reason of contentation, but some will say, how much shall we have before we be contented, the Apostle answereth in the next verse: if we have meat and clothing, we are therewithal contented. Again, if they be rich, the same Apostle showeth how they shall bear their wealth in these words: Charge them that are rich in this world, that they be not high minded, neither trust in their uncertain riches, but in the living God, which giveth us all things to enjoy abundantly; that they distribute to other, that they be rich in good works, that they be willing to give, and easy to be entreated; laying up for themselves a good foundation against the time to come, that they may lay hold on eternal life. Out of the which words we must observe these things. First, that

1 Tim. 6.6-8

1 Tim. 6.17

18

19

Ruth Chapter 4. verses 11,12

riches must not make men proud, for they are the gift of God, but our rich men scorn and disdain their poor brethren of Christ, commanding and oppressing them both by word and deed, in most odious and shameful manner. Secondly, they must not put any confidence in their wealth, but repose their trust in the living God, who gave it to them, and to whom they shall give an account for using and abusing it, for to put trust in their wealth, is to think they may do with it what they please. Thirdly, they must distribute willingly, liberally, and daily, for as they are rich in substance, so they must be rich in good works, that is, they must excel other in giving, as they do in possession. Fourthly, that those men which do thus bestow their wealth, have laid the foundation of their salvation, and lay hold on eternal life. This is the way to keep wealth after the word of God, and whosoever doeth otherwise either in marriage or unmarriage, doth hoard up but rust to torment him, the canker to consume him, the care to molest him, and vengeance against the day of vengeance, eternally to condemn him.

Lastly, in departing from his wealth, first, if he have wronged any man, he must follow the example of *Zacchaeus*, restore four-fold, and he shall be blameless for that, spend liberally upon his family in good sort, after the counsel of *Solomon*, for this pinching of servants and families favoreth not of God, nor of Religion, nor of humanity, the brute beasts condemn it: but spend nothing in waste, for thou art but steward of thy goods, now you know a steward must give an account to his master. Finally, that which thou reservest, give to thy children, as *Abraham*, and all the godly did to their posterity: and whosoever followeth this counsel, shall be guiltless for misspending, clear from evil keeping, free from wrong getting, and acquitted from the dreadful reckoning which all the world shall make one day to the Lord for abusing his benefits. Now let us give thanks to God.

Luke 19.8

Prov. 5.15-17

The Fourteenth Lecture

Ruth Chapter 4. verses 12-14

12 *And that thy house be like the house of* Pharez, *whom* Tamar *bare unto* Judah, *of the seed which the Lord shall give thee of this young woman.*

13 *So* Boaz *took* Ruth, *and she was his wife, and when he went in unto her, the Lord gave that she conceived, and bare a son.*

14 *And the women said unto* Naomi, *Blessed be the Lord, which hath not left thee this day without a kinsman, and his name shall be continued in Israel.*

15 *And this shall bring thy life again, and cherish thine old age, for thy daughter in law which loveth thee hath borne him, which is better to thee than seven sons.*

We have showed you the last Sabbath, that this twelfth verse is a part of the prayer of the elders and people at the marriage of *Boaz* and *Ruth*, for in the first part they prayed for the fruitfulness of the woman, but in this they commend unto God the blessing for their posterity, and because we then divided it, we will first of all handle it, and then proceed to that which followeth.

First, therefore out of this second part in their prayer, we gather another duty of the godly in praying for children, which is, to desire in some measure the blessings of this world, either riches or honor upon them:

which in this place, these Jews do unfeignedly pray for
the house, or posterity of *Boaz*, when they say, and that
thy house may be like the house of *Pharez*, who had the
birthright of *Judah*, whose posterity was the noblest of
all the family, from whom also descended this *Boaz*, as
appeareth by the end of this Chapter, which flourishing estate, as it had continued in the progeny of *Pharez*
for six generations, so they wish it might follow in his
posterity for many more, neither is this special in this
place, but also dispersed thorough all the Scripture, for
we know what promise the Lord made unto *Abraham*,
that unto his seed he would give all the land of *Canaan*,
as a comfort unto him, to think that his posterity should
be so well provided for, whereby they might not only be
continued, but richly advanced as the Lords of the earth.
The like was it that he promised to *David*, that he should
alway have a son to sit on his seat, not simply a son, but
a son to sit on his seat, as if the Lord had said, thou shalt
alway have the kingdom in the possession of thy posterity, and they shall reign as Kings for evermore. So on
the contrary, it is a curse when the name of houses are
put out, their memory forgotten, their wealth dispersed,
their honor abased, and their children like vagabonds
upon the earth. It was also a special promise to the people of the Jews, that if they observed the statutes of the
Lord, then should they and their seed be able to lend to
other, but they should not need to borrow of any.

Gen. 12.4

2 Sam. 7.12

Psal. 109.8-12

Deut. 28.12

These things considered by the example of those
promises of the Lord, and the persons of these fathers,
we have an excellent way described for the maintenance
of our possession, in the name of our posterity: which is
this, to commend it by prayer to the tuition of the eternal God, for that which he hath promised, may we pray
for, the same way, that maketh barren women to become
fruitful, the increase of the earth to multiply, the heavens
to give their rain, countries to be delivered from sword,
famine, and pestilence, and pulleth down all the bless-

ings of God upon us, is also the appointed means for
the continuance of worldly families. But how long, how
long shall I persuade the world before they believe it?
do they not spend their days in worldly devises, to compass the earth by multitudes of purchasings, which are
always travailing abroad in restless journeys, buy many
bargains to augment their substance, using all lawful
and unlawful means for to increase their wealth, and
enlarge their possessions, that their posterity might be
honorable when they are dead, their children advanced
by money, not by virtue, maintained by pride, not by humility, reign like kings in all manner of pleasure upon
the earth, while the fathers are tormented in hell for
their wrongful oppressions; thus men pray on the world
as the Eagles on the altars, and the birds on *Abraham's*
sacrifice, but not to the Lord, as the young Ravens that
call upon him, who being left of their own parents, are
fed by the Lord, that his kindness might be manifested
to our children, as well as to birds, and that their welfare
dependeth upon the blessing of God, not the benefit of
elders, the favor of our Maker, not the covetousness of
our fathers. Against these it is that the Prophet cryeth   Isa. 5.8,9
and curseth, because they join house to house, land to
land, field to field, inheritance to inheritance, that themselves might reign alone upon the earth: this is the care
of them, which are suddenly from the dust to the chair
of wealth advanced, from slavery to honor, from beggary
to riches, that they might (as the Prophet saith) build   Psal. 49.12
fair houses, encroach greater compass of lands, that their
names might be famous upon the earth.

But who is he that maketh any ordinary and
daily prayer unto the Lord, that his substance might
be by his blessing increased, with his favor preserved,
and to his glory bestowed. Nay, nay, if none had no
more wealth than that which they had gotten by prayer,
their glorious shows should in little space grow as bare
as the trees in the winter, when they have neither fruit

nor leaves to cover them. This I speak not to the discredit of any wealthy persons, but show them the way to attain the end of their desire, the continuance of their posterity in godliness and wealth, which is by prayer.

Luke 22.32 For as Christ prayed for *Peter,* that his faith should not fail him; so parents must pray for their posterity, that their names may not decay in them. If any think when their barns are enlarged, their corn gathered, they filled, health enjoyed, wealth increased, and rest obtained, that either souls or children shall have the greater rest, like that fool in the Gospel, their marks are much amiss, for

Luke 12.16-18 wealth and issue are lost both in an hour. Look upon the example of *Job,* the death of his children, and decay of his wealth. Again, none must be hereby emboldened, to present their prayers before the face of the Almighty, for the maintenance of their children in worldly vanity, to make that the only end of all their desire, which is, to be more careful for the shoe than the foot, for the raiment than the body, and for the body than the soul: but this must be their direction, as the Lord commanded the

Deut. 28.12
Psal. 144.12-14 Jews, if they kept his statutes, then should their oxen be strong to labor, their sheep bring forth thousands and ten thousands in their streets, their daughters like the polished corners of the Temple, and their sons as their fruitful garners, which never are empty. For ungodly *Haman* was hanged, though he were the prince of princ-

Esther 7.10 es, but godly *Mordecai* was advanced, which was as poor as the basest. *Shebna* was deprived of his office, because he was wicked, when godly *Eliakim* was promoted to his

Isa. 22.20 place: even so it is not honor, but the fear of God that bringeth and sustaineth honor, that you must pray for your children: Kings for ungodliness were deprived of their seats and thrones of majesty, whereunto they were born, much more will the Lord execute his judgments of poverty and slavery upon those that would be advanced, and yet are wicked; for *Solomon* saith, that the prosperity of fools slayeth them, and the crown doth not endure from generation to generation, yet the fear of the Lord abideth forever.

Secondly, by this verse we may note, when they expressly make mention of *Tamar* the mother of *Pharez*, and wish the posterity of *Boaz* to be like his, the great blessing of God upon that incestuous birth; for we know the history, how that *Tamar* was the daughter in law of *Judah*, the wife and widow of his eldest son, dissembling herself to be a whore, by her apparel and place, had the company of her father in law, by whom she was conceived of two sons, the elder was this *Pharez*, and the younger *Zarah*: yet we see how the Lord doth magnify this *Pharez* with a glorious and godly posterity. By the which he teacheth us these two profitable lessons, that the sins of the faithful are forgiven, though they be never so great. We see this *Judah* an excellent man, yet overcome in this action, had not any such plague inflicted on him, as *Ruben* his eldest brother, or *Simeon* and *Levi*, but he which covered and omitted that sin of *Abraham* with *Hagar*, of *Jacob* with *Bilhah* and *Zilpah*, of this *Judah* with *Tamar*, *Lot* with his own daughters, and such like; will also forgive all the defaults of the godly unto the end of the world. By the which we gather exceeding comfort, when we come to this persuasion, that there is no condemnation to them that are in Jesus Christ, that the gates of hell shall not prevail against the mercies of the Lord, that the victory of our faith shall conquer the world, when *Noah* shall be cleansed from his drunkenness, *Moses* and *Aaron* from their doubting, *Miriam* from her murmuring, *David* from his murder, *Peter* from his denial of Christ, and all because the Lord will cover the sins of his Saints, be they never so great, when he punisheth the faults of many thousand wicked persons with eternal damnation, although they have not sinned with the like transgression.

Secondly, by this we learn, that the Lord doth not punish the children for the parents' faults, if they

Gen. 38.18,29

commit not the like themselves: for this *Pharez* begotten
in incest, was blessed by the Lord, not only with temporal glory in himself and his issue, but also with this,
that he was made one of the fathers of Christ. And this
teacheth us, that this upbraiding of men for their birth,
be they base born or free born, is no fruit of the word of
God, but the malice of the Devil, which first deceived
the parents, and now would discredit the child. Let it
not therefore, beloved, be any speech in our mouths, to
shoot at them whom the Lord hath wounded by nature,
any thought of our hearts to envy their welfare, were
their parentage never so base, but pray for them, that
though they proceed not of a sanctified birth, yet they
may grow up to a sanctified and holy life, to make a godly and a blessed end. And finally, let us be encouraged
unto Religion by the favor of God, which dealeth thus
mercifully with his Saints, never suffering anything to be
laid to the charge of his chosen, stopping the mouth of
the Devil himself, that he never rise in judgment against
the faithful, or bring any little sin of theirs into the remembrance of God, but washing them all in the laver
of regeneration, the blood of his son, and will give them
white robes cleansed from all filthiness, that they may be
chaste virgins for the Lord's service, and feed at his own
table for evermore: this consideration made *David* to cry
out, and say, *Oh when shall I come and appear before the
presence of God?* It made *Simeon* to say, *Now Lord let
thy servant depart in peace*: it caused *Paul* to utter these
words, *I desire to be dissolved, and to be with Christ*: for
blessed are the people that are in such a case, yea, blessed
are the people whose God is the Lord. Thus much for
this verse. Now let us go to the verse following.

In these three verses following, the holy Ghost
declareth the blessing of God upon this marriage of *Boaz*
and *Ruth*. The words contain in them two parts, the first
part is of *Boaz*, verse 13. the second is of the women
that were present at the travail of *Ruth*. The first part

Lecture 14

showeth, how *Boaz* taking *Ruth*, and using her as his wife, had the blessing of God, in conceiving and bearing him a son: the other part of the women, is their rejoicing with *Naomi* for this fruitfulness of *Ruth*; it comprehendeth two parts, the first, their thanksgiving to God, verse 14. in these words, *Blessed be God*: secondly, the matter of their thanksgiving in the words following: first, for *Boaz* his sake, in that God had left him to be *Naomi's* kinsman: secondly, because this child of *Ruth's* her loving daughter in law, should renew her years, and cherish her old age: of these parts let us briefly speak in order.

So Boaz took. After the solemnity of this marriage, in the presence of the people, and their prayers ended, which they poured forth in the behalf of both these parties and their posterity, *Boaz* proceedeth to the end of this action, and taketh *Ruth* to his house to be his wife, as a duty of a kind and a godly husband. For all this while we must imagine that *Ruth* was absent from the place of this communication, and according to the counsel of her mother, sat waiting at home, for some prosperous news, and praying, no doubt, for a joyful success of this desired marriage, out of this we gather. Chap. 3.18

First, the duty of all godly husbands, which is to take their wives and dwell with them, as this *Boaz* doth *Ruth*, for it is no doubt, but that he presently went to the house of her mother, and thence took her, bringing her to his own house, that there they might live and love together. This phrase of Scripture we may find used in many places, as in the history of *Isaac*, how he took *Rebekah* his wife, and brought her into the tent of *Sara* his mother, and was comforted after his mother's death, where the holy Ghost doth not only declare the kindness of *Isaac*, but also the commodity of dwelling with a wife, for the presence of *Rebekah* caused her husband to forget the death of his mother; as if he had said, the presence of a wife is greater than the comfort of a mother. For this cause *Peter* exhorteth that husbands should dwell with Gen. 24.67 Rebecca Rebecca 1 Pet. 3.7

Ruth Chapter 4. verses 12-15

their wives, like men of understanding, giving honor to their wives, as to weaker vessels, because they are the heirs of the same grace, and that their prayers be not hindered, as if he had said, they must dwell together, and they must pray together, for as Christ is alway present with his Church, so husbands must keep the company of their wives.

This point being evident both by reason and Religion, it condemneth the wandering abroad of many idle husbands, some which are never satisfied with riches, by markets and merchandise, traveling in the world, deprive their wives of their due benevolence; others for their pleasure walk from country to country, spending their days in pleasant disport among carnal and suspicious companions, leave wife and family, to the sea of this world, like children in a ship, without guide or mariner; many are present, but to the discommodity and discomfort of their poor wives and children, oh how do any of these persons take their wives with godly minds either to dwell or pray together? How can the vine prosper when the root is uncovered, and how can women be comforted, when their cover is taken from them, I mean their husbands, as *Abimelech* the king of Gerar told unto *Sara*, Is not the body dead without a head? yea if it be but a minute of an hour: do not then our wandering youths murder the body of their own family, being absent about unnecessary business, sometime for the space of many months? Is not the body maimed if it want but the least member, yea, but a finger, how is then those households wounded, where the chiefest parts, either husbands or wives, be wanting and wandering abroad, and finally, what is this but to divorce themselves for a season without any lawful cause, to put asunder them whom the Lord hath joined together, to break the fellowship of holy wedlock, to despise the society of godly marriage, to lay open themselves to the temptations of the devils, and to thrust both bodies and souls into danger of damnation? This I speak not, as if all absence from either party (with consent for a time about necessary business) were utterly unlawful: for so *Jacob, Moses, Aaron, David,* and the Apostles, should be faulty; but I speak against this willful departing of one from the other, without either consent of man or wife, conscience of the law of God, or regard to their own persons, for the company of these twain is greater than parents or children, for which the Apostle saith, that if one be a believing person, and the other an infidel, yet they must not depart if they be willing to dwell with them, and he giveth no liberty for breaking their company, except it be to pray the more fervently, and wisheth also that if they do so, yet it must be but for a season, that Satan tempt them not, so great regard must be had of the fellowship in marriage, that the zeal of prayer, the worship of God, the love of our own parents, the increase of wealth, and the pleasures of the world, must not separate, without the voice of both parties, and yet the time must be but short for the avoiding the temptation of Satan, and the danger of their own damnation.

1 Cor. 7.13

Verse 5

Secondly, by this we may gather, who is the author and sender of children, which is the Lord: for this Scripture saith, that *the Lord gave her to conceive,* for as *Paul* saith of the corn that is cast into the earth, that it increaseth neither by the planter nor yet the waterer, but by the Lord: so must we say by the seed of mankind, that it lieth neither in the husband nor in the wife, but in the blessing of God: for which cause, when *Rachel* said to her husband *Jacob,* give me children or else I die; he answered her in anger, am I in God's stead, that kept thee from the fruit of thy womb? as if he had said, it is God that sendeth issue, and not man: therefore *David* saith, that children are the possession of the Lord, and the fruit of the womb is his reward. By the which we are taught many excellent and worthy lessons: first, that seeing they come from the author of every good gift, we have a ready

1 Cor. 3.6

Gen. 30.1,2

Psal. 127.3

way where to ask them, when we want them: for as when
we want wisdom, the Apostle saith, we must ask wisdom
at the hand of God: so when we want children, we must
ask children at the hand of God. When *Rebekah* was
barren, by her husband's prayer she was made fruitful:
so barren women by their husband's prayers have been
made the mothers of many children. *Hannah* obtained
by her prayer at the Temple, not only *Samuel*, but also
three other sons and two daughters. Oh let us not be
vexed then for many children, but let everyone ask confidently by the will of God, and they shall receive (if it
so please him) plentifully to their own desire. Secondly,
seeing children come of the Lord, we are taught to use
them as the blessings of God, and as the child by nature should first know his mother that bare him, so we
by instruction should first teach our children the fear of
God that gave them; it is far better for many children
that they had never been born, except their parents had
more knowledge to till their minds with the immortal
seed of God his holy word, than to look upon the sun, as
the condemned person which cometh out of prison, and
so goeth to execution, in like manner children, without
the knowledge of the fear of God, do come from the
womb of their mothers, which is their prison, to the fire
of hell, which is the place of execution. Oh my beloved,
look upon your tender children, and so often as you see
them, you behold the blessings of God upon you, make
much of their souls by praying for their salvation: you
have brought them into the world, leave them not to the
Devil.

       Thirdly, seeing children are the gift of God, those
which have children, have greater account to make, than
those which have none, for of him to whom much is
given, shall much be required, and they to whom the
Lord hath given children and servants, lands and cattle,
shall answer for every one of these to the Lord: therefore
parents must finish their reckoning, which they must

Gen. 25.21
Rebecca

1 Sam. 2.21

give to the Lord, and let not one farthing of their debt be omitted, for he will plague them as well for not doing their duties to their own children, as graceless children for contemning of God. And this one consideration should mitigate the desire of posterity, because, if they abuse them, their own damnation shall be the greater, if they be unruly, they bring nothing but sorrow to their parents: if they be godly, the world will hate them, and if they be wicked the Devil will have them. Were it not a pitiful sight to see the father burned, for murdering his son, how much more grievous is it to see both father and son, mother and daughter, husband and wife, master and servant, mistress and maids, pastors and people, to go all to damnation together, because the former did not guide the later: oh, would God that the desire to escape this judgment, would sink into the hearts of all, that we might every one addict our lives to holiness, our minds to knowledge, our bodies to obedience, our hearts to understanding, our children to instruction, our servants to religion, and all our souls to salvation.

Thirdly, by this we gather, that it is a greater blessing to be the mother of a son, than the parent of a daughter, if it so please God to send them: for in this place the holy Ghost saith, that *the Lord gave her, and she conceived and brought forth a son*, as if he had said, the Lord gave her, her own desire, and the best issue, which was a man-child: for this cause our Savior saith, that a woman forgetteth her pains in travail, so soon as a man-child is born into the world. Therefore is it that the Lord promised *Abraham* a son, that he gave *Zacharias* and *Elizabeth* a son, and finally therefore the Lord calleth us all his sons, as a father rejoiceth more for a son, so the Lord rejoiceth in the salvation of the faithful. By this we are taught to magnify the name of the Almighty, for everyone his benefits in their degree, and if we want any, by prayer to crave it at the hands of God, always remembering that we leave the end of our desires to be

John 16.20
Gen. 18.10

Luke 1.13

Ruth Chapter 4. verses 12-15

agreeable to his will. And here we see the prayer of the
people in the former verse to be in part fulfilled, when
the Lord did so soon bless this good old man, by giving
him a son: for it is no doubt but the holy Ghost doth so
presently after their prayer add her conception and his
birth, that he might stir us up with greater zeal, to desire
the prayers of the faithful, which are always available in
the presence of the Lord. Come therefore my brethren,
and let us fulfill the desire of the Lord, and account more
of the petitions of the godly, than all the possessions of
the wealthy: by prayer the earth is made fruitful, and the
heavens drop down abundance: by prayer famine is removed, war appeased, the wrath of God pacified, and the
health of the body recovered, by prayer wisdom is increased, faith confirmed, remission of sins obtained, the
barren woman made a fruitful mother of many children,
the days of life lengthened, peace of countries and consciences prolonged, and the kingdom of heaven eternally
inherited. Therefore those which cannot pray, abhor the
presence of God, are weary of our assemblies, forsake
sermons and congregations, depart from the fellowship
of the faithful, and have their sins sealed up, their lives
accursed, and their souls everlastingly condemned.

And the women. Now we must proceed to the
second part of this Scripture, wherein is declared what
issue and effect this wrought in other, for so soon as
the child was born, it did not only bring comfort to the
parents, but also joy and gladness to the godly citizens
of Bethlehem: among whom these women are reported by the holy Ghost (which no doubt, were present at
the delivery of *Ruth*) to magnify the name of God, for
this so great a benefit bestowed upon the old woman:
although her children were dead, yet her name might
be recovered by her loving daughter in law. By this we
first of all observe the duty of all the faithful, which is to
rejoice with them that rejoice, and to weep with them
that weep: for as there godly Jewish women rejoice with

Rom. 12.12,
15

Naomi for the fruitfulness of *Ruth*, so must we everyone be like affected for the blessings that are poured
upon our brethren. The like unto this, may we read of
the neighbors and kindred of *Elizabeth*, hearing of the
wonderful mercy of God unto her, they rejoiced with   Luke 1.58
her. This teacheth us the same duty, that the joy of our
brethren should be our rejoicing, and their sorrow our
lamentation, for there is no fellowship, but there must be
a feeling of the same joys or miseries, not only in public affairs, which respect the whole commonwealth, but
also in private business, the benefit of every particular
person. The head is sore when the stomach is sick, the
hand is grieved when the foot is maimed, and every part
of the body being in prosperity, rejoiceth together. For
this cause *Paul* biddeth us to endure all things with the
same mind, meaning that every man's mind should be
like his brother's either in sorrow or rejoicing. But is   Rom. 12.16
this the fellowship that reigneth among us in these days?
or rather are we not merriest when our neighbors are
tormented? and doth it not grieve us to see others to
prosper beside us? yes surely, for there is no more hearty
and unfeigned friendship among men in our days, than
is between the hawk and the bird, when either of them
is taken, the other rejoiceth. This is the cause that men
are no more accounted of, after wealth faileth, friendship
withdraweth when they stand in most need, and least
pity is in the greatest extremity. Every tree is green in
the Spring, every bird will sing in Summer, and every
false-hearted Christian, will fawn upon their brethren in
prosperity, but be ashamed of their want in adversity:
yea, there never wanteth privy repiners and grudgers, at
the wealth and welfare of everyone: for some say, it is
too much if their neighbors' corn increase, others say it
is too little, when they are vexed and troubled by loss of
their goods, and this maketh many meddlers in other
men's matters, many backbiters for other men's welfare,
many envy that any should have their shares as good as

Ruth Chapter 4. verses 12-15

themselves, like him in the Gospel, whose eye was evil because the Lord's hand was good, and as all the waves of the sea do beat upon the shore, so all the brains of the world do breathe against the prosperous.

Secondly, the manner of their rejoicing must be considered, which the holy Ghost hath set down in these words, *Blessed be the Lord*: wherein they testify perfect joy, both to the Lord, by praising him, and giving thanks; and also to *Naomi*, unto whom nothing could be more acceptable, than to hear the name of God to be blessed for her sake. To bless in the Scripture, whensoever it is referred to God, signifieth to praise or to give thanks: as when *Zacharias* saith, *Blessed be the Lord God of Israel, for he hath visited and redeemed his people*; that is, praised be the Lord God of Israel. Likewise the Apostle *Paul* saith, *Blessed be God the Father of our Lord Jesus Christ, the Father of mercies, and the God of all consolation*, that is, praised be God. And in another place he saith, *If thou bless with the Spirit, how shall he that occupieth the room of the unlearned, say Amen to thy thanksgiving*: that is, if thou give thanks with the Spirit. In this place it is of the first sense, as if these women had said, We praise thee O God, that thou hast looked on the misery of *Naomi*, and hast reserved her a kinsman, by whom the name of the dead might be raised upon the inheritance, and his own honor continued in God's people. By the which we are taught what manner of joy the faithful are to have for their brethren, namely, such as may redound to the praise of God, according to the saying of the Apostle, that he which rejoiceth, must rejoice in the Lord: for as bodily exercise profiteth little, so carnal joy profiteth less, such as is the framing of vain songs, giving over our labors, and to rejoice in pastimes, and such as is used in ringing of bells, and the like sort, being only for man and not for God. Therefore here we have an excellent manner of rejoicing, when God is glorified by our mirth. Thus we read *Moses* and *Aaron* with

Luke 1.68

2 Cor. 1.3

1 Cor. 14.16

1 Cor. 1.31

Exod. 15

their sister *Miriam* did, after they came out of Egypt. Thus did *Deborah* and *Barak* after the victory against *Sisera*. Thus did the women after the victory of *Saul* and *David*, when they came from the slaughter of the Philistines. Thus did *Zacharias* when his tongue was restored unto him. Thus did the children of Jerusalem cry when Christ came riding upon the Ass. Thus do the faithful rejoice after the destruction of Rome's Antichrist, singing, Praised be God, salvation and honor and glory and power to our Lord God: And the Lord crieth out of heaven unto us, Praise the Lord all ye his servants, and whosoever fear him both small and great. Therefore beloved, seeing it becometh the just to be thankful, let us praise the Lord both evening and morning, and let us not see a sparrow to light on the ground, without some praise to God, by whose providence all things are governed, by whose will all things are ordered, for whose glory are all things appointed; that we should evermore give thanks to him that sitteth on the highest heavens, and ruleth the mightiest princes, appointing the measure for the sea, and calling the whole world to judgment, in whose presence is light and life for evermore.

Judg. 5
1 Sam. 18.6

Luke 1.68
Luke 19.38
Rev. 19.1,2,5

Thirdly, the matter of their thanksgiving, must be considered, for they praise God, because he had kept a kinsman alive for *Naomi*, whose name should be continued in the people of God; so that in plain words they commend the kindness of God, because he had so provided for this godly *Naomi*, as she might be comforted by his means, and his name continued by her daughter, and all three eased by this one child. By the which we are taught these two profitable lessons: first, that we must magnify God for the life of our friends; so do these Jews for the life of *Boaz*, by whom the Lord brought such great comfort to both these destitute and desolate widows, for as we are sorry for their deaths, when it is too late, so must we be thankful for their life, when yet they are with us: the son for the life of his father, and the father for

Ruth Chapter 4. verses 12-15

the son, the wife for her husband, and the husband for his wife, the servant for his master, the subjects for their prince, the people for their teachers, and the daughters for their mothers. There are few of these, but they bring much benefit unto us, and no small comfort doth arise by their presence, which we shall better perceive when we want them, than now we enjoy them, and for these the Apostle also willeth us to pray, and one cause of these
1 Tim. 2.1 two miracles upon *Lazarus* and *Dorcas*, was that their life might be prolonged with the church of God, and more kindness showed to their godly friends: Secondly, by this all those that are able to bestow any kindness upon other, are taught their duties to their own kindred, that especially they be careful for the relief of their poverty, the maintenance of their dignity, the preservation of their honesty, and the nourishing of their own flesh, for unto that end hath the Lord increased their substance, continued their name, prolonged their days, and advanced their seats, that they may be more able to do for their poor brethren which are commended to them by the Lord, committed by the world, and compelled by nature, which are bone of their bone, and flesh of their flesh, that they might be maintained as your own selves: When *David* was made king he advanced his sister's sons and his kinsmen: when *Saul* was king, he advanced *Abner* and other his friends; and we know that many of Christ's Apostles were his kinsmen: unto the which
1 Tim. 5.4 end *Paul* exhorteth, that poor widows be provided for by their friends, that the Church be not charged with them. This condemneth the forgetfulness of many in our age, which being in wealth, will scant acknowledge their poor kindred, whereby they show themselves like unnatural beasts, as if the Lord were not able to bring them down to the footstool in the place of the other, that they might cry and not be heard.

And this shall. In this verse is the second part of their joy, insomuch as now *Ruth* hath brought forth

a son, it is better to *Naomi* than seven sons, for seven
is taken for many, and not for any definite number, as
when *David* saith, that he praiseth God seven times a   Psal. 119.164
day, that is, many times every day. Also they protest in
this verse, that it rejoiceth them to see *Naomi* so comforted with the birth of this child, as that now her life
is restored, whereas before it was dying like an old stub,
which had no green twigs upon it, but now this one being shot forth, she reviveth and gathereth comfort in
her old years. By this we see the duty of parents, which
is to rejoice when their children increase, and they
see their children's children: these Jewish women, no
doubt, but spake by the experience of their own days,
that as a woman lying at the point of death, being recovered, is joyful and thankful for the same: even so old
persons have new lives in their children's children; for
which cause they ought to be thankful to the Lord, for
the comfort of their children, who may likewise rejoice
when they see their parents delight in their offspring.
Thus, no doubt, but *Abraham* did, when he saw *Esau*
and *Jacob*, his son *Isaac's* children, being born about fifteen years before his death: this did *Jacob* when he saw   Gen. 48.10,11
Manasseh and *Ephraim*, his son *Joseph's* children, kissing
and embracing them, and saying, I had not thought to
see thy face any more, but the Lord hath let me see thy
seed and posterity, as if he had said, I thank God for seeing thee, but I rejoice that I see thy children also. And
truly, this I am sure will godly aged parents do, who have
these for their examples, of faith and conversation, that
they might with more thankfulness praise the Lord, who
letteth them see their children's children, and with greater comfort rejoice in them, that were born of their own
bodies, but with greatest joy and most willing minds
commend their withered age, and all worn years to the
hands of the Lord, who hath multiplied their seed in this
life, and will glorify themselves in the life to come. Now
let us give praise to God.

Ruth Chapter 4. verses 12-15

The Fifteenth Lecture

Ruth Chapter 4. verses 16,17

16 *And Naomi took the child and laid it in her lap, and became nurse unto it.*

17 *And the women her neighbors gave it a name, saying, there is a child born to* Naomi, *and called the name thereof* Obed: *the same was the father of* Jesse *the father of* David.

In the former words we heard the last Sabbath, the prayer and thanksgiving of the people, or the women of Bethlehem, for the birth of this son of *Boaz*, and the comfort of *Naomi*: but now in these words the holy Ghost proceedeth to the education and circumcision of the child in these two verses: wherein the holy Ghost delivereth unto us these things: first, that Naomi took the care of the education of the child, verse 16. Secondly, the naming of the child by the neighbors, the women of Bethlehem, which they gave unto it by occasion of their own words, when they said in the fifteenth verse, that he should cherish her, namely, *Naomi*, and therefore they call him *Obed*, which signifieth serving; thereby signifying, that he should serve for the comfort of *Naomi*: of these parts let us briefly speak in order, as the Spirit of God shall give utterance, and the time permit.

And Naomi *took the child.* After the mercy of God in the blessing of *Ruth* with a son, who was the only heir unto the house of *Elimelech*, the husband of *Naomi*, which brought no small joy to the old woman, to see her name and the name of her family revived in the birth of this son, when it was utterly decayed in the sight of the world, for she was old and a stranger in *Moab*, and had no hope of any more children, neither was it likely that her daughters in law (their husbands being dead) would return from their country and kindred unto a strange people, with whom they had small acquaintance, even none at all, *Naomi* their mother in law excepted, so that the hope of her posterity being buried in Moab, the life of her family must needs decay in Bethlehem. Therefore her return to her own country, was a favor of God unto her, and raising up the mind of *Ruth* to be partaker of her journey, and companion in her travail, was an especial comfort to her wearied age, but providing so honorable a marriage for her, and making her so fruitful a wife in short time, was the life of *Naomi's* death, the renewing of her family, the restoring of her hope, and the resurrection of her dead sons, for the continuance of their names, in the gate of their places: and therefore, she like a joyful and thankful grandmother, for discharge of her conscience, love of the infant, and ease of her daughter, becometh a fellow nurse for the better education of the child, out of the which we note.

First, that as we have heard how the miseries of *Naomi* were cast upon her together, so now the mercies of God are multiplied in the same in greater measure: For then her woe was begun by the death of her husband, continued through her long dwelling with the wicked *Moabites*, and redoubled through the death of her two sons: so now it falleth again, as the darkness departeth at the dawning of the day, and giveth place to the light of the Sun, so her miseries are repealed, first, with the loving and constant fellowship of her daughter in law *Ruth*, who was as a careful husband to her, in laboring for her living, and a blessed child to increase her posterity: Again, she now was in quiet, dwelling among the people of God, enjoying the company of the faithful, and the fellowship of her friends: moreover, her posterity is restored in the fruitfulness of *Ruth*, and she, even she herself liveth to see the day when all this falleth upon her, to the endless comfort of her withered age, and present praise of the name of God. Thus we see it a righteous thing with God, first to wound, and then to heal; first to strike, and then to stroke: first to cast down, and then to lift up: for this is certainly the cup of all the faithful, that they must taste of many bitter afflictions, before they come to the possession of eternal blessedness, yea of worldly misery, they must sustain some cross, before they can be thankful enough for that which they quietly enjoy. So we read of *Job*, how in one day he had his corn burnt, his cattle stolen, and his children slain: this was bitter unto him for many days, yet in the end he was restored two for one, and saw more sons and more beautiful daughters, yea, his children's children to his unspeakable comfort. The like may be said of innocent *Joseph*, he was rebuked by his father, hated and sold by his brethren, imprisoned by his master, forgotten by *Pharaoh's* butler, all these were no small discouragements to so young a man, yet in the end he was advanced to the highest step of honor, as a recompense for all the tribulations he had endured. I may also add this of *David*, being persecuted by *Saul*, betrayed by the inhabitants of *Keilah*, driven to the *Philistines* his sworn enemies, to crave a dwelling of them, seeing many martyred for his sake, in the end had the possession of the kingdom of Judah, and after of Israel, which was the gift of the Lord, the reward of his afflictions, and his religion. By the which we may see the hope of the godly: not that which they feel, but that which they may lawfully look for, the ease of their pains, the remedy of their grief, the comfort of their troubles, and the end of their misery to be speedily redressed, if with patience they look and wait for the pleasure of the

Job 1.14-17
Job 42.12,13

Gen. 37.10,11

Ruth Chapter 4. verses 16,17

Lord.

Psal. 3

Therefore the godly say with *David*, if ten thousand compass them round about, they will not be afraid, for the Lord is the eye witness of all their miseries: the hot furnace of Babylon feareth them not: the Lion's den cannot drive them to dishonor God, if flames of fire consume their bodies to ashes, the darts of Satan pierce their souls to the quick, the reproaches of the world destroy their names, and the enemies of God spoil their substance, yet they are not left destitute, for their faith overcometh the world, their patience, all their afflictions, and their love of God, their desire of earthly prosperity. All which caused the Apostle to say, that hope was the anchor of the soul, meaning that as the anchor stayeth the ship in the midst of all the waves, though they be never so great and huge: in like manner the hope of the godly keepeth them in the bark of Christ's Church, among the thousands of worldly tribulations: For *David* saith, great are the troubles of the righteous: but the Lord delivereth them out of all, as if he had said, the righteous and godly are afflicted to this end, that the Lord might show his power in their deliverance: And in another place he complaining of his sufferings, and the sorrow of his soul: yet concludeth with this figurative speech: Why art thou so sad, O my soul? and why art thou cast down within me? trust still in the Lord, for by him I have deliverance against all my pains and grief. Even so do I say to all my poor brethren in the world: why are you so sad? if you want maintenance, the earth is the Lord's: If friendship, the hearts of kings are in his hands, as the rivers of waters: if liberty, he can break asunder the iron gates, and deliver the prisoners from their tormentors: if health, in his presence there is joy and life for evermore: if children, he maketh the barren woman to bring forth many children: if apparel, he clothed the Lilies above the royalty of *Solomon*: if meat, he can multiply the least morsels into the greatest measures: and finally, if defense, he giveth

Heb. 6.19

Psal. 13.1
Psal. 43.5

his royal Angels charge over the poorest of the godly, that the violence of princes, and the force of the Devil himself, shall never go beyond the decree and purpose of the Lord? Therefore if gripes of grief, and torments of sorrow do lodge with us all the night, yet joy shall come in the morning, when the poor shall be restored, the sick recovered, the sorrowful comforted, the faithful rewarded, and the wicked eternally plagued.

Secondly, by this verse we also gather a worthy example of a godly grandmother, which for the ease of her daughter, the love of the infant, and the thankfulness she owed to God, she became a fellow nurse unto this young son of *Boaz*: for although the words of the Scripture be these, that *she became nurse unto the child*; yet the meaning is not, that she took it from the mother, but that her tender care over it was such, that during the weakness of *Ruth*, and absence of his mother, she laid it in her lap, and was as careful for it, as any nurse that was hired to that duty: for *Naomi* could not be a nurse in these old days of hers, without husband or milk: which we know is the chiefest nourishment for young children, and therefore a nurse in this place, is taken for one that had a great care to procure the welfare and ease of the child.

By the which we note another duty of aged parents, which live to see their children's children, namely that they be as nurses unto them, to be as careful for them as their own, for therefore the Lord suffereth them to see the increase of their seed, that they might cover and nourish it in their own presence. For this cause we may read, that the sons of *Manassas*, and his son's Gen. 50.23 sons were brought up on the knees of *Joseph*, their great grandfather, for this laying in the lap or on the knee, signifieth a most tender care over the infants, that they be always not only in the presence, but also in the hands of their grandparents, as *Rachel* when she gave her maid *Bilhah* unto *Jacob*, and said that she might bring forth

Ruth Chapter 4. verses 16,17

Gen. 30.3

upon her knees: that is, she would be as careful in the nourishment of them, as if they were her own. Then by this they are taught their duties, upon whom the Lord hath vouchsafed to bestow this blessing, that they see their children's children, namely, that it is required at their hands, that they provide for their education, good instruction, and bringing up: for they may say as *Laban* said to his daughters' children, that they are their own, and therefore the care of the bringing up dependeth upon them: we see the little twigs at the top to be nourished as well by the root, as the bows that grow out of the body of the tree, even so grandparents provide as well for the maintenance of their children's issue, as for their own: so that in all kindness they must be entreated, in all wisdom be instructed, with all carefulness be corrected, and with all Religion be governed: for alas, if the twigs fail, there can be no fruit, and if your seed be corrupt, there will come but a hard harvest, so if your children's children be not overseen by you that are parents and rulers of both, your name will decay, your family die, and your posterity be utterly forgotten.

Thirdly, in this place we may profitably enquire, about the nursing of children, seeing *Naomi* is said to be the nurse of this child of *Ruth*: Whether it be lawful at all to put out children to nurse from their own mother, or whether the care of parents be not to bring up their children in their infancy, in their own persons or presence, or else commit the tuition of them to other. Unto the first question I answer, that every woman being in health of body and mind, is bound by the word of God to nurse her own children, and the reasons for the confirmation hereof are these, first because the Lord in the creation of their bodies, hath given to every woman breasts, which are the means whereby children suck their nourishment: and therefore either the Lord created their breasts in vain, or else they sin, if they set them not to work: if any say, that the Lord did give the breasts not for any necessity that they are bound so to do, but that they might be furnished with the means if they had the pleasure to do it, to whom I answer by the like example, the Lord hath given to every one hands to work, eyes to see, ears to hear, and tongues to speak; is it in the choice of men, to cut off their hands, to pull out their eyes, to stop up their ears, and to keep their tongues in silence all their life, and never use them, as many women do their natural breasts? I think not, for if they should, they must deface the workmanship of God; dismember their own bodies, and murder the parts of mankind.

Therefore as the Lord hath given to everyone hands, everyone must work, or else he is accursed, unless they will be idols: of whom *David* speaketh, they have hands and handle not, eyes and see not, ears and hear not, feet and walk not, noses and smell not, and such are women that have plentiful breasts, and yet give no suck. Secondly, the example of all the godly confirm it, as we see in *Sarah*, which nursed her son *Isaac*: in the mother of *Moses*, which was careful that her child should be nursed by no other than herself: in *Manoah's* wife the mother of *Sampson*: so did *Bathsheba* the mother of king *Solomon*, being a queen in Israel the wife of king *David*; yet she thought it her duty to take her own child and nurse it: I will speak nothing of *Hannah*, of *Elizabeth* the wife of *Zacharias* and mother of *John Baptist*: of the virgin *Mary*, which gave suck to the Lord of glory, Jesus Christ her savior: and of the mother of *David*, all which are as patterns of natural affection, for all the godly women in the world to imitate, and what blessing was poured upon their children, who knoweth not. Therefore either women must follow their godly examples, or show some charter of their liberty above these, or proclaim open disobedience to God, and the godly, because they swerve from his holy word, and their most pure and worthy example: but it is better to obey God than men, and to be ruled by the troublesome lives

Gen. 21.7
Exod. 2.8,9

Judg. 13.4,14

Song of Sol. 8.1

1 Sam. 1.23
Luke 1.80
Luke 2.7
Psal. 22.9

Ruth Chapter 4. verses 16,17

of the faithful, than by the peaceable, and pleasant devises of all the gentlewomen in the world whatsoever.

Rom. 1.30

Thirdly, it is a sign of the want of love and natural affection in the parents (as the Apostle speaketh) when the mothers do not bestow the labor to give their own children their natural milk: for if they had the same natural feeling of their duties to their children, they could not (having no occasion) commit the nourishing of their children to strangers, who can never be so inwardly kind to the infants, as the mothers are, or either ought to be: therefore, although though they pretend a kind of sorrow for their children's absence or departing from them, yet it is like the lamentation of *Esau*, which wept when he could not get the blessing, whereas he sold it before, and was the only cause of his own reprobation: so women weep at the departure of their children: whereas it lieth in their own power to keep them in their own possession, and more thankful would the child be in his heart to his mother, if she had bestowed the labor to nurse him.

Fourthly, it is not so natural for the child to be nursed where he was not born, for the same body whereof he had his being, is most fit for his feeding, as we see a plant doth best prosper when it is grafted where it sprung up first of all, than being removed into another ground, so the bodies of children do grow more freely, and like more cheerfully with their own mother's milk, than with all the world beside, and the ancientest Physicians say, that it were also better for the mothers if they gave themselves to this labor, therefore they do but hinder their own infants, born of their own bodies, and as it were keep them from their natural welfare, when they give them to be made another nature, which is by their nursing and feeding. These causes and more also being duly and carefully considered, you shall find it a greater sin, to give your children to other to be nursed, than heretofore you conceived of it, so that you must for this one thing, condemn the use of your breasts, (which were the creation of God, and the practice of the ancient godly women, which were every way as noble as any alive) forsake the tender love that a mother ought to bear to her innocent babe, bring your children's bodies to a second, yea, a contrary disposition and complexion, and stop up the plentiful conduits of streaming milk in your breasts, to the loss and hindrance of your own health: Therefore, if any have any power to perform this natural duty to their children, let them practice it: for all the carnal reasons of the world must not prevail against the least collection of the word of God. But some will say, admit that any through negligence do put their children to be nursed of other, doth the fault only rest in the parents, and nothing in the nurse? to whom I answer, if it be unlawful for the parents to give, it is also unlawful for the nurse to take: so that whatsoever is said against the one, may also be brought against the other. But in causes of weakness in the woman, danger to the child, or sickness in either of both; it is not only a duty of necessity, but of conscience, to nourish and cherish the children of other.

Therefore, although the mothers had the nursing of their children, yet there were others also like peti-nurses, which had some especial care in the keeping of the children, as we may read of the nurse of *Rebecca*, Gen. 24.19 which was the true use of nurses for the ease of their mother, to take the custody of the children in all things, save only in giving them suck, and therefore is it, that we may read in ancient histories, that one child had many nurses, that is, many to attend the welfare and nourishment of the infant: of this sort was *Naomi* at this present, who took upon her some care of this son of *Boaz*, that they both might be more diligent for the education thereof. Now for the other question, whether it be lawful for the parents during, all the time of the infancy thereof, if the mother be not able to give it suck, to commit

Ruth Chapter 4. verses 16,17

their children to other to be brought up: I answer, that every man and woman are bound to see their children's first instruction, that is, if it be possible, to have them in their keeping at their first entrance into knowledge, and when they are first of all capable of any goodness. So we read *Isaac* remained with his father *Abraham* in the time of infancy, when God commanded *Ishmael* to be cast out: so *Jacob* kept little *Benjamin* with him: neither would he depart from him unto any, till *Simeon* was bound in Egypt: so we read of the king *Joash*, whom his aunt *Jehosheba* hid from the rage of *Athaliah*, who was brought up in the house of her husband *Jehoiada*, where he was most worthily instructed in the fear of the Lord: so we read our Savior Christ kept, till he was twelve years old, with his mother and supposed father, and after he had been at Jerusalem, he was obedient to them till the year of his preaching, which was when he came to the age of thirty years. Therefore the conclusion of all this is, that neither the nursing nor instruction of our children must be deferred to other, at the least so as we seem not but to be many ways as careful for them, as if they were in our presence, to be evermore mindful for the wealth of their bodies, and health of their souls.

Gen. 21.12,13
Gen. 24.4
2 Kings 11.2,3

Fourthly, and lastly, by these words we may gather, how great and excellent is this work, the bringing up of children, for which the Lord hath expressed in his Word, that it is required that many should be applied, for in this place we see *Naomi* and *Ruth* bestow their labors for the education of this new born babe: and we have heard that *Rebecca* had a nurse that came with her from her father's house to the land where *Abraham* dwelt; which signifieth unto us, that neither their infancy can be unfed, nor their youth unruled; for this is not so base a work as many think it, that one is enough, if not too much, to take the care of their children, for we know they are easily drawn to many inconveniences, neither can the parents be present to foresee all, but if any be

helpers in this business, their care is much eased, their
children less endangered, their welfare better provided,
and the parent's duty better discharged. Every flock hath
a keeper beside the owner, every garden hath a dresser,
beside the master; and if it be possible, let every child
have an overseer beside the parents, for alas, the silly
infant is soon cast into the fire, falleth into the water,
overturned with the wind, and every beast is ready to
work his destruction: all which may be wisely prevented,
though not with the presence, yet with the counsel and
care of the parents, by providing such careful persons to
be their guides, as may also defend them when they are
absent.

And the women her neighbors. In this verse is the
second part, which concerneth the naming of the child,
where the holy Ghost doth declare unto us the persons
that named the child to be the women of Bethlehem, the
neighbors of *Naomi*, which no doubt was then given to
the child, at the eighth day, which was the circumcision,
according as we see in the history of *John Baptist*, after
the law of the Lord, calling him by the name of *Obed*,
which signifieth serving, or a servant; showing how he
should serve for the comfort of *Naomi*, *Boaz*, and his
mother.

By this we first of all note and observe, that it
is the duty of the faithful to be helpers one to another
in the service of God, and admonition of their duties:
for here the child being circumcised, was accompanied
with many godly women, whose device they used, and
followed in the naming of the child. Indeed we may often read that the parents gave names to their children,
sometimes the fathers, sometimes the mothers, and
sometimes the Lord himself, as in many persons we
may perceive, but we never read that the people were so
kind to help in this matter, and to further the duty of any
godly minded (only this place excepted) so that these
women are a most godly example for all the faithful to

Ruth Chapter 4. verses 16,17

behold, how they must further and help one another in the cause of Religion: for the naming of children in old time was very excellent, when they were careful by their earthly and outward titles, to admonish them of their inward and heavenly duties. And that which these did in this one, must we do also in all other duties, to draw more and more to the love of Religion: as we read the Apostles did one another, when they came to the first knowledge of the Messiah: for as a little leaven seasoneth a whole lump; even so a few godly persons may draw a great many to Religion. Therefore this one duty of all other, belongeth to the flock of Christ, that they help one another in the works of Christianity. When the ruler of the Temple his daughter was sick, for the little child he went to our Savior, by which means he recovered her life, this was the duty of a godly father: when the man sick of the palsy could not come to Christ, four of his neighbors brought him to his presence, and the Lord forgave him: this was charity and the duty of neighbors: When *Dorcas* was dead, the women sent for *Peter*, who being come, she was restored to life. And thus parents must help forward their children, neighbors, their fellows, and every man one another: if they want knowledge, let us teach them knowledge out of the pure word of God: if they cannot pray, let us pray with them, and for them, to the Almighty God; if they travel to hear the Word, let us travel with them to encourage their carefulness: but of this matter we have often spoken. Now let us give praise to God.

The end of the Fifteenth Lecture.

The Sixteenth Lecture

Ruth Chapter 4. verses 18-22

18 *These are the generations of* Pharez: Pharez *begat* Hezron.
19 Hezron *begat* Ram: Ram *begat* Amminadab:
20 Amminadab *begat* Nahshon: Nahshon *begat* Salmon.
21 Salmon *begat* Boaz: Boaz *begat* Obed.
22 Obed *begat* Jesse, Jesse *begat* David.

Now by the merciful kindness of the Lord, we are come to the last part of this history, and the conclusion of this Chapter, where the holy Ghost describeth unto us the kindred of *Boaz*, even all the generations, from *Pharez* to king *David*: showing unto us the increase of these Jews from their dwelling in the land of Canaan, before they went into Egypt, until the time that *David* was anointed and appointed king in Israel: we may, for the easier handling of these words, divide them into these two parts: The first is, those persons that were the progenitors, ancestors, or fathers of *Boaz*, in the eighteenth, nineteenth, and twentieth verses, which are set down to be *Pharez* the first, *Hezron* the second, *Ram* the third, *Amminadab* the fourth, *Nahshon* the fifth, and *Salmon* the sixth, who was the immediate and natural father of *Boaz*. The second part is the progeny, offspring, and children of *Boaz*, which succeeded him; first, *Obed*: secondly, *Jesse*, and thirdly, *David* the king. Of these parts and persons, let us briefly speak, so much as serveth for the exposition of the Scripture, and the satisfying of the time, through the assistance and help of the Spirit of God.

These are the generations. Now that the holy Ghost had declared unto us this history of *Ruth*, though briefly and in a few words, yet in ample and large circumstances, for the understanding of his mind: at the end hereof he annexeth the kindred of the persons, whom it chiefly concerneth, that he might show unto us, that they were no mean or base persons, for whom this history was compiled, but such as descended of the noblest family in all the world, who were the appointed fathers of many kings, and that which is most of all, the persons, of whose seed, our Savior Jesus Christ took the beginning and substance of his human nature. And therefore in this place we must declare the causes that moved the holy Ghost to be so careful in the rehearsing of the genealogies of the fathers; for we must not imagine, that he mustereth not the names of those ancient persons, to work any wonder in our minds at the recital of them, or that the Scripture could have been perfect without the several generations therein described: but we must know that there were diverse necessary and weighty causes by the judgment of the ancientest and most approved writers, which moved the Spirit of God to intersert these genealogies.

First, therefore according to the condition of all mankind, there is equally described the generations both of the godly and ungodly in the Scriptures, for this cause to show the multiplication of mankind: of this sort are the generations of *Adam, Seth* and *Cain* reported by *Moses*, that hearing the number of mankind so quickly multiplied, we might the more earnestly give praise unto God: Again, the genealogies of the sons of *Noah* are described unto us: to show the replenishing of the earth, the destruction of countries, and the restoring of the world: But to come nearer unto the matter, we must take

Gen. 5

Gen. 10

this for a general rule, that the genealogies of the wicked
are reported in the Scripture for to show the blessing and
love of God upon the godly and righteous men: as for
example, the Lord reckoneth up the posterity of *Ishmael*, Gen. 25.13,16
the son of the bond-woman, showing us how great a
people he became, and how many Dukes or princes pro-
ceeded out of his loins; to show unto us the promise and
covenant which he made to his father *Abraham*, that he Gen. 21.13
should be a great people, was fulfilled, and this served to
magnify and exalt the name of godly *Abraham*. We read
that the Lord bestoweth a great genealogy upon wicked
Esau or *Edom*, numbering or reckoning up his sons, and Gen. 36
his sons' sons, his kingdom, and the kings of his seed
that reigned after him, for no other end, but to report
and manifest the blessing upon godly *Isaac* and *Rebecca*
his parents, according to the oracle that he gave to his
mother, when she demanded and enquired the cause of
the struggling or striving in her womb. The like may
be said of godless *Ham* for *Noah* his father's sake, of the
sons of *Jacob* for *Israel's* sake, of *Ephraim* and *Manassas*
for *Joseph's* sake. By the which we gather, and note this
excellent doctrine, that if the wicked have any good, it
is for the sake of their godly and righteous parents or
friends.

We see they should not have so much as a name
in the Book of God, were it not for the cause of the righteous and godly: we read that when the Sodomites were
overcome in war, their people lead captives, and their
goods spoiled by the company of Chedorlaomer, then Gen. 14.15
for *Lot's* sake, the Lord stirred up *Abraham*, and armed
him with men and courage, who won the victory, recovered the spoil, brought back the prisoners, restored their
goods, and gave them all liberty, for godly *Lot's* sake,
who was shortly after despised by them, but they for
their wickedness were burned in brimstone, when righteous *Lot* was delivered from them. If *Joseph* had not
been, they had had no corn in Egypt. If *Moses* had not

Ruth Chapter 4. verses 18-22

been, the Lord had often destroyed the Israelites, while they wandered and wavered in the wilderness. For *Jacob's* sake, the Lord increased the flocks of *Laban*; For *Joseph's* sake, he blessed the affairs of *Potiphar*; for *Paul's* sake, he saved all them that suffered shipwreck at Miletum. Even so also he blessed the house of *Obededom*, because the ark was kept therein, and at this day giveth greatest peace to those countries, where his Gospel is promoted. Let the Atheists think if there were none that feared God, they should quickly be condemned, let the drunkards know, if there were not some temperate persons, their bodies should be quickly consumed, let the covetous wretches assure themselves, if there were not some liberal men, their own goods would turn to their death: let the profaners of Sabbaths remember, that if there were not some sanctifiers thereof, their delightful vanities would long ago have wrought their sorrowful destinies: let the contentious plaintiffs be certified, that if there were not some peaceable Christians among them, their wealth had long ago been wasted, for the prayers of the faithful are like the walled Cities against the rage of enemies, to keep the vengeance of the Lord from falling upon us: as the blood of the Lamb spotted upon the posts of the Israelites' houses, caused the angel to pass by them: when all the first-born in Egypt were slain, even so the blood of the Lamb of God, which is shed in the hearts of the godly, maketh his messengers of death to depart from our country and kingdom.

    If there were not a remnant among us, that are in league with the Lord, that daily are the hearers of his Word, the beseechers for his mercy, and as the ambassadors of peace to dissuade him from punishing our contempt of his Word with condemnation, our abuse of his creatures into pining famine, our wantonness and peace into lamentable wars, our riotous lives into foreign captivity, and our pampered bodies, to the slaughter of the sword. You, even you, that blaspheme the name of God,

Of Religion   357

if there were not a number that reprove your abomina-
tions, the heavens would rain down stones to revenge
your accursed tongues: you, even you, that spend the
Sabbaths in dancing and playing, if there were not a
company that refrain your pollutions, you had been cut
off from your pleasure with some fearful death, before
you had passed these many days of security: you, even
you, that think the preaching of the Gospel like the voice
of one that singeth, whereunto you owe no more obedience, than ear-service: if there were not a remnant that
heard the Word of power, which they believe is able to
save their souls, you had been many years since, suffering the reward of such impious infidelity. What stayeth
the Lord from coming to judgment, but the faithful and
elect company: what keepeth you in your possessions,
revenues, and lands, but the poor Saints of God, who
are hardly admitted to the tables of your servants, who
prayeth for the increase of your wealth, the prosperity
of your lives, the feeding of your bodies, and the continuance of your honor, but these despised persons, who
have entered a covenant for your daily welfare with the
King of heaven and earth.

They are the flock, for whose sake you have your
wool to clothe you, and your milk to feed you; they are
the Bees, for whose sake you enjoy the honey for your
delight, and the honeycomb for the pleasure of your
meat; they are the birds, which have built up your palaces and houses of rest, for the defense of your weakness;
they are the oxen that bring your corn to your barns,
and your store into your garners; they are the beasts, that
bear you out of the dangers in safety, and deliver your
lives from trouble. Finally, there is not a usurer, but he
hath his money for their sake; there is not a Gentleman,
but he hath his lands for their sake; there is not a Prince,
but he hath his Crown for their sake; there is not a rich
man, but he hath his wealth for their sake; there is not
a Minister, but he preacheth for their sake: and there

Ruth Chapter 4. verses 18-22

should be no peace, prosperity, or plenty, if it were not for them, for the Angels are their servants, the earth is their maintenance, and heaven is their inheritance. Be assured therefore, beloved, if righteous *Lot* go out of Sodom, or godly *Noah* into his Ark, then fire will fall from heaven, and the depths will open their fountains of water to burn and destroy the world: even so, if the Lord take away the righteous from among us, then, even then presently, shall follow the destruction of our country, the consuming of our kingdom, the confusion of the world, and the condemning of the reprobate, and therefore let us make much of them, in whom we see any hope of Religion, for they are the right heirs of the world, and you that have their lands, are but overseers of their father's testaments, and therefore shall give an account of your possessions to them when they come to age, and be answerable for every farthing which you spent not upon them.

Secondly, another cause of the genealogies, or recital of generations in the Scriptures, is for the Chronologies or noting of several times, wherein every worthy thing was done, and how the world grew in years, and the mercy of God in sparing the wicked lives of so many godless men, and choosing but one family among all the world, with whom he would establish his covenant: for this cause in the genealogy of *Adam*, we read how long he and every one of his children lived, to show how long the Lord suffered the wicked before he brought the flood, and in what age of the world the same overflowed, which by the genealogies there set down, appeareth to be in the year of the world one thousand six hundred fifty and six, when *Noah* was six hundred years old. Again we read in the genealogy of *Shem*, by the supputation [*reckoning*] of the years therein mentioned, how long after the flood, *Abraham* was called from his country, and received the covenant of promise, concerning the incarnation of Jesus Christ, and the salvation of the world. The same may

Gen. 5

Gen. 11

Gen. 12.3
Gen. 17.24

be said of the often repetition of the age of *Abraham*, as at his calling, at the time of his circumcision, at the birth of *Isaac*, and at his death, which giveth a great light to every part of the Scripture, for thereby the occasions of many excellent histories are taken, the darkest places are opened, the faithful are confirmed, and the Church of God instructed of her age, of her continuance, of her members, and of her condition, which is subject to many and often changes. Sometimes her glory is greater, as in the first age, sometime lesser, as in *Abraham's* time, sometime afflicted, as the estate of *Jacob* in Egypt, and all his children testifieth: sometimes without any known and public ministry, or offices, as till *Aaron's* days, sometime without any civil or politic government, as in the time of all the Patriarchs, sometime without peace in persecution, as in the time of the *Judges*, wherein these persons here named, lived, and sometime in most flourishing estate, as under *David, Solomon, Asa, Josiah*, and such like. By the which we gather, that it never standeth in one stay, but either increaseth or decreaseth, ebbeth or floweth, riseth or falleth, waxeth or waneth: therefore herein lieth the great comfort of the godly even in these troublesome days (but yet the best that ever are to be looked for in this earth) wherein they see the ancient to depart, and new men in their room, one generation cometh, and another goeth, iniquity advanced, coldness in religion embraced, dissimulation and hypocrisy maintained, wars and persecution threatened to the Gospel, schisms defended, errors invented, the world blinded, the truth declined, godliness defaced, and the Church of God disquieted, with a thousand greater calamities, this all the fathers suffered before us, and this we their children must also abide; only herein let us rejoice, that we shall be accounted worthy to suffer for Christ, and that our names are written in the kingdom of heaven.

Thirdly and lastly, the especial cause of this genealogy, and of all the fathers and children of *Abraham*

Ruth Chapter 4. verses 18-22

in one kindred, was for to show the natural descent of
Christ from *Adam*, and so forth unto the virgin *Mary*:
for seeing he was to be incarnated, it behooved that his
parentage should be described from the beginning of the
world: for this cause *Luke* the Evangelist, gathered together the several descriptions of all the genealogies pertaining to Christ, throughout all the whole Scripture, as
a necessary ground of the Gospel, to declare the kindred
of our Savior from the beginning of the world, whereof
these persons mentioned in this place are a part, from
whence he took them into his number.

     Now least any man should think, that the birth
of Christ should be obscure, and the taking upon him
the flesh of mankind, should be uncertain, as well to
convince all errors that arose about his humanity, as to
testify the nobility of his birth, and worthiness of his
parentage, the persons of whom he descended, are in
many books of the Scripture severally named, and not
without great commendation. For this family of Christ
had many and special blessings, which were the arms of
the same, by which it was distinguished from all other.
In *Adam* it had this promise, that the seed of the woman
should break the Serpent's head; meaning, that Christ
which should be born of a woman, should overcome the
force of the Devil. In *Noah* it had this promise, that the
covenant of God should be established with him and his
seed, meaning that his promise which he had made unto
Adam, should be performed in his posterity, which was
for the coming of Christ. This promise was renewed
unto *Abraham*, unto *Isaac*, and unto *Jacob*, and most
plainly unto *Judah*, the third son of *Jacob*, who was the
father and grandfather of this *Pharez*, that the Scepter
shall not depart from *Judah*, nor the lawgiver from between his feet, until *Shiloh* come, and the people shall be
gathered unto him: and again unto *David* he swore, that
the fruit of his body should sit upon his Throne, both
which promises or prophesies respect the coming and

Luke 3.23

Gen. 3.15

Gen. 9.9

Gen. 29.10

Psal. 132.11

the reign of Christ.

By this then we first of all gather the scope of the whole Scripture, namely, that above all other it respecteth Jesus Christ the Son of God, and Savior of the world, the Prince of peace, the mighty King, and the great Counselor. For this cause, he himself speaketh to the Jews, *Search the Scriptures, for in them you think to have eternal life, and they are they that testify of me.* Again, *John* speaketh in the end of his Gospel, that the Scripture was written that we might believe in Christ. And we read that *Apollos* did mightily confound the Jews, proving by the Scriptures that Jesus was Christ. But most evident and plain is that of the Disciples going to Emmaus, and Jesus overtaking them by the way, it is said, that he began at *Moses* and all the Prophets, showing them, that Christ ought so to suffer, and that redemption and remission of sins, might be preached in his name to all the world. By the which it is most easy to be gathered, and doth necessarily follow, that the sum, drift, and scope of the Scripture, dependeth upon Christ. First, because all the godly that are named therein, were either his Fathers according to the flesh, or else the singular types prefiguring his person, such was *Melchizedek, Joseph, Moses,* all the Judges, *Samuel,* and the Prophets, which although they were not of his natural linage, (*Melchizedek* excepted) yet they did most lively represent him, *Moses* and the Judges in this, that as they delivered the people from earthly captivity, so should he redeem them from everlasting calamity. *Samuel* and the Prophets in this, that as they instructed the Jews in the law of the Lord, which was given by *Moses,* so Christ should put his law in the inward parts of the Church, and teach them the Gospel of truth, their redemption wrought by himself, the law of righteousness, the words of eternal life. *Aaron* and his fellows in this, that as they sacrificed for the sins of the people with bullocks and beasts, and sprinkled the blood with hyssop for their outward cleansing, so Christ sacrificeth his

John 5.39

John 20.31

Acts 18.28

Luke 24.27-46

Ruth Chapter 4. verses 18-22

own body, and cleanseth from sin, through the sprinkling of his own blood. *David* and the Kings in this, that as they ruled the people by their temporal laws conquering their enemies, and giving them rest and worldly honor, so Christ doth reign with the spiritual law of his Word, triumphing over hell, death, and Satan, leading captivity captive, ascending up on high, receiving gifts for men, delivering his Church from their adversary the Devil, bestowing upon them spiritual peace and liberty, giving them the honors of his Ministry, Word, and Sacraments in this life present, and Crowns of glory in the life to come. Thus if we look upon the Judges, they show us our redemption. If we look upon the Kings, they show us our salvation. If we look upon the Prophets, they show us our instruction. If we look upon the Priests, they show us our reconciliation, and if we look upon the very names of the fathers of Christ which are described in the old Testament, they teach us that our names are also described in heaven, and this is the profit we reap by the generation or genealogy of the faithful, to confirm unto us the true humanity of our Savior.

So that herein most lively appeareth the dignity of the Scriptures, and the majesty of Christ, one mutually looking on another, as the sun doth the stars, and the stars the sun, for as the excellency of the sun appeareth by the glory of the stars, to whom it giveth light, so the majesty of Christ is manifest by the Scriptures, to whom he giveth credit: On the other side, as the glory of the stars is magnified because it is the light of the sun, so the credit of the Scriptures is exalted, because they concern the Son of God. If the doings of earthly men be but painted in some pamphlets, tragedies, or books of Chronicles, we account them famous, because their actions are commended in print, what shall we then say of the Son of God, whose works excel the worthiest enterprises of all the world together, and are recorded by the holy Ghost, the eternal God of truth, throughout all the sacred books of his eternal word, far above the credit of worldly commendations, is not his majesty incomparable? Do we buy the books of earthly men's devises, to read the feigned and doubtful adventures of Princes long since in their graves, and shall we suffer this book of the heavenly stratagems of our Savior lie asleep in the shops? Compare their worthiness together, you shall find the difference as great, as is between the light of the sun, and a little rotten wood glistering in the dark. They overcame some worldly Princes, but he overcame the Prince of the whole world: they through a multitude of earthly soldiers, but he through himself alone an infinite number of infernal powers: they invented politic laws for their peaceable government, but he giveth spiritual precepts, and ruleth by them the hearts of men himself: they had the heads of many noble persons uncovered at their presence, but he hath the tongues and knees of all them in heaven, in earth, and under the earth, bowing unto him, yea, the Angels do him reverence, for he is their head: they prepared names of Ships to cut the seas, but he could command the waters to bear him up when he walked upon them: they had their glory in gold, silver, precious stones, and soft apparel, but he being on earth, had his countenance like the brightness of the sun, and his garments as white as the light; they could dig in the earth to find treasures for their maintenance; but he commanded the fishes of the sea to render him his want: they were able upon infinite charges, to keep great families: but he without any charge fed five thousand men, besides women and children with a few barley loaves and two fishes, and caused much more to be taken up, than at the first was divided among them, finally they were able to destroy the bodies of men; but he is able to destroy both body and soul, they showed themselves in outward glory, but he shall show himself in flaming fire, to render vengeance to all them that have not obeyed his Gospel.

Ruth Chapter 4. verses 18-22

Therefore here must we learn the majesty of Christ even in the Scriptures, who was promised to these Fathers, appeared in their flesh, satisfied for our sins, to whom all the Scriptures give witness, that he shall be the judge of Princes, and subjects, living and dead. Unto whom we must give reverence, as to his Majesty appertaineth, for even now he beholdeth with what fear we hear his word, with what love we receive it, with what hunger we desire it, and with what conscience we will practice it. Oh come let us kiss the Son lest he be angry, let us wash his feet with the tears of our eyes, and wipe them with the hairs of our head. Let us sue to him, for he is the Judge we are the rebels, he the Savior, and we the slaves. Against him only have we sinned by contemning his Majesty, profaning his Sabbaths, blaspheming his honor, disobeying his Gospel, and treading the pardon of our souls under the feet of our pleasures; therefore while we have time, let us love his truth, receive his Gospel, believe his word, sanctify his Sabbaths, magnify his name, reverence his Ministers and repent us of our sins.

Pharez begat Hezron. Now after the causes of the Genealogies described and the use of them, gathered out of the word of God and godly writers, we must proceed to the special persons here mentioned, for whose sake the former hath been spoken; we showed you in the beginning that these generations were some of them before Boaz, and some after him, as his children, and this we must put you again in mind of, that here is handled the Genealogy of Christ. In the which this seemeth doubtful that he beginneth with *Pharez*, what should move him thereunto, seeing (as already we showed you) that this *Pharez* was an incestuous birth: and therefore to common reason, it seemeth much more commendable that he should have been utterly blot out of the note of these Fathers, or else the Genealogy should have been farther repeated as from *Abraham* or *Noah*, that so the consideration of his birth might have been hindered, through the

company of other godly Fathers. Unto which I briefly
answer, that for this cause he beginneth at *Pharez*, for
the better understanding of the Prayers of the Elders, in
the twelfth verse, which desired that the house of *Boaz*
might be like the house of *Pharez*, whom *Tamar* bare
unto *Judah*, wherefore at the end of this History the Author annexeth the description of the house of *Pharez* and
of *Boaz*, for whom they prayed, unto the third generation. So that in those days, most commendable was the
posterity of *Pharez*, for they were the chief of the tribe of
Judah, because this *Pharez* was by nature the heir of the
birth right of *Judah*, because he was the Son of *Tamar*,
the widow of *Judah* his eldest Son. Again, the Scripture
is not wont to cover the faults of the dearest children of
God, neither doth the holy Ghost ever conceal the sins
of the godly. It telleth us of the drunkenness of *Noah*, the
incest of *Lot*, the unlawful oath that *Joseph* swore to his
brethren, (by the life of *Pharaoh*) the adultery of *David*,
the distrust of king *Asa*, the fellowship that good king *Je-
hoshaphat* had with wicked *Ahab*, and *Peter's* denial. At
all these the Spirit of God never standeth, but indicteth
them of their sins, though he give them their pardon by
Christ.

But we must know further, that the Spirit of God
so ruled the pen-writers of the Scriptures, that he suffered them not to omit the grievous sins of themselves
their fathers and children: as for example, *Levi* was the
great grandfather of *Moses*, which was the first writer
of the Scripture, yet he setteth down the curse that the
Lord pronounced by *Jacob* against him for the slaughter of the Shechemites. Likewise it is held of everyone
that *Job* was the writer of his own History, yet how doth
he lay open his own corruptions, cursing his birth, accusing God of injustice, and desiring to plead with him.
Moreover, *Samuel* wrote his own History, especially the
greatest part of the first book, yet he layeth out the corruptions of his Sons in the government of the people and

Exod. 20
Gen. 49.7

Job 4

Ruth Chapter 4. verses 18-22

how wicked they were, for whose sake the people were driven to desire a King, the like may be said of many other, whose cursed sins are by themselves detected, being not ashamed to confess them, as they were not to commit them, but thus the godly are their own Judges to condemn their own sins, for they know if they condemn themselves, they shall not be condemned of God. They say with the prodigal Son that they have sinned against heaven and against earth, and are no more worthy to be called the sons of God: they say with Paul, that they are the greatest of all sinners, and therefore have received the greater mercy: they say with the man in the Gospel, *I am not worthy that thou shouldest come into my house*: and evermore they lay the worst side of their garments outward, that they might be more vile in their own eyes, more fearful to sin, more loving to God his mercies, more humble in the world, and more hunger for righteousness.

Cast away therefore if you be the children of God, this shame to acknowledge the infirmities where withal you are infected, for he that confesseth not his sins, even to his brethren, can never confess the mercies of God to himself. He that commendeth a Physician, telleth what dangerous sickness he delivered him out, and he that will commend Christ the Physician of our souls, must tell what sins his soul was sick of, and how his Savior hath delivered him: but yet alway remember that no man is bound upon necessity to declare his particular sins, except when his conscience is grieved for them, that he receive comfort, or when he must satisfy the injury he hath done to his neighbors. But we must learn not once to despise any penitent sinners, but rather embrace them or lay them in our own bosoms; they are the sheep which wandered, but now is found; the groat [*silver coin*] which was lost, but now is recovered; and the branches which were dead, and now are green, for the Angels rejoice for them; Christ died for them, heaven is prepared for them, and we must pray for them. We have heard already that this *Pharez* was the incestuous Son of *Judah*: now if any ask why the Lord would take any part of such ungodly beginnings, I answer with *Paul*, that Christ came to save sinners, that is, he was   I Tim. 1.15 incarnated of incestuous progenitors, to show unto us that he could save such; of adulterous births, to show unto us that he could save the children of adultery, of Gentiles such as *Ruth*, *Rahab* and *Bathsheba* was, that he might show unto us, he was the appointed Savior of the Gentiles, because he vouchsafed to take his nature from them: for thus it becometh him to fulfill all righteousness, to destroy the gates of Hell, to deliver his members from the thraldom of Satan, to gather together in one, from the East and West, North and South, all the children of *Abraham*, to enjoy the presence of his Majesty, the inheritance of his kingdom, and the end of their faith, the salvation of their souls.

   Pharez begat Hezron. Now we will briefly give you the exposition of the names and so make an end of this History. *Pharez* or rather *Peretz* in Hebrew signifieth a division; and the occasion of this name was, because of the two twins in the womb of *Tamar*, he first of all brake forth, and therefore they called him a division, from the time of his birth, he was born in the land of Canaan. *Hezron* or *Chetzron*, which was also born in   Gen. 38.29 the land of Canaan, and the Son of *Peretz*, who was born   Gen. 46.12 about the time, that the Israelites went into Egypt, and signifieth in our English tongue, the arrow of joy; for till the Israelites went into Egypt, they endured a great famine, which *Ezekiel* calleth the arrow of famine, and when they were delivered from this famine, by going into Egypt for corn, this child being then born, he was called the arrow of joy, as the famine is called the arrow of sorrow, as a remembrance of the mercy of God to them, in giving them bread. *Ram* was the Son of *Hezron*, and was born in Egypt, about the time of *Jacob's* death, when the

Ruth Chapter 4. verses 18-22

children of Israel began to be hated of the Egyptians; and therefore they called him *Ram*: which signifieth in our English tongue, cast down, or cast off, because they then began to be afflicted, and saw (no doubt) great misery like to fall upon them, and they should be cast down so soon as either the king or *Joseph* should be dead. *Amminadab* the Son of *Ram*, was also born in Egypt, about the time of *Joseph's* death, when he told the Israelites, that the Lord would visit them, and deliver them from the Egyptians, and it signifieth in our English tongue a people that would be free, being compounded of two words; wherein the Israelites testify the hope of their deliverance, that although they were now in thraldom, yet they should be in freedom again. *Nahshon* or *Nachschon*, the Son of *Amminadab*, was also born in Egypt a little before the departure of the Israelites, when they cried grievously to the Lord for their affliction which they endured in Egypt under the Taxmasters, and it signifieth a crying or complaining, thereby noting in the name of the child that he was born in affliction, which might put him in mind of his Father's misery, this man when the children of Israel were gone out of Egypt, and pitched their tents

Gen. 50.24   in wilderness of Sinai; was by election or appointment
Numb. 1.1,7 of God, made the Prince of the whole Tribe, *Salmon* or *Shalmon* the Son of *Nachschon*, was born after the Israelites were departed from Egypt, while they wandered in the desert and were delivered from the Amalekites and other their enemies; and his name signifieth peaceable, because they lived then peaceably, being freed from the Egyptians and other calamities, this man married with the victualer *Rahab* of Jericho, of whom he begat *Boaz*.
             Boaz signifieth in strength, who was born about the time
Matt. 1.5   of the deliverance of the Jews, from the tyranny of the
Judg. 3.16   Moabites by the hand of lame *Ehud*: by which means they got strength, and remained a long time in peace. *Obed* signifieth a servant, who was born as we see in *Ephrata Bethlehem*, his mother being *Ruth* the Moabi-

tess, the women gave him this name, because he should serve for the raising up of *Elimelech's* family, the restoring of *Naomi's* life, and the comfort of his parents, *Boaz* and *Ruth*. *Ischai*; or *Jesse*, the Son of *Obed*, signifieth an oblation, and was born about the days of *Jephthah*; and it may be had, his name given by reason of the vow of *Jephthah*, when he went against the Ammonites, that he would offer the first living thing that met him after he returned with the victory, whereupon his daughter meeting him, she lived in perpetual virginity. *David* the youngest Son of *Jesse*, who no doubt was born in the time of *Heli*, signifieth beloved, because commonly the youngest are best loved, or else his name did prophesy that he should be so loved of God, with whom he would establish his covenant concerning Christ, and advance him to the kingdom. By which we may plainly see, that this History was written after he was chosen from his brethren and anointed to be king after Saul, or else the eldest Son of *Jesse*, should have been named because the birth-right belonged to him.

Lastly, by this we may gather, that the foundation of the Gospel must be searched for in the old Testament for this Genealogy, as all the other of Christ is taken from thence, and the Apostle defining the Gospel, saith that God had promised it before by the Prophets, in the holy Scriptures, that is in the old Testament: and therefore it was needful, for *Mathew* to begin his Gospel with the Genealogy of Christ, from *Abraham* and *David* who had most lively promises of his incarnation; also *Mark* and *Luke* begin with *John Baptist* who was the promised *Elijah*, and the forerunner of Christ according as before it was prophesied: and *John* fetcheth it from the creation and beginning of the world, as it appeareth in the entrance of his Gospel. By which we may see the hope of the Fathers for the coming of Christ, to be the same with ours, and had the lively promises thereof revealed in the law and the Prophets. Secondly, the heavenly agreement

Rom. 1.2

Ruth Chapter 4. verses 18-22

that is between the old Testament and the new, for there he was promised, thence he was proved to be the Messiah, all the Prophets give witness unto him, now he is exhibited, humbled, and advanced to the highest degree, the government, heaven and earth: sitting at the right hand of God, making intercession for his Saints, working in the calling of his servants, with the ministry of his word, disposing all things to the damnation of the wicked, and the salvation of the godly. Now let us give praise to God.

FINIS.

www.ingramcontent.com/pod-product-compliance
Lightning Source LLC
Chambersburg PA
CBHW032033080426
42733CB00006B/67